EFFECTIVE SCHOOL DISTRICT LEADERSHIP

SUNY Series, Educational Leadership
Daniel L. Duke, Editor

EFFECTIVE SCHOOL DISTRICT LEADERSHIP

Transforming Politics into Education

edited by

Kenneth Leithwood

STATE UNIVERSITY OF NEW YORK PRESS

Published by
State University of New York Press, Albany

Production by Susan Geraghty
Marketing by Theresa Abad Swierzowski

Printed in the United States of America

For information, address State University of New York Press,
State University Plaza, Albany, N.Y., 12246

Library of Congress Cataloging-in-Publication Data

Effective school district leadership : transforming politics into
    education / Kenneth Leithwood, editor.
        p.   cm.—(SUNY series, educational leadership)
    Includes essays based on research funded by the Social Sciences
and Humanities Research Council of Canada.
    "The majority of the chapters in this book are the outcome of a
project undertaken by a group of faculty, research staff, and
students in the Department of Educational Administration at the
Ontario Institute for Studies in Education"—CIP galley.
    Includes bibliographical references and index.
    ISBN 0-7914-2253-4 — ISBN 0-7914-2254-2 (pbk.)
    1. School superintendents—Ontario. 2. Educationa leadership-
-Ontario. 3. School management and organization—Ontario.
I. Leithwood, Kenneth A. II. Ontario Institute for Studies in
Education. Dept. of Educational Administration. III. Series: SUNY
series in educational leadership.
LB2831.726.C2E33 1995
371.2'011'09713—dc20   94-3955
                                                              CIP

10 9 8 7 6 5 4 3 2 1

CONTENTS

ACKNOWLEDGMENTS

Of the twelve chapters published in this text, seven are based on research that was funded by the Social Sciences and Humanities Research Council of Canada. We appreciate this support.

Three chapters were written by authors who are not members of OISE. We are especially graeful to Frances Wills, Kent Peterson, Joe Murphy, Edward Holdaway, and Anthony Genge for their willingness to have their work included in this volume.

Vashty Hawkins was an invaluable aide in the preparation of this manuscript.

PREFACE

Most chapters in this book are the outcome of a project undertaken by a group of faculty, research staff, and students in the Department of Educational Administration at the Ontario Institute for Studies in Education (OISE). This is the second phase of their work, the first having been published in *Understanding School System Administration* (Leithwood and Musella 1991). And that volume itself was something of a sequel, at least for several of us, to an earlier text, undertaken by an association of senior school administrators in Ontario, entitled *The Canadian School Superintendent* (Boich, Farquhar, and Leithwood 1989). This text, then, is the third in a "trilogy," as I have come to think of these three volumes.

In the case of the immediately preceding text and the present text, the work of OISE members has been substantially enriched by reports of research done by those in other institutions and jurisdictions. In the present text, important chapters have been contributed by Derek Allison, Patricia Allison, and Helen McHenry using evidence collected in Ontario; by Frances Wills and Kent Peterson, based on their research in Maine; by Joseph Murphy, based on his research in Kentucky; and by Ted Holdaway and Anthony Genge, their research having been carried out in Alberta.

The research reported by OISE faculty, staff, and students was accomplished over a period of about three years. Sometimes this research involved remarkable levels of collaboration that few of us had directly experienced before. In other cases, in something like the "cooperative play" of two-year-olds, we sat in the same sandbox but played independently. As I think the resulting work indicates, there is a place for scholarly collaboration and there is also a place for independent thinking.

In our previous text, *Understanding School System Administration,* we tried to represent the rich complexity of CEOs' thinking and behavior, and of the context of their work. We made no attempt to assess or prejudge the value of the ways the CEOs included in our studies worked. The current text differs in one important respect: It is primarily concerned with the practices of those who appear to be exceptionally effective at what they do. Little evidence is available about the nature of effective CEO practices or their causes and consequences. While we make no claims to having encompassed this topic in any comprehensive way, we hope that we have substantially pushed forward the understanding of what effective education CEOs do and why they do it.

REFERENCES

Boich, J., Farquhar, R., and Leithwood, K. (Eds.). (1989) *The Canadian School Superintendent*. Toronto: OISE Press.

Leithwood, K., & Musella, D. (Eds.) (1991). *Understanding School System Administration*. London: Falmer Press.

CHAPTER 1

Introduction:
Transforming Politics into Education

Kenneth Leithwood

THE THEME

Medieval alchemists were the source of great expectations. Clearly, the world had more lead than it felt it needed and not nearly enough gold. Eventually, of course, these alchemists had to admit defeat and turn their minds toward more mundane and, very likely, more socially redeeming challenges—finding antidotes for stomach gas, cures for foot fungus, that sort of thing. Many of their customers, I expect, were pleased with these modest improvements to their quality of life. And, as a consequence, some of the more astute of these alchemists ended up with a lot of gold of their own.

For present purposes, the most relevant of the morals to this story is that sometimes the goals you set for yourself turn out to be less desirable than the ones you trip over after discovering the impossibility of achieving the ones originally in mind (there is, I think, an ancient Chinese *curse*, something along the lines of "May your fondest dreams come true"). This is not a moral taken much to heart in public talk about either individual or organizational goals. It seems so—uninspired? lacking in vision? opportunistic? But most of us privately will admit that a large proportion of what we count as "successes" in our lives are judged in relation to these "tripped over" goals.

Which brings us, of course, to school superintendents and the nature of their work. By all accounts, this work is overwhelmingly

1

"political." For example, the most common conflict superintendents cope with, highlighted by Blumberg's (1985) study, mostly
arises from the friction between different stakeholder interests:
"politics" as the managed reduction of conflict. Crowson and
Morris (1991) note superintendents' overwhelming preoccupa-
tion with the characteristics, histories, and needs of their local
communities: "politics" as realization of the general will and common good. Similarly, Wirt's (1991) study demonstrates just how
short is the rope that binds superintendents' initiatives to the
agenda of their elected boards: "politics" as the authoritative allocation of values. As these examples suggest, we will attach no formal or singular definition to the meaning of politics in this text.
But usually what we describe as political work involves creating
defensible guidelines for action out of competing, values-based
interests.[1]

Superintendents, we are told, were not always as oriented to
politics as they appear to be at present (Tyack and Hansot 1982;
Boich, Farquhar, and Leithwood 1989). Large-district superintendents might be more politically oriented than their small-district
colleagues are (Wolf 1990; Jones 1987), and males more than
females (Bell and Chase 1989). Nonetheless, this orientation has
given rise to a fair bit of handwringing because it seems so uncon-
nected to the provision of instructional services to students.
Whereas the role of modern superintendents, then, has typically
been described as that of a politician (as well as negotiator and
statesman—see Wimpleberg 1986), some believe that there ought
to be a parallel for superintendents to the instructional leadership
role widely advocated for school principals (Wirt 1991; Wimpleberg 1986; Murphy and Hallinger 1986; Jones 1987; Coleman
and LaRocque 1990).

This is where the moral of the alchemy story becomes relevant.
Instructional leadership is not an appropriate image for the superintendents' role (indeed it is no longer suitable even for principals,
as I have argued elsewhere—Leithwood 1992). Why? Because
when, organizationally, you are as remote from classrooms as
superintendents are, the functions evoked by the phrase *instructional leadership* are necessarily carried out more effectively by
others; the chances that the superintendent of a moderate-size district will directly influence the instructional experiences of students is about the same as the alchemist's chances of producing
gold from lead.

Of course, the meaning of "instructional leadership" has never been well defined. In many instances it seems to be a synonym for "good" leadership, according to Cuban's (1988) description of how the meaning of instructional leadership applied to the superintendency has evolved to the present. But I am using the phrase to denote a form of leadership that is designed to affect classroom instruction quite directly, through, for example, supervision, coaching, staff development, modeling and other such means of influencing teachers' thinking and practice. Leadership that indirectly constrains teachers' choices or frames their work needs to be called something else.

Take the case of superintendents' instructional leadership as described by Murphy and Hallinger (1986) and Peterson, Murphy, and Hallinger (1987). In one of the very few rigorous empirical studies available on this matter, the practices of superintendents in twelve successful school districts[2] in California were examined. The work of these administrators was described, in sum, as

> active involvement in . . . establishing district direction in the areas of curriculum and instruction, in ensuring consistency and coordination among technical case operations, and in monitoring internal processes and inspecting outcomes. (Peterson, Murphy, and Hallinger, 1987, p. 228)

These superintendents ran *very* tight ships. To be instructional leaders, they had to rely heavily on bureaucratic controls and were themselves actively involved, for example, in hiring and in specifying texts to be used in schools. Indeed, in 75 percent of the cases the superintendents even prescribed to teachers *the one best form of instruction!* (They lived in Madeline Hunter country, after all.)

In the mid 1980s when these data were reported, such superintendents' practices seemed a natural outgrowth of what was being learned at the time about the structure and leadership of effective schools. In retrospect, however, the California study might better have characterized the role of the twelve superintendents as master bureaucrat than as instructional leader. Standardized achievement data notwithstanding, what they produced doesn't look much like gold to me. Indeed, few people today who are familiar with what has been learned recently about conditions for teacher growth, the importance of collaborative cultures, the need for teachers to possess a large repertoire of instructional techniques, or the positive consequences of collaborative decision making at the school level would advocate many of the practices ascribed to those twelve superintendents. Instead, their close evaluation of teachers and administrators, based on criterion-referenced student achievement data, can be seen from our present vantage point as a major impediment to organizational risk-taking and productive innovation. Of course, at the time almost no one in education had even heard of organizational learning (e.g., Levitt and March 1988; Senge 1990), total quality management (Sashkin and Kiser 1992), or transformational leadership (e.g., Burns 1978; Bass 1985). We were still of the view that doing what we had always done, but doing it "harder," would suffice.

Since that time, many people have come instead to the view that what is needed is a more profound restructuring of our educational organizations. Furthermore, the conceptions of restructuring that seem most promising at the present time depend on significant changes in organizational governance, changes based, in large measure, on a profoundly new understanding of power. In *The Prince*, Machiavelli (1640/1981) deduced what he claimed is a general rule:

> that whoever is responsible for another's becoming powerful ruins himself, because this power is brought into being either by ingenuity or by force, and both of these are suspect to the one who has become powerful. (p. 44)

Machiavelli's conception of power, in this general rule, is rooted in the ability to control others—through money, force, law, and the like. Bureaucratic organization depends on the exercise of power conceived of in this way. Current efforts to restructure organizations in order to "debureaucratize" them, in contrast, bring with them a conception of power referred to by Dunlap and Goldman (1991) as "facilitative." Such power springs from the expertise or capacity to accomplish some purpose valued by the organization and its clients. Facilitative power is "the ability to help others achieve a set of ends that may be shared, negotiated, or complementary without being either identical or antithetical" (Dunlap, Goldman, and Conley 1993, p. 70).

More than ever before, the way forward seems to depend on establishing authentic partnerships with school communities and other stakeholders. More than ever before, a restructuring agenda stresses the political role of the superintendent. But this is not a defensive political role as it has often been in the past, premised on maintaining the power to control or to ward off external threats to the organization. It entails, rather, proactively trans- *CMC* forming the values, aspirations and interests of the increasingly diverse constituents served by today's schools into a set of sophisticated educational services that address those values, aspirations, and interests. It is the exercise of facilitative power, transforming politics into education.

Lest we think that superintendents are being asked to do something unique, it is instructive to consider the context of CEOs in large private corporations at the present time. The 11 January 1993 issue of *Fortune* magazine carried the theme title, "The King is Dead: Why More Boards Are Waking Up and Pushing Out the CEO." Stimulated by the recent fall from power of many CEOs in such industry giants as General Motors (Robert Stempel), IBM (John Ackers), American Express (James Robinson), Digital Equipment (Kenneth Olsen), and Compaq Computers (Joseph Canion), the cover story (Stewart 1993) asserted that there was a common central cause. In the words of one source cited in the story, this cause was "a sea change in the relationship among management, boards and shareholder" (p. 34).

Why? If we are to believe the *Fortune* analyst, it is due in part to the growth of such institutional investors as pension and mutual funds. They have created a form of concentrated, collective shareholder power that could not exist as long as most shareholders acted only as individuals. Without such collective power, management effectively could not be called to account except by their boards of directors, boards that CEOs themselves often chaired! Furthermore, these institutional investors have become so large that their holdings are dispersed broadly throughout the market. Under these circumstances, it is often easier for these investors to use their power to improve poorly performing companies than to find alternative companies in which to invest.

Reflecting on what this sea change will mean for CEOs in the future, another source cited in this article suggested that "the CEO will look less like an employer and more like a congressman, trying to represent his various constituents and, to the extent he succeeds, being re-elected" (p. 34). To be successful, these CEOs will need to seek out and communicate with their employers (shareholders). Rather than complain that shareholders don't know the business, CEOs must teach them about that business: "Sharehold-

c restructuring efforts in ed = similar to private co.
✓ letting "share holders" know about co., including
"board" to solve probs.

6   KENNETH LEITHWOOD

ers deserve extensive information about training, customer satisfaction, R&D, quality, and strategy" (p. 40). These CEOs also will need to use their boards effectively to help solve their organizations' toughest problems. These new functions prescribed for private-sector CEOs are remarkably analogous to what educational restructuring means, for example, to the superintendents presently involved in Kentucky's major educational restructuring efforts (Murphy 1993).

Some will claim that transforming politics into education is just another form of alchemy. But I suspect it is more "doable" than providing instructional leadership. Superintendents have a lot of experience with politics. Politics seems a natural part of the job as it is usually defined. Among the most frequent contacts superintendents have on the job are interactions with their political masters. So, starting with the politics of the job and trying to fashion education from it is more like using the rudder of a boat to steer the best course down the river than using the paddle against the current. This theme of transforming politics into education is central to most of the chapters in the text, in one way or another. More precisely, available evidence suggests that typical superintendents have great difficulty transforming politics into anything other than more politics. The impact of these superintendents on their districts seems marginal, at best: As Cuban (1988, p. 129) observes, "The evidence paints the superintendent as no Superman; instead what we see is more like a frazzled Clark Kent struggling to get out of a phone booth." So the chapters mostly concern how effective superintendents manage this transformation.

Having made this case for a political theme in understanding effective superintendents' work, several caveats are in order. First, the research reported in subsequent chapters addresses this theme "unevenly" (as one of the book reviewers put it). This is clearly so, especially if one focuses on the issues explicitly addressed in each chapter: Some explicitly are concerned with politics, others are not. But each has something substantial to say about one or more conceptions of politics, even when that was not the stated intention of the authors. This was a theme, we admit, that was "discovered" through reading the completed chapters, not a framework uniformly guiding the research on which all chapters are based from the outset. That a political theme should emerge so clearly, even when not explicitly intended, speaks to its pervasiveness and importance.

WHAT "EFFECTIVE" MEANS (ACTUALLY): RUMINATIONS ON METHOD

"Effective" school district leadership—how is that different from "ordinary" or "ineffective" leadership? At minimum, the term *effective* evokes notions of leadership that is exceptional, perhaps worth emulating, often in rare supply, or widely valued. The legacy of "effective schools" research has created a predisposition on the part of many educators to define effectiveness in terms of student performance. Schools are effective when their students perform beyond expectation. Or when the performance of same-age cohorts of students gets better over time. Or when differences in achievement within a school among groups of students defined by their ethnicity or SES significantly diminish. In all these cases, student performance is the bottom line.

But as we are numbingly aware by now, this legacy still leaves unresolved the problem of which areas of student performance really count. Is exceptional performance in basic skills enough? If not, what other kinds of performances should be considered? How are we to judge the effectiveness of a school, for example, in which students perform much above average on tests of spelling and grammar but much below average on the quality of their expository writing? For some, the answer to these questions is further complicated by school context: Exceptional performance of basic skills, they claim, is a high standard for some kids in some schools. For others, nothing less than the acquisition of higher-order thinking skills for all students will do (the concepts of equity and effectiveness are hard to keep separate).

Quite aside from the problem of settling on which student performances matter in judging a school's effectiveness, even the effective-schools movement allows for less "bottom line" solutions to the problem. There are, of course, the "correlates" of effective schools; strong instructional leadership, academic goals, high performance expectations, and the like. Would we judge a school to be effective if it showed strong evidence of these correlates? Would we also have to see evidence of better-than-expected student performance? Most of us would probably say that it depends. If the school shows signs of "moving" (to use Rosen-holtz's 1989 term) by incorporating features likely to pay off for students in the long run, perhaps some would be willing to claim that the school was effective.

Suffice it to say, then, that finding a defensible basis on which to make a judgment about a *school's* effectiveness is no easy mat-ter (we have not exhausted the complexities). This is the case even though most of us will quickly agree that, of course, the central purpose of a school is to contribute to its students' growth. And schools have a direct effect on the experience of students. What then of a *leader's* effectiveness? And not just the leader of a school but of a *school district*, an organizational entity with no direct effects on the tangible experiences of students. As Yukl (1989) points out, virtually all leadership effects are indirect: Leadership practices influence or are mediated by aspects of the organization, which in turn affect the achievement of its central goals. The more removed the leadership position is from the direct delivery of ser-vices to clients, the longer the chain of mediating variables linking leadership practices with the achievement of central organiza-tional goals.

So if we think the task of settling on a robust basis for defining a school's effectiveness is a bit treacherous, imagine the challenge in finding something comparable for defining effective district leadership. Such was the challenge faced by the authors of many of the chapters in this book. The purpose of this preamble, then, is to enhance your sensitivity to the scope of the challenge and to put to rest the idea that there are clearly defensible responses to this challenge, if only the authors had possessed the wit to use them.

Among the seven chapters that depend in one way or another on a definition of leadership effectiveness, four different approaches are to be found. The reputation of the CEO was the most frequently used approach. Reputation among other CEOs and/or experts in the study of leadership was the basis for sample selection in chapters by Holdaway and Genge (chapter 2), Allison, Allison and McHenry (chapter 3), Townsend (chapters 7 and 8), and Leithwood and Steinbach (chapter 4). As a second approach, Musella (chapter 9) compared the practices of two new CEOs with prescriptions for effective practice culled from relevant liter-ature and concluded, from the close match, that they were effec-tive. Wills and Peterson (chapter 5), using a third approach, selected for their study CEOs of districts that were judged by state officials to have "good planning processes," processes central to state-mandated reforms. Finally, while Holmes's study (chapter 10) did not require judgments to be made about the effectiveness of individual CEOs, it was premised on the argument that significant differences in the educational values of CEOs and those publics served by their districts jeopardize CEOs' effectiveness.

Each of these four methods has significant limitations, most of which are identified by the authors. But it is important to remember that other plausible methods will also be limited. This probably argues for the accumulation of a significant corpus of research using different methods before succumbing to any smug convictions of having discovered the truth.

THE CHAPTERS

Chapters 2 through 11 report the results of original, recently completed, empirical research. Each of these chapters addresses, more or less directly, effective school system leadership and our secondary theme, transforming politics into education. Holdaway and Genge (chapter 2) begin by providing us with a broad picture of the work of thirteen effective superintendents: what their priorities are, how they judge their own and their districts' effectiveness, what they do to influence that effectiveness, and so on. In the course of chapter 2, we find that political matters are the most frequently identified source of constraints on what superintendents do, and that effective superintendents interact very frequently with members of their boards, particularly the chairs of those boards. Acknowledging the time and effort superintendents devote to their elected masters, Allison, Allison, and McHenry (chapter 3) unpack the nature of the working relationships between effective superintendents and board chairpersons. This is evidence, previously unavailable, about the extent and nature of this crucial relationship and how it influences decisions about the educational programs provided by schools.

Of course, politics is by no means confined to arenas officially designated as political in the sense of public authorities who allocate scarce resources. For example, community members, union representatives, teachers, and other groups have unique interests that they often advocate and seek support for. These interests frequently call for responses from central office leaders under circumstances that jeopardize competing interests. In chapter 4, Leithwood, Steinbach, and Raun describe how such "problems" get solved by superintendents with their immediate administrative teams; at the same time this chapter interrogates such group problem-solving settings for evidence of the exercise of facilitative power by superintendents.

The studies by Wills and Peterson (chapter 5) and by Murphy (chapter 6) were conducted in a second arena not formally designated as political (the public's elected officials deciding who gets what)—the superficially bureaucratic arena of district responses to state mandates. We learn from these studies how unique district contexts and superintendents' personal interpretations of environmental uncertainty have the power to produce enormously varied responses to the same state mandate. We also learn how state-initiated restructuring efforts are dramatically increasing superintendents' use of facilitative power.

This same theme, developing a less bureaucratic, more interpretive understanding of the relationship between state or provincial policy and the practices of district (and other) leaders is pushed considerably further along in chapters 7 and 8, by Townsend; indeed, Townsend characterizes what is described in these two chapters as (1) an inventory of persons' storylines about intergovernmental relations, (2) a case study that wallows in local color and provincial color, and (3) a behavioral inquiry into interactions between district and provincial managers. As with some of the other writers, Townsend makes an effort to bring more humanity into the policy process.

The three remaining chapters pursue issues critical to superintendent effectiveness but contribute more indirectly to the central theme of the book than do the preceding chapters. How superintendents, new ones in particular, systematically can bring about significant changes in school district culture is the problem addressed by Musella in chapter 9. Carefully attending to the needs of different interest groups is part of the solution to this problem. In chapter 10, Holmes raises the thorny dilemma of values and leadership. Offering evidence that the educational values of superintendents are substantially different from those of the publics served by their districts, this chapter sensitizes us to the changes that will be required in district leadership in order to serve the increasingly diverse interests of school communities.

In chapter 11, Lawton, Scane, and Wang explore school district structures within which leadership is exercised. Chapter 11 sums up the case for flatter school district organizations in response to the current restructuring agenda and provides evidence of such flattening in one large, provincial jurisdiction. Finally, in chapter 12, I offer a framework for developing a more comprehensive understanding of the superintendency and illustrate the utility of the framework with reference not only to the chapters in this text but to a selection of additional literature on district leadership, also.

NOTES

1. I am indebted to Richard Townsend for clarifying my own understanding of the range of meanings the term *politics* might have.
2. An instructionally effective district was "one in which there were high overall levels of achievement across subject areas, growth in achievement over time, and consistency in achievement across all subpopulations of students" (Peterson, Murphy, and Hallinger 1987, p. 216).

REFERENCES

Bass, B. (1985). *Leadership and performance beyond expectations.* New York: Free Press.

Bell, C., & Chase, S. (1989, April). *Women as educational leaders: Resistance and conformity.* Paper presented at the annual meeting of the American Educational Research Association, San Francisco.

Blumberg, A. (1985). *The school superintendent: Living with conflict.* New York: Teachers College Press.

Boich, J., Farquhar, R., & Leithwood, K. (1989). *The Canadian school superintendent.* Toronto: OISE Press.

Burns, J. (1978). *Leadership.* New York: Harper & Row.

Coleman, P., & LaRocque, L. (1990). *Struggling to be good enough.* New York: Falmer Press.

Crowson, R., & Morris, V. C. (1991). The superintendency and school leadership. In P. Thurston & P. Zodhiates (Eds.), *Advances in educational administration: Volume 2. School leadership.* London: JAI Press.

Cuban, L. (1988). *The managerial imperative and the practice of leadership in schools.* Albany: State University of New York Press.

Dunlap, D., & Goldman, P. (1991). Rethinking power in schools. *Educational Administration Quarterly, 27*(1), 5–29.

Dunlap, D., Goldman, P., & Conley. (1993). Facilitative power and nonstandardized solutions to school site restructuring. *Educational Administration Quarterly, 29*(1), 69–92.

Jones, B. (1987). *Teacher and principal perceptions of instructional climate and the instructional leadership of superintendents in selected Ohio school districts*. Unpublished doctoral dissertation, Miami University, Oxford, Ohio.

Leithwood, K. (1992). The move toward transformational leadership. *Educational Leadership, 49*(5), 8–12.

Levitt, B., & March, J. (1988). Organizational learning. *Annual Review of Sociology, 14*, 319–340.

Machiavelli, N. (1981). *The prince*. (G. Bull, trans.). London: Penguin Books. (Original work published 1640.)

Murphy, J. (1993). *Restructuring in Kentucky: The changing role of the superintendent and the district office*. Mimeo, Vanderbilt University, Nashville, Tennessee.

Murphy, J., & Hallinger, P. (1986). The superintendent as instructional leader: Findings from effective school districts. *Journal of Educational Administration, 24*(2), 213–36.

Peterson, K., Murphy, J., & Hallinger, P. (1987). Superintendents' perceptions of the control and coordination of the technical core in effective school districts. *Educational Administration Quarterly, 23*(1), 79–95.

Sashkin, M., & Kiser, K. (1992). *Total quality management*. Seabrook, MD: Ducochon Press.

Stewart, T. (1993). The King is dead: Why more boards are waking up and pushing out the CEO. *Fortune*, January 11, p. 34.

Tyack, D., & Hansot, E. (1982). *Managers of virtue*. New York: Basic Books.

Wimpleberg, R. (1986). The dilemma of instructional leadership and a central role for central office. In W. Greenfield (Ed.), *Instructional leadership*. Boston: Allyn & Bacon.

Wirt, F. M. (1991). The missing link in instructional leadership: The superintendent, conflict and maintenance. In P. Thurston & P. Zodhiates (Eds.), *Advances in educational administration: Vol. 2. School leadership*. London: JAI Press.

Wolf, E. (1990). The school superintendent in the reform era: Perceptions of practitioners, principals, and pundits. *Peabody Journal of Education, 65*(4), 9–30.

Yukl, G. (1989). *Leadership in organizations* (2nd Edition). Englewood Cliffs, NJ: Prentice Hall.

CHAPTER 2

How Effective Superintendents Understand Their Own Work

Edward A. Holdaway and Anthony Genge

As chief executive officers (CEOs) of their school systems, super-intendents occupy key positions in formal organizations. Many are responsible for large budgets, and for considerable numbers of different classes of employees, and are able to exert substantial influence on the effectiveness of their schools. Although they are usually far removed from classrooms, their actions can have an important, indirect effect upon student performance.

Recent research on the improvement of education has been focused more on principals and schools than on chief executive officers (CEOs) and school systems. However, in response to urgings by many (e.g., Allison 1989; Boich, Farquhar, and Leithwood 1989; Bridges 1982; Hoyle 1988; and Murphy and Hallinger 1986), some researchers in both Canada and the United States are now directing some of their efforts toward examinations of the work of CEOs (see, for example, Roberts 1991; and Hord 1991).

As with principals and their schools, CEOs have been viewed as pivotal with regard to increasing the effectiveness of their school systems. (See, for example, Aplin and Daresh 1984; Crowson and Morris 1990; March and Miklos 1983; Wissler and Ortiz 1988.) The idea that CEO involvement in instructional programs can result in increasing system effectiveness is finding support in some recent studies.

The major purpose of this study (Genge 1991) was to obtain the perceptions of effective CEOs concerning their leadership role and the actions they take to increase the effectiveness of their school systems. These perceptions were expected to provide important information about effective school system leadership and its relationships with other variables. Several researchers have recently identified that a need exists for a more detailed examination about how CEOs increase the effectiveness of their organizations. For example, Boich, Farquhar, and Leithwood (1989) concluded that "in spite of the intimate relationship between school districts and their leadership, the nature and evaluation of the superintendency has been largely neglected by scholars, writers, and those responsible for professional preparation" (p. 1).

Hoyle (1988) claimed that "the role of superintendents is one of the least thoroughly researched roles in educational administration" (p. 8). Also, Murphy and Hallinger (1986) observed that "research on the superintendency is remarkably thin, while research on the leadership role of the superintendent is sparser still" (p. 214). Similarly, Allison (1989) asserted that "further and more detailed examinations of the work and work environment of chief school officers would appear worthwhile" (p. 306). Crowson and Morris (1990) concluded that "there has been surprisingly little inquiry into how superintendents handle the internal organizational affairs of their school districts" (p. 7). Holloway (1990) concluded that still relatively few researchers are specifically interested in superintendents' behavior. Consequently, a need exists for researchers to assist school system administrators in developing a clearer idea of what they can do that will "make a difference." Research and literature from both Canada and the United States were relevant to this study because the organizational arrangements of school systems in the two countries are very similar.

REVIEW

The consolidation of school districts in Canada from the 1940s through the 1960s led, more than did any other trend, to professionalization of the superintendency (Boich, Farquhar, and Leithwood 1989, p. 3). This was assisted by a shift in authority over many matters, including the hiring of the CEO by the school districts rather than by provincial departments of education. CEOs of large school systems have become corporate executives rather than public servants. Furthermore, school principals and teachers have gained substantial influence over decisions affecting schools.

In an early process study, Holdaway (1969) examined the interactions that occurred at meetings of thirteen school boards in Alberta. He concluded that superintendents were perceived as potentially influential, that their effectiveness at meetings heavily depended upon expectations held for them, and that they behaved in widely different ways at board meetings. This suggested that many different styles of operation are potentially useful but situationally dependent.

Competencies required by provincially appointed superintendents in Alberta were studied by Campbell and Holdaway (1970). The fifty-six superintendents who participated emphasized the importance of being able to understand human behavior: The fifty-three board chairs who participated were most concerned about the superintendents' ability to supervise educational activities and personnel.

In the report of his inquiry into the Alberta school superintendency, Downey (1976) noted that "many uncertainties, ambiguities, misperceptions, and even conflicts attend the superintendent's role and position in the local school system" (p. 31). Shortly after Downey's report was released, Ingram and Miklos (1977) conducted the study, commissioned by Alberta Education, *Guidelines for Employment of School Superintendents*; they emphasized the superintendent's role in executive, managerial, educational, and public relations functions, as well as in policy development, and saw the superintendent as being extremely important in maintaining effective relationships (pp. 22–23, 31, 65). The Alberta School Act (1988) establishes the superintendent as chief executive officer of the school board, but does not further specify his or her duties.

In a time-on-task study, Duignan (1979) observed eight Alberta superintendents for a period of thirty-four days in order to describe their administrative behavior. Superintendents' behavior, he concluded, was not as planned and organized as the literature at that time suggested. Furthermore, superintendents in this study acted both internally and externally as "spokesman, arbitrator, mediator and politician," (p. 210). Duignan also reported a set of commonly agreed upon superintendent tasks, based on a review of others' research. These included public relations activities; advising the board; budget preparation; instructional improvement and evaluation; personnel selection, development, and evaluation; pupil accounting; managing, or advising on, property, equipment, and supplies; and policy development and execution.

In another Alberta study, Cymbol (1986) found that superintendents were both expected and perceived to perform a wide range of tasks. Both trustees and superintendents attached great significance to an educational leader role that involved working with professional staff in providing high-quality education to students. Green (1988) concluded that the important tasks performed by Alberta superintendents were policy development, evaluation, working with trustees, public relations, managing staff, and business management. He found that the size of the school system was associated with "significant differences in task expectations" (p. 199). Except for the lack of focus on instructional leadership, Green's and Duignan's lists of tasks were similar.

Based on evidence collected in Ontario, McLeod (1984) reported that

> confusion as to whether the senior administrator should perform as a 'mover or shaker' or as a functionary often leads to disillusionment and mutual distrust. . . . Without realizing it, the chief executive's frustration and suspicion closely approximate that which he creates in school trustees who resent his perception that they should be prevented from 'dabbling in administration' or from 'tampering with the curriculum.' (p. 187)

Allison (1989), in analyzing data to determine the roles and responsibilities of central office administrative positions in Ontario, concluded that CEOs were "overwhelmingly generalist in nature" (p. 304) and that they were system-focused rather than school-focused.

In addition to the primarily Canadian studies reviewed to this point, a number of studies carried out in the United States and reported at the 1990 annual meeting of the American Educational Research Association provided relevant background to the present study. These included, for example, Armstrong's (1990) study of superintendents' communications networks in Washington and Idaho, Johnson's (1990) study of the activities of twelve newly appointed superintendents, and Holloway's (1990) examination of the interactions of six superintendents with school board members outside board meetings. Together these studies supported the value of contingency theory in understanding superintendents' work, and demonstrated the value of focusing intensively on the work of a small number of superintendents.

A useful starting point for this study was Georgopoulous and Tannenbaum's (1957) definition of organizational effectiveness: "the extent to which an organization, given certain resources and means, fulfills its objectives without incapacitating its means and resources and without placing undue strain upon its members" (pp. 536–37). CEOs' effectiveness was best defined as the extent to which CEOs fulfill organizational goals while simultaneously facilitating fulfillment of personal needs.

RESEARCH QUESTIONS

The general question pursued in this study was, How do effective CEOs administer their school systems? In which activities, by what methods, and in which interactions do CEOs become involved in performing their roles? More specifically, the study asked these questions:

1. What are the most important priorities of CEOs, and how are these achieved?

2. What is meant by the term *effective educational leadership,* and how is this reflected by CEOs in school systems?

3. What criteria (benchmarks, indicators) are used by CEOs to judge the overall effectiveness of their school systems?

4. What factors contribute to the effectiveness of CEOs?

5. What criteria do CEOs use to judge their own and others' effectiveness?

6. What are the major constraints (barriers, obstacles) that tend to reduce the effectiveness of CEOs, and how are these constraints overcome?

7. What is the nature of CEOs' interactions with each important stakeholder group?

8. What are the CEOs' most important bases of influence when they deal with board members and with other educators?

9. What are CEOs' most important personal values, and how do they reflect these in their school systems?

10. How does holding the position of CEO affect their personal lives?

11. What are the major sources of satisfaction and dissatisfaction of the most effective CEOs?

METHODOLOGY

Selection of Sample

All 63 Alberta CEOs who were full-time, not on leave, responsible for only one school system, and in their current position for at least two years, were eligible to be selected for the study. Members of a panel of 14 judges—eight from the central and regional offices of Alberta Education (the provincial department of education), and three each from the senior staff of the Alberta Teachers' Association and the Alberta School Trustees' Association—participated in the selection. Previous studies by Aplin and Daresh (1984), Hoyle (1988), Murphy and Hallinger (1986), and Peters and Waterman (1982) also used similar panels for subject selection. Judges were presented with the list of eligible CEOs and the names of their school systems, and were free to use whatever criteria they wished to use in identification of the "most organizationally effective superintendents." (Had the researchers provided a list of criteria, the responses might have been unduly biased toward CEOs who performed well on those criteria; further, some important criteria may have been omitted from the list.) Forty-one CEOs received recommendations from one or more judges. The 15 who received the highest number of recommendations (from 6 to 10) were asked to participate in the study. These did not include CEOs of the four largest systems, who were eliminated because their systems were vastly different from the other systems in the province and because their anonymity could not be guaranteed.

All 15 CEOs who received the highest frequency of endorsements agreed to participate in the research. Our claim is not that these were the *only* effective CEOs in the province, but rather that the 15 selected were the most effective *as perceived by a panel of judges.* Only 13 of the 15 CEOs actually participated in the study, because two from public school districts consented to be involved in a final pilot study. The 13 CEOs in the final sample were employed in four public school districts, two separate (Roman Catholic) school districts, two school divisions, and five counties.

They should most appropriately be referred to as "13 of the most effective CEOs in Alberta."

School districts employing the selected CEOs had a mean enrollment of approximately 4,000 students. The mean number of teachers and schools in the systems were 230 and 12.3, while the mean number of years of experience as superintendents of the participants was 11.5. The two smallest systems did not engage the services of assistant superintendents, whereas the larger systems employed a number of assistant superintendents. Male and female CEOs were included in the population, although only masculine gender nomenclature is used throughout this paper, to preserve anonymity. For the same reason, the ranges of the variables identified above are not included.

After interviews with the 13 CEOs had been conducted and analyzed, the 14 judges were contacted and asked to identify the three behavioral characteristics possessed by the most effective school superintendents in Alberta. This strategy was suggested by two noninvolved educators who had read the preliminary report. The frequencies of mention of the behavioral characteristics provided by the 12 judges who responded were as follows: Behaves ethically (8), Has interpersonal skills (6), Communicates effectively (4), Articulates a vision (3), Learns about and demonstrates knowledge of educational developments (3), Advocates education strongly (2), Solicits and utilizes input (2), Is decisive (2), Is sensitive to others (2), Takes risks (1), Is politically astute (1), Is intelligent (1), and Is consistent (1). The highest numbers of first mentions were obtained by Behaves ethically (5), Has interpersonal skills (3), and Articulates a vision (2).

Development of Instruments

A semistructured, open-ended interview schedule consisting of seventeen questions was developed based on matters considered relevant in the literature. The preliminary instrument was presented to two practicing CEOs and two professors for initial feedback. A refined instrument was pilot-tested with two of the CEOs identified by the judges and refined a final time.

After analyses of the interview protocols and system documents had been completed, a follow-up interview questionnaire was developed to obtain some clarification, additional information, and general reactions to information presented in eight tables.

Collection of Data

Interviews, ranging in length from 75 to 135 minutes, were conducted by one or other of the two researchers. These interviews were tape-recorded, and typed transcripts were prepared.

CEOs also were asked to provide the following documents: district mission and goal statements; principal, teacher, and student evaluation policies; annual board reports for the previous year; district newsletters from the previous year; agendas and minutes from central office and principals' meetings for the previous year; and their districts' organizational chart.

Analyses

Interview protocols were analyzed by one researcher. Numerous readings of the transcripts and repeated listenings to the original tapes were undertaken to identify commonalities, differences, and major themes and subthemes, as was done by Allison (1989). The second researcher spot-checked the coding of the first researcher. When coding problems arose, these were discussed until consensus was reached. Documents were examined for additional insight and to check upon information provided by the interviews.

Reliability and Validity

The reliability of the interview coding was addressed by having the two researchers arrive at a consensus solution when coding difficulty was experienced. Whether the CEOs would answer the same questions differently at another time is open to conjecture. Use of a follow-up interview allowed CEOs to reflect upon their earlier positions. In general, a high degree of stability was noted between responses of individuals in the two interviews.

Did we actually obtain accurate information about how the most effective CEOs think and act? We had to assume that the expert judges had selected a group of superintendents who were considered to be highly effective. We also had to assume that the CEOs were truthful.

RESULTS

In this section, results are reported in response to each of our specific research questions, using information provided from both the initial and the follow-up interviews.

Highest Priorities of CEOs

Respondents were asked to identify their three highest priorities. These were classified as system priorities, personnel priorities, and instructional priorities and were mentioned 13, 20, and 6 times, respectively. CEOs usually emphasized that their priorities were in rank order — that is, the first-mentioned priority was their first priority. Consequently, responses were weighted (3 for priority 1; 2 for priority 2; and 1 for priority 3), producing weighted totals of 31 (system priorities), 32 (personnel priorities), and 15 (instructional priorities). However, the first priorities mentioned had a distribution of 7 for the system, 2 for personnel, and 4 for instructional. Across categories, the unweighted individual priorities that were identified as a first priority by at least one CEO were planning (3 mentions), providing appropriate programs (3), developing a mission statement (2), fulfilling the role of CEO (1), identifying needs (1), maintaining good relationships (1), setting roles (1), and focusing on teaching and learning (1). When weighted, the highest totals were obtained for planning (10 points), providing appropriate programs (9), developing a mission statement (6), communicating effectively (5), and maintaining good relationships (5). When developing a mission statement, identifying needs, and setting goals were viewed as integral aspects of the planning process, planning emerged as by far the most commonly identified priority area.

CEOs were then asked to identify the methods they used to achieve their priorities. A large number of methods were mentioned only once. Holding a retreat with the board was mentioned by three superintendents. Similar diversity was obtained for the methods used to achieve personnel and instructional priorities. To demonstrate this diversity, the following methods were identified as functions involved in "top-down" planning: Examine the futurist literature; examine emergent trends by environmental scanning; hold a retreat with the board; assess where we are, where we want to be, and how to get there; establish three-year priorities; and engage the whole system (i.e., community and staff) in developing plans at all levels.

CEOs were also asked to identify their educational program priorities; no specific number was requested. The number of priorities identified ranged from one to five. These responses were classified into academic (12 mentions), special needs (9), social

(8), technological (3), and spiritual (1). Five mentions were obtained for each of the following subpriorities: implementing the programs of Alberta Education properly, providing programs for special-needs students, and developing programs to alleviate social problems. Two mentions were obtained for each of the following priorities: ensuring that all students are literate, developing communication skills, and delivering programs or technology.

Leadership Behaviors

Because reputationally effective CEOs had been identified, obtaining their perceptions about how they provided educational leadership seemed to be particularly pertinent. Fifty responses were obtained; each superintendent provided 1 to 7 responses. All superintendents mentioned being action-oriented and being an effective delegator. Being an example (6 mentions), involving all stakeholders (5), and providing people with adequate and relevant information (4) were the next most frequently identified behaviors.

System Effectiveness Criteria

Because we assumed that the effectiveness of CEOs is closely related to system effectiveness, respondents were asked to identify criteria that they used in judging the effectiveness of their own school systems. Each respondent provided from three to ten criteria. The most frequent responses, 55 in total, related to student performance. All 13 CEOs identified level of student performance on both provincial achievement tests and provincial grade 12 diploma examinations. The level of student performance on teacher-made tests and the Canadian Test of Basic Skills were each mentioned three times. Nine also identified level of student satisfaction on surveys as a criterion.

The next most frequently mentioned categories of criteria related to (a) staff satisfaction and performance, and (b) public satisfaction, which were mentioned 25 and 22 times, respectively. Ten CEOs identified levels of staff satisfaction determined by surveys, while 6 listed the degree to which there is peace and harmony. Other effectiveness criteria were mentioned less frequently: Three identified the results of school evaluations, and two the degree to which the board accomplishes its priorities.

Factors Contributing to CEOs' Effectiveness

CEOs identified from two to seven factors contributing to their effectiveness. These were categorized into personal and situational factors. The most common personal factor was having skills in dealing with people (6 mentions), having a sense of direction (3), having a sound knowledge base (3), and being politically astute (2). Situational factors were less frequently identified; having an action-oriented board was the most common response in this category, identified by 2 CEOs.

CEO Effectiveness Criteria

With respect to judging the effectiveness of CEOs, each respondent identified three to eight criteria. Most frequently mentioned were annual formal board evaluations (12), formal and informal feedback from parents (11), informal feedback from teachers (10), informal feedback from principals (9), informal feedback from trustees (8), and informal feedback from central office staff (8). These responses did not identify actual criteria. Consequently, in the follow-up interview, the CEOs were asked to provide examples of more specific criteria; these included achievement of board priorities, provision of sound advice, respect, trust, and board confidence. However, in the initial interviews, CEOs clearly placed considerable weight upon the opinions of board members and feedback from all relevant constituent groups and less weight upon the criteria that people use in making their judgments.

Constraints upon CEOs' Effectiveness

Most interviewees identified three constraints upon their effectiveness, providing a total of 34 responses. Cited most frequently were political constraints, especially those related to the school board (6 mentions), time constraints (5), financial constraints (5), and constraints associated with an oversized agenda (4). Bureaucracy and change received 2 mentions. Ten constraints were mentioned once each.

CEOs' Interactions

CEOs interacted quite frequently with their chairpersons, who expected to be kept informed of developments and problems.

These discussions occurred mainly in the area of the school system office, but also at conferences and workshops. Meetings of CEOs with their chairs were especially important prior to board meetings. Considerable interaction also occurred with individual trustees. However, social interactions were far less frequent, both with chairpersons and other trustees. [These results mirror findings reported in chapter 3.—Editor]

As could be expected, the CEOs were continually in contact with other central office staff members. Also, nearly all visited principals, and to a lesser extent teachers and students, as frequently as their schedules allowed. In their role as the key administrator, these CEOs also communicated as much as possible with their support staff, service clubs, and professional associations.

Bases of CEOs' Influence

CEOs attempted to influence board members by relying on knowledge/information (9 mentions), trust (8), experience (7), and openness and honesty (5). They influenced other educators by using the same approaches but also by showing that their opinions were valued, asking them to perform tasks, demonstrating desirable performance, providing time to reach a decision, being credible, providing needed resources, and being supportive.

Values

Interviewees were asked to identify their most important personal values and how these were incorporated into their behavior. From 2 to 5 values were listed by each, for a total of 47. The most frequently mentioned were integrity (8), honesty (7), people's contributions/strengths (5), and education/children (4). Three mentions were obtained by each of hard work, family, and positive attitudes, and two each by respect of others, teamwork, and sincerity.

Effect of Job on CEOs' Personal Lives

Most CEOs reflected first upon the negative effects of their job on their personal lives; these mainly related to the reduction in the quality of their family life because of the job's time requirements, especially with respect to night meetings. Many clearly were concerned about the impact on their spouses and children, although to some extent this was offset by family support and increased quality of the time that their families did spend together. Nearly all found the job to be quite stressful. When specifically asked about positive effects, CEOs mentioned opportunities to do more because of a higher salary, the flexibility of scheduling their work, and the ability to attend conferences and build a network of contacts.

CEOs' Satisfaction and Dissatisfaction

When asked to name the three aspects of their work that provided them with the greatest satisfaction and the three that provided the greatest dissatisfaction, by far the most commonly identified source of satisfaction was the inherent variety of the position (7 mentions). Three mentions were obtained for each of problem-solving, the work itself, positive feedback, and seeing a project implemented successfully. Two mentions each were given for having staff or students succeed, doing your work well, feeling that you are doing something worthwhile, having an enthusiastic staff, seeing that the system is meeting its goals, observing happy teachers, and having a community supportive of education. Six other sources of satisfaction were each mentioned once.

Concerning dissatisfiers, workload variables were the most common—four cited lack of time, two identified the large amount of paperwork, and two the multitude of jobs to be done. The level of provincial funding for education and the presence of employees with poor attitudes were each reported three times. Political actions affecting the education of students was mentioned by two CEOs. Seventeen other sources of dissatisfaction also surfaced, including hungry students, loss of confidence in an individual, and the inability to provide support to all who need it.

Overall Categorizations

The underlying orientation of each CEO was assessed by examining each interview transcript holistically. This analysis, undertaken by a third researcher in conjunction with one of the original researchers, proved to be a challenging task because the interview questions and their answers covered a wide range of topics and activities. Nevertheless, these analyses of orientation or overall emphasis are offered with reasonable confidence because of the consistency with which these factors appeared throughout the interviews. Underlying orientations included these: efficiency/ action/management by objectives (4 CEOs); people orientation (3); team approach (2); vision (1); sensitivity to needs (1); educational advocacy (1); and suitable programs (1). These thrusts obviously were quite diverse, but their listing here should not be taken to mean that they were completely mutually exclusive.

SUMMARY AND DISCUSSION

Responses to the specific questions raised by the study can be summed up as follows:

1. Planning was the priority most frequently mentioned by the CEOs. Their highest educational priorities were proper implementation of government programs, provision of programs for students with special needs, and development of programs to help alleviate social problems. A wide variety of methods was used to achieve the CEOs' priorities.

2. The main behaviors used by these CEOs to demonstrate educational leadership were being action-oriented and being an effective delegator.

3. The effectiveness of their school systems was judged mainly by student performance and satisfaction of staff, students, and the public.

4. Having skills in dealing with people, having a sense of direction, and having a sound knowledge base were the factors most frequently mentioned as contributing to CEOs' effectiveness.

5. The effectiveness of CEOs was judged mainly by annual formal board evaluations, which assessed matters such as achievement of board priorities, and feedback from constituent groups.

6. The main constraints upon effectiveness were related to politics, lack of time, shortage of finances, and the number of tasks to be performed.

7. CEOs interacted frequently with board chairs, other trustees, other central office staff, principals, and community groups.

8. The most important bases of CEOs' influence were knowledge/information, trust, experience, and openness and honesty.

9. The values most important to them were integrity, honesty, people's contributions/strengths, and education/children.

10. CEOs were inclined to identify more negative than positive effects of their jobs upon their personal lives; reduced time available for being with their families was mentioned most frequently.

11. The most frequently identified source of satisfaction was the variety of tasks involved in the CEO's job; for dissatisfaction, the workload emerged first.

The CEOs were acutely aware of their political environment, had clear understandings of their relationships with their school boards, saw the need to communicate effectively with relevant publics, and intentionally made time available to visit their schools. Their responses also reinforced conclusions drawn in previous research concerning the ambiguous, demanding, influential, and pivotal nature of the role of the CEOs of school systems. However, variety was a source of satisfaction to these CEOs. Previous research has suggested that (a) CEOs can have a substantial influence on their systems; (b) quite different CEO leadership styles can lead to effective outcomes; (c) personal interactions, including those with trustees are extremely important for CEOs; and (d) CEOs tend to be educational generalists and tend to focus upon the school system more than upon individual schools. Evidence from this study supports these findings. In addition, there emerged three general themes—a sense of vision, the importance of people, and the need to be visible—that warrant more-extended discussion.

Developing Visions. CEOs in this study had a clear vision for their systems that they were able to translate into mission statements, goals, and objectives, all with a student focus. They readily identified priorities for the facilitation and achievement of this vision and were very involved in many operational aspects of their systems. Large amounts of information were collected about their school systems, and they were able to organize the information into patterns or configurations relevant to their vision.

Importance of People. Concern for and about people emerged as a dominant theme. This did not mean that the CEOs were always "nice" to people; it meant being honest and open, even at the risk of sometimes being critical. They believed that people wanted to be involved and to participate in decision making and that this involvement would lead to feelings of ownership in the enterprise. Feelings of ownership were developed by promoting involvement and teamwork, and by valuing the worth and dignity of every individual who had an interest in the organization. Some advocated that universities should provide superintendents with training and background knowledge in the "softer dimensions" of leadership, to help them with this role.

CEOs' priorities were not achieved in isolation; the active involvement and commitment of many constituent groups were required. In the "big picture," individuals and groups external to the organization seemed to play significant roles. The input and involvement of parents, business organizations, community service organizations, and churches were actively sought. These groups often were significant players in the formulation of vision for a system.

Being Visible. CEOs were profoundly interested in curriculum and instructional matters. These interests led them to spend considerable time in schools interacting with principals, teachers, and students on everyday activities. Superintendents indicated that, to perform their tasks properly, they needed to visit and be visible at school sites.

Researchers have recognized the need to establish strong systems for principals (see, for example, Sapone 1983; Aplin and Daresh 1984; Murphy and Hallinger 1986; Roberts 1991). Superintendents in this study averaged seven hours per week in schools. During these visits they nearly always met with principals and discussed a variety of issues. In addition, they visited classrooms and interacted with teachers and students. Similar findings were reported by Murphy, Hallinger, and Peterson (1985); especially consistent with this study were the oral and visual aspects of the supervisory process. Superintendents felt it desirable to be on school sites, to perform informal monitoring, and to offer advice and support to principals on a continuing basis. Principals, as

Gunn and Holdaway (1986) recommended, "were left to run schools as they saw fit," but they received the expert advice and support of superintendents. This finding appears to be at variance with Hannaway and Sproull (1978–79), Peterson (1984), and Crowson and Morris (1990), who reported an "administrative distancing" between central offices and school sites.

Several important implications for research and practice are evident from this study. With respect to research, other studies could benefit from examining how the more effective CEOs actually influence the effectiveness of their school systems as organizations, especially with regard to their planning and communication activities. Their direct influence upon subsystems, especially schools; the effect of various constraints upon CEOs' effectiveness; and differences in the behavior of the more effective and less effective CEOs.

Twelve implications and recommendations for CEOs' practices are warranted by the study:

1. CEOs should recognize that their roles have symbolic importance in creating priorities and values throughout their school systems.

2. An important aspect of CEOs' work involves focusing on schools and emphasizing the centrality of the teaching-learning process.

3. Open communication with individuals and groups is essential if CEOs are to obtain their commitment.

4. CEOs should ensure that the roles of various actors in their systems are clearly understood. This especially involves the separation of roles of trustees and CEOs concerning policy development and administration. Although this separation is not a new concern, it is still important and deserves continuing attention.

5. Several writers have characterized the CEO's position as a lonely one, but the numerous consultations held by CEOs in this study led us to question this characterization.

6. Appropriate, distinctive performance indicators should be identified for each CEO.

7. CEOs need to be visible and accessible to principals and teachers.

8. CEOs should actively represent the interests of the school system in the community.

9. CEOs should focus on important matters and delegate all others.

10. Effective CEOs will in future need to be more consultative and less directive.

11. Although much of the work of CEOs is fragmented, they need to have a clear focus and established goals.

12. CEOs should ensure that appropriate attention is paid to the evaluation and development of their principals.

These implications and recommendations are based upon research with a small sample of CEOs, identified as being among the most effective in one Canadian province. Despite the limited size of the sample, many crucial issues emerged that should be addressed by all CEOs. Of special importance would appear to be the relationships among the effectiveness of CEOs, of their school systems, and of their schools. Although the study yielded defensible implications and recommendations, most of these still tend to be rather general; the ways in which these general recommendations are operationalized in particular settings remains the preserve of professional judgment.

NOTES

An earlier version of this paper was presented at the annual conference of the Canadian Association for the Study of Educational Administration held at Kingston, Ontario, June 1991. The financial support provided for this study by the Scholarship and Research Awards Committee of the Faculty of Education, University of Alberta, is gratefully acknowledged. Substantial help was provided by the following people: David Jones, with the analyses; Tracey Kremer, with typing the manuscript; and Eva Radford, in reviewing earlier drafts.

The financial support provided for this study by the Scholarship and Research Awards Committee of the Faculty of Education, University of Alberta, is gratefully acknowledged. Substantial help was provided by the following people: David Jones, with the analyses; Tracey Kremer, with typing the manuscript; and Eva Radford, in reviewing earlier drafts.

REFERENCES

Allison, D. J. (1989). Exploring the work of school chiefs: The case of the Ontario director of education. *Alberta Journal of Educational Research, 25*(4), 292–307.

Aplin, N. D., & Daresh, J. C. (1984). The superintendent as an educational leader. *Planning and Changing, 15*(4), 209–18.

Armstrong, M. A. (1990, April). *An examination of public school superintendents interpersonal networks in Washington and Idaho.* Paper presented at the annual meeting of the American Educational Research Association, Boston.

Boich, J. W., Farquhar, R. H., & Leithwood, K. A. (1989). *The Canadian school superintendent.* Toronto: OISE Press.

Bridges, E. M. (1982). Research on the school administrator: The state of the art, 1967–1980. *Educational Administration Quarterly, 18*(3), 12–33.

Campbell, L. A., & Holdaway, E. A. (1970). Perceptions of competencies required by superintendents. *Canadian Administrator, 9*(7), 31–34.

Crowson, R. L., & Morris, V. C. (1990, April). *The superintendency and school leadership.* Paper presented at the annual meeting of the American Educational Research Association, Boston.

Cymbol, S. (1986). *The role of the locally appointed superintendent of schools in Alberta.* Unpublished master's thesis, University of Alberta, Edmonton.

Downey, L. W. (1976). *The school superintendency in Alberta—1976: A report of an inquiry.* Edmonton: Alberta Education.

Duignan, P. A. (1979). *Administrative behavior of school superintendents: A descriptive study.* Unpublished doctoral dissertation, University of Alberta, Edmonton.

Genge, A. (1991). *Effective school superintendents.* Unpublished doctoral dissertation, University of Alberta, Edmonton.

Georgopoulous, B. S., & Tannenbaum, A. S. (1957). A study of organizational effectiveness. *American Sociological Review, 22*(5), 534–40.

Green, W. J. (1988). *Role of the superintendent.* Unpublished doctoral dissertation, University of Alberta, Edmonton.

Gunn, J. A., & Holdaway, E. A. (1986). Perceptions of effectiveness, influence and satisfaction of senior high school principals. *Educational Administration Quarterly, 22*(2), 43–62.

Hannaway, J., & Sproull, L.S. (1978–79). Who's running the show? Coordination and control in educational organizations. *Administrators' Notebook, 27*(9), 1–4.

Holdaway, E. A. (1969). Superintendents and school board meetings. *Canadian Administrator, 8*(7), 27–30.

32   EDWARD A. HOLDAWAY AND ANTHONY GENGE

Holloway, W. H. (1990, April). *The superintendency: Interactions with board members outside the school board meeting.* Paper presented at the annual meeting of the American Educational Research Association, Boston.

Hord, S. M. (1991, April). *District level executives' perceptions about providing leadership for excellence.* Paper presented at the annual meeting of the American Educational Research Association, Chicago.

Hoyle, J. R. (1988, February). *The 21st-century superintendent: A great motivator. Paul B. Salmon memorial lecture.* Paper presented at the annual meeting of the American Association of School Administrators, Las Vegas.

Ingram, E., & Miklos, E. (1977). *Guidelines for employment of school superintendents.* Edmonton: University of Alberta, Department of Educational Administration.

Johnson, S. M. (1990, April). *A study of new superintendents.* Paper presented at the annual meeting of the American Educational Research Association, Boston.

March, M. E., & Miklos, E. (1983). Dynamics of control over educational decisions. *Alberta Journal of Educational Research, 29*(1), 1–14.

McLeod, G. T. (1984). The work of school board chief executive officers. *Canadian Journal of Education, 9*(2), 171–90.

Murphy, J., & Hallinger, P. (1986). The superintendent as instructional leader: Findings from effective school districts. *Journal of Educational Administration, 4*(2), 213–36.

Peters, T. J., & Waterman, R. H. (1982). *In search of excellence.* New York: Warner.

Peterson, K. D. (1984). Mechanisms of administrative control over managers in educational organizations. *Administrative Science Quarterly, 29*, 573–97.

Roberts, L. M. (1991, April). *Constructing a practical framework for the superintendent's leadership role in school reform.* Paper presented at the annual meeting of the American Educational Research Association, Chicago.

Sapone, C. V. (1983). A research review: Perceptions on characteristics of effective schools. *NASSP Bulletin, 67*(465), 66–70.

Wissler, D. F., & Ortiz, F. I. (1988). *The superintendent's leadership in school reform.* New York: Falmer Press.

CHAPTER 3

Chiefs and Chairs: Working Relationships between Effective CEOs and Board of Education Chairpersons

Derek J. Allison, Patricia A. Allison, and Helen A. McHenry

Although the literature reveals a continuing fascination with relationships between school boards and their superintendents, surprisingly little attention has been given to examining how chief superintendents and board chairpersons interact with each other in attending to their respective responsibilities. This omission seems at least partly attributable to historical and organizational factors in the evolution of the superintendency in the United States, from whence the great bulk of the pertinent literature emanates. This literature is typically predicated on assumptions rooted in the continuing struggle between expert and political control over schools that has dominated educational administration in the United States throughout this century (e.g., Allison 1991b; Blumberg 1985; Callahan 1962; Carlson 1972; Tyack 1976; Tyack and Hansot, 1982). Not surprisingly, perhaps, this literature tends to view matters from the perspective of superintendents, with boards typically being treated as faceless, often fickle, political entities. Apart from other limitations, such an approach predisposes readers and researchers to overlook both the existence and the role of board chairpersons, implicitly precluding investigations of how they might or do work together with their senior administrators in attending to organizational affairs.

But the literature of educational administration is not alone in overlooking the dynamics of this relationship. In his recent study of CEOs and chairpersons of National Health Service organizations in the United Kingdom, Stewart (1991) pointed to the lack of attention given in the broader literature to "the relationship between chairmen and chief executives in terms of what they actually do, and how they affect each others role" (p. 511). This more general neglect is curious given the theoretical importance of the two positions and the practical desirability of establishing and maintaining efficient links between administrative and governance subsystems in organizations, particularly service organizations financed by public funds. The importance of such links has recently been highlighted by Carver (1991) in his discussion of effective boards in profit and nonprofit organizations. In common with the broader literature, however, Carver offers little comment, description, or analysis regarding the nature of effective working relationships between chiefs and chairs.

This chapter reports a study that specifically investigated working relationships between reputationally effective chief administrators and the chairpersons of their boards. Earlier work (Allison 1991a; Allison and Allison 1988; Hickcox and Stapleton 1970; McLeod 1984) pointed to the importance of this relationship, and the broader project in which this study was embedded provided an opportunity for closer investigation.

FRAMEWORK

Following Weber (1922/1978), Parsons (1960), and Thompson (1967), all but the smallest formal organizations contain distinct technical, administrative, and governance subsystems. Additional specialized subsystems can be identified in some organizations (e.g., Mintzberg 1979), but these three generic subsystems appear to be common to all modern organizations of at least medium size and complexity. The technical subsystem contains the productive apparatus and core technology of the organization. In school systems this includes schools, classrooms, students, curriculum, and, although this remains an open theoretical and empirical question, perhaps teachers (Allison 1980, 1983).

Administrative subsystems regulate organizational operations and member behavior. This subsystem was the focus of Weber's (1978) now-classic discussion of bureaucracy. In accord with Weber's observations, administrative positions in contemporary organizations are normally occupied by individuals appointed under contract who hold formal qualifications certifying appropriate technical competence. Also in accord with Weber's analysis, positions in administrative subsystems are organized in a formal hierarchy. In contemporary school systems the administrative subsystem is composed of superintendents, principals, and possibly teachers. Although actual titles and duties vary, the dominant position in this hierarchy will be referred to in this chapter by the generic titles of *CEO* or *chief*.

Governance subsystems are formally responsible for establishing policy, supervising the financial affairs of the organization, and hiring, monitoring, and, when necessary, dismissing administrative officials. The degree to which the governance subsystem of any particular organization actually determines policy and exerts direct control over these and related functions is empirically variable, but its formal responsibility for these matters is normally clearly specified in relevant charter legislation or other pertinent legal documents. Wide variation is evident nonetheless in both the form and the assigned powers of governance subsystems, a characteristic that may have encouraged both Weber and Parsons to elide detailed discussion of this element of formal organization. As a general rule, however, governance subsystems appear to be constituted so as to represent the interests of the clients, shareholders, owners, or other formal beneficiaries of the organization. Typically, members of governance subsystems are elected or appointed to represent such interests. Governance subsystems are thus essentially political arenas, with members being required to meet in formal conclave in order to decide questions and enact policy. Governing subsystems are known by a wide variety of names, (e.g., *cabinets, councils, soviets*), but the most common contemporary term is boards, as in *board of directors, board of governors,* or *board of trustees.* In Canada and the United States governance subsystems of public school systems normally take the form of an elected or appointed board of trustees who are understood to represent the interests of the community or communities served by the school system.

Because members of governance subsystems must meet in formal session in order to actually govern the organization, it is convenient and common for one member to be designated to coordinate and preside at meetings, and to represent the board at other times. For members of governance subsystems who hold such responsibilities, the term *chair* or *chairperson* will be used in the balance of this paper, although other titles, such as *president* or *director*, are also in common use. The generic office of chair, it is worth noting, represents the only formal hierarchical distinction normally present in governance subsystems.

The preceding outline defines the broad conceptual framework for the study reported here. How CEOs and chairs understand each other's roles and work, and how they work with each other, were the general questions for the study. It seems evident that the CEO, as the superordinate administrator, senior employee, and formal leader of an organization, will necessarily have a special relationship with the governance subsystem. As the chief administrative official, she or he is accountable to the board for the overall operation, health, and success of the organization. The CEO also provides the main conduit for the flow of information and expectations between the administrative and the governance subsystems. In this respect, members of the governance subsystem can legitimately expect their CEO to provide, on the basis of his or her particular expertise, timely and sensible advice on policy needs and options, procedural matters, and difficult governance decisions.

Yet this is an implicitly difficult relationship, fraught for both parties with complex dangers that are exacerbated in the absence of shared understandings of respective roles and responsibilities. These inherent difficulties and dangers are compounded by the temporary-system characteristics of governing boards, which officially exist only during the comparatively brief periods when the members are assembled in formal conclave. In this context, the chairpersons occupy a position that enables them to play a potentially crucial role in helping form and modulate the relationship between the CEO and the governing board. They can be available for consultation when the corporate board is not in session, and they are in a position to inform the CEO about political concerns and pressures and other pertinent matters. Chairs also provide a convenient "back channel" through which CEOs can keep board members informed about organizational affairs, and a sounding board against which CEOs can test ideas and options before taking action.

The form and manner in which chiefs and chairs structure and conduct their working relationships thus assumes both theoretical and practical importance. Each is in a position to substantially help or hinder the other and, thus, the overall operation of the organization. Formal and conventional role expectations for each position, however, may preclude the easy establishment of cooperative relationships within the official arenas of the organization, encouraging chiefs and chairs to deal with each other in the no-man's-land, as it were, between the borders of the bureaucracy and the board.

The Literature

This conceptual framework obviously oversimplifies organizational realities. In business organizations, for example, it is not uncommon for the positions of chair and CEO to be combined into a single office, bearing a title like *managing director*. This practice has attracted continuing attention in the broader literature (Brown 1976; Puckey 1968) and prompted Chitayat (1985) to undertake one of the few focused studies of working relationships between CEOs and chairs. In the Israeli business and service organizations that provided the setting for Chitayat's study, CEOs were expected to initiate strategic directions and decisions, subject to final review and approval of their boards. Chitayat was able to distinguish separate functions for CEOs and chairs, but he concluded there were no compelling reasons for the two roles to be separated within the kinds of organizations studied. He observed, nonetheless, that the most common reason for separating the two functions is a "need for checks and balances on the CEO" (p. 69). He also noted that this need can have a more pressing priority in state-owned companies, where there is a more obvious concern with "reviewing and controlling the CEO's activities in order to ensure the proper use of resources and the flow of information" (p. 69). In cases where the positions of CEO and chair are separated, Chitayat stressed the implicit complementarity of the two roles, and thus the desirability of establishing good working relationships.

The only other prior study of working relationships between CEOs and chairs located in the literature was Stewart's (1991). In this case, there was a clear separation between functions of CEOs and chairs in the National Health organizations studied in the United Kingdom. Chairs were appointed to their offices by the secretary of state for the government department concerned, and usually they were retired individuals who had amassed considerable business, administrative, or political experience. Stewart's findings highlighted the crucial importance of the complementary roles that chairs and CEOs define and play for themselves at the intersection of the administrative and governance subsystems. He identified five distinct, but not necessarily exclusive, roles played by chairs: partner, where the chair works closely with the CEO; executive, where the chair gives explicit instructions to the CEO; mentor, with the chair acting as coach and counselor; consultant, where the chair waits to be asked for advice; and distant, where the chair's actions are restricted to presiding at formal meetings and attending official functions. Stewart concluded that "a relationship that worked as partnership seemed to make for a synergy of effort" that was beneficial for both CEOs and chairs and the organization as a whole, but noted that the possibility of attaining this "will depend upon whether at least one of the two thinks of the relationship in that way" (p. 525). He cautioned, however, that chairs who work closely with CEOs might find it difficult to "retain sufficient detachment to appraise" the interests of constituents represented by the governance subsystem (p. 524).

The importance of the relationship between the CEO and the chair in publicly funded school systems has already been observed. In their report of a conference examining the role of board chairs, Hickcox and Stapleton (1970) stressed the crucial importance of the relationship between chairs and CEOs but offered little comment on the nature of this relationship. Some insight into the relationship is provided in brief articles by Isherwood and his colleagues reporting the results of a Canadian survey of trustees and superintendents (Isherwood et al. 1984; Isherwood and Osgoode 1986). Two main points were stressed in these reports: First, chairs and chiefs often work together in developing and setting the agenda for formal board meetings; second, trustees, and thus presumably chairs, expect their CEOs to keep them informed about developing issues and concerns so that there will be no "surprises." These two points are also noted in a survey of Ontario supervisory officers conducted by Fullan, Park, and Williams (1987), and in analyses of the work of Ontario directors of education (CEOs) offered by Allison and Allison (1988), Allison (1991a), and McLeod (1984). These sources all confirm the importance of good working relationships between school system chiefs and their chairs, but none explored the details of such relationships.

METHOD

This study was part of the larger study of chief executive officers in education, aspects of which are reported in some other chapters in this book. As part of this larger study, all Ontario directors were asked (by letter) to nominate the ten most effective directors in the province. Responses were combined, and the ten most frequently nominated directors were invited to participate in the study.

The Ontario Education Act clearly designates directors of education as chief executive officers of their boards, and specifies that directors "shall, within policies established by the board, develop and maintain an effective organization and the programs required to implement such policies." Trustees are locally elected to Ontario school boards every three years. Each year, the trustees of each board elect a chairperson from among themselves. Chairs are allowed to serve consecutive terms. The Education Act is silent regarding the duties and role of chairs of boards of education.

The ten directors selected for the study were interviewed a number of times to gather data relating to components of the larger project. In a general interview concerning leadership and leadership style, directors were specifically asked about their working relationships with the chairs of their elected boards. In addition, this interview included several more general questions, the answers to which were expected to further illuminate a director's working relationship with the chair. Chairs were interviewed only once, using an interview schedule that asked them to reflect specifically on the role of chair and their working relationship with the director.

When the student enrollments in the ten systems represented by these chairs and chiefs were compared, they fell evenly into two size groups. Five boards can be considered relatively small by Ontario standards, their student populations all less than 20,000 (ranging from approximately 8,000 students to approximately

18,000 students). The other five boards were distinctly larger, with student populations all above 40,000 (ranging from approximately 42,000 students to almost 60,000 students). This fortuitous and remarkably distinct dichotomization made it possible to treat organizational size as a variable in our analyses.

RESULTS

Personal and Demographic Characteristics

Of the ten chairs, four were women and six were men. Three of the four women were chairs of smaller boards; only one large board had a female Chair. Only one of the women reported being employed in another capacity in addition to her position as chair, but all of the men reported that they held other full-time jobs, except for one who had recently retired. The type of employment reported was frequently related to education: One chair was a secondary teacher (in another school system), one a psychologist, one a college administrator, and one a social worker.

All chairs had considerable experience as trustees. The shortest tenure as a trustee was six years, the longest seventeen, with the median being ten years. The average number of years in the role of chair was three, but total experience-in-role was not necessarily continuous, most experienced chairs having completed several one-or-two year terms of office. Three chairs had no prior experience in the role.

Although it is possible to describe a "typical" chair in this study, it is more accurate to describe two: the typical chair of a smaller board, and the typical chair of a larger board. In smaller boards the chair was typically a woman, not otherwise employed outside the home, who had been a trustee for eleven years and chair for just over one year. In the larger boards, the chair was typically a man with a full-time job, probably in a field related to education, who had been a trustee for twelve years and chair for just over two years.

In comparison, the chiefs were a remarkably homogeneous group. Except for one, all were males; all had worked their way up through the administrative hierarchy by serving as vice-principals, principals, and supervisory officers (assistant superintendents) before being appointed to the directorship. Half had originally taught in elementary schools, half in secondary. All had worked as educators for more than twenty years, most for more than one board, although usually in a subordinate administrative position rather than as director. This is consistent with the findings of an earlier study of Ontario central office senior administrators (referred to in Ontario as "supervisory officers") (Fullan et al. 1987): Whereas such administrators were almost invariably hired from inside the system, directors of education were often hired from outside. The major difference between the directors in this study was experience in role, the median being four years, with a range extending from one to twenty-two years. The "typical" director in this study is nonetheless easier to describe than the typical chair, the relevant descriptive data being substantially similar to that obtained in a larger 1987 sample (Allison and Allison 1988; Fullan et al. 1987). Thus, a director in this study was typically a male, ex-principal, ex-supervisory officer, who had followed a relatively mobile career trajectory and moved into the directorship less than six years ago.

The Role and Work of Chairs

Chairs were asked to identify differences between being a trustee and being chair. Three spoke of a change in focus: As individual trustees they represented a particular constituency and aired their personal views; as chairs they felt constrained to think of the good of the entire system and to be "more careful" in their speech to ensure that the views they expressed reflected "the consensus of the board." Three chairs also mentioned that since assuming the role of chair they had become much closer to the administration in general and the director in particular. This closeness was described as being manifest in both a new working relationship and a better understanding of different perspectives, responsibilities, and strengths. The most commonly stated difference, however, reported by five of the chairs, from both large and small systems, was the increased workload and time commitment.

A number of questions were asked about the amount of time spent on specific tasks and in the role generally. Overall no chair reported spending less than fifteen hours on the job in an average week, and no chair reported spending substantially more than forty hours. There was, however, a marked relationship between the number of hours-in-role reported by chairs and organizational size: Chairs from larger boards all reported spending twenty or more hours a week, while three of the five reported that they spent an average of forty hours or more attending to board business in an average week. On the other hand, none of the chairs from smaller boards reported spending forty hours a week on the job: Two estimated that they usually spent between twenty to forty hours, and three less than twenty hours per week, attending to official business. This makes sense, since it is likely that the role of the chair will be more demanding in larger and more complex systems. At the same time, chairs of larger systems likely had less time available for the demands of the role, since they characteristically also had full-time jobs.

Chairs were asked specifically whether they felt that the role of chair should be regarded as a full-time commitment. Half of them felt that the role could easily become a full-time job if the incumbent chose to make it so, but most were convinced that this would not be a good idea. Said one chair, "There is a line between policy and administration and if trustees have too much time, they tend to meddle in administration." Several also mentioned that trustees are paid a part-time stipend, and most boards could not afford to pay for a full-time chair. Several chairs pointed out that flexibility of time was more important than quantity.

Chairs were asked to talk about the specific tasks they performed. All reported that one of their most important tasks was to represent the board at official and ceremonial functions. Most chairs (8) made a distinction between their ceremonial role and their role as the board's official spokesperson. The next most commonly identified task, mentioned by seven chairs, was sitting on board committees; in many systems the chair was an ex officio member of all or almost all board committees. Five chairs identified tasks best described as providing liaison between the trustees and the administrative subsystem, usually through the CEO.

There was no clear pattern evident in the amount of time given by the chairs to different tasks within the role. Time allocations seemed to be largely idiosyncratic and situational, although organizational factors did appear to have an effect. For example, three chairs from larger systems reported spending substantial amounts of time in official and ceremonial functions, whereas three chairs from smaller boards reported spending more time in relatively informal meetings.

Most of the chairs, at some time during the interview, commented on the importance of reaching a clear understanding with the director about their respective roles: "If a particular partner . . . does not understand their role then you have a problem. Things work as well as the people who are in the positions." Chairs generally summarized the distinction between the two roles as that of policy and implementation: Chairs were seen as being responsible for policy, and chiefs for implementing the policies through management of the system. Indeed, it was chairs rather than directors who typically voiced concerns about the inadvisability of having trustees in general—and chairs in particular—interfering in administrative matters.

Most directors also spoke of establishing and maintaining mutually understood role definitions as a very important aspect of the relationship with the chair. It was evident, however, that although most directors seemed to have a very clear view of what the respective roles of chiefs and chairs were, these views, although highly congruent over matters of major definition, were not entirely congruent with one another in terms of actual detail. Some chiefs, for example, felt that it was part of the chair's role to represent the system to the public, whereas others felt that they should do this themselves. The determining variable in most cases appeared to be the personalities and strengths of the individuals involved. Directors were generally sensitive and responsive to the need for flexibility implied in this respect, many commenting on or offering examples of how they adapted aspects of their work to better accommodate the strengths or interests of an incoming chair.

Importance of the Working Relationship

All of the chairs agreed emphatically that their relationship with the Director was very important. They used words such as *vital, critical, essential,* and *absolutely key,* and spoke of the desirability of a mutually supportive partnership based on honesty, trust, openness, and respect. Directors were asked a more indirect question, in which they were required to rank their most important working relationships. All of the directors in larger boards listed their relationship with the chair first. Four directors in smaller boards ranked the chair as the second most important working relationship—one listed his secretary first, one ranked "staff" first, and two ranked their supervisory officers (assistant superintendents) first. The remaining director ranked the chair fourth, after supervisory officers, principals, and support staff.

Generally, directors spoke very positively of their relationships with their chairs. Many talked about reaching a mutual agreement (one specifically described this as making "a pact") with the chair, the terms of which would clarify that they depended on the chair to run the political side of the operation while they managed the administrative side of things. Directors typically said their chairs were supportive and helpful and provided "a pipeline to the community."

Frequency of Meetings

All of the chairs reported frequent meetings with their chiefs. Some of these meetings were part of larger meetings, such as administrative or executive council meetings, but most chairs reported informal meetings throughout the week, making this the most common forum for communication between chiefs and chairs. Seven chairs had offices of their own in the board headquarters and reported that they dropped into the building regularly throughout the work week, often at unusual hours such as very early in the morning, during lunch, or after work. Brief, unscheduled meetings with the chief typically occurred during these visits. In addition to these face-to-face contacts, most chairs reported that they communicated with the chiefs frequently by telephone. Characteristically either of them might initiate the call, but the purpose was usually to inform the other about a single occurrence or item of new information; typically the calls were short. Other forms of communication, such as memos, e-mail, or fax, were unpopular and only rarely resorted to.

Whereas chairs were asked to estimate the frequency of meetings with the directors, the latter were asked to go over their appointment books for the past month as part of a question that dealt with the full spectrum of the director's work. A complicating factor of this approach was that some directors did not record regular meetings with the chair as appointments; one, for example, did not record his regular breakfast meetings with the chair every Wednesday morning. Nonetheless, the directors' diaries contained an average of four scheduled meetings with the chair over the four week period surveyed. In addition, all directors indicated that they frequently met informally with their chairs. The directors of one large board and one small board reported that these informal meetings would take place virtually every day. One director of a large board reported that he normally spoke informally with his chair at least once a day, while three directors reported speaking with their chairs at least three times a week. The average seemed to be practically daily contact, either face-to-face or by telephone.

Content of Meetings

Seven of the chairs reported that the most consistent subject discussed in their meetings with the director was the form and content of the agenda for the next regular board meeting. In some systems the chair and the director set this agenda by themselves; in others the board agenda was determined by a complex process involving different administrative groups and committees. In one large system, the chair and director discussed the agenda, but the chair decided on the formal agenda after consulting with others. Two chairs described their discussions of the board agenda with their chiefs as "rehearsals" for the formal meeting, going over each item in detail, anticipating questions and preparing answers.

Other than discussing the board agenda, the most common topics of discussion during chairs' frequent informal meetings with their directors concerned "issues that have come up." This description subsumes anything related to the system or its personnel. The implied purpose of these discussions was twofold: To ensure that both participants were kept well informed, and to avert or minimize potential problems. Chiefs and chairs agreed that many such problems eventually amounted to nothing but some invariably became very significant issues, and it was important that these not come as a surprise to either party. These discussions were apparently very frank: When chairs were asked if there was anything they would consider inappropriate for private discussion with their director, nine out of ten replied that nothing was proscribed; the tenth said that he would not discuss trustee problems with the chief unless they got out of hand.

Directors were more detailed in their descriptions of the topics discussed in their meetings with chairs. Like the chairs, they reported that they talked about problems, concerns, and issues, including everything from personnel problems, complaints and political "hot spots" to the behavior of trustees: a "confidential sharing" of potential problems. Nine directors also mentioned the task of constructing the agenda for the board meeting and reviewing strategies and policies. Three directors also mentioned that they talked with their chairs about provincial matters, "new ideas in education," and possible future trends. These directors were particularly concerned with keeping their chairs as up-to-date as possible in the broader field of education as well as in their own systems.

DISCUSSION

Findings from this study endorse the importance of the working relationship between chiefs and chairs, but also illustrate the many ways in which this relationship can be organized. Such variation appears attributable to the personalities and circumstances of the chairs. This was illustrated very clearly by one director, who said,

> The previous Chair phoned or dropped in to talk over matters informally. The new Chair has a different organizational plan. He makes lists of things to talk about, in person, and the meetings tend to be somewhat less casual and more formal.

In this and other cases, the personality and the occupation of the chair influenced both the nature of interactions with the director and the aspects of the role on which the chairs opted to concentrate, reflecting similar findings by Chitayat (1985) and Stewart (1991).

There were, however, certain common characteristics with respect to the nature of the working relationships. Chairs and directors interacted frequently, often informally, and shared a mutual trust and respect. They conferred about the official agenda for forthcoming board meetings, but also discussed emergent concerns and issues affecting the organization. The breadth of topics discussed in private is perhaps surprising; apparently no potentially important development in or around the organization was "out of bounds." This offers impressive testimony to the degree of trust and confidence that most of these CEOs and chairs had in each other's competence and discretion. It also illustrates the importance of the CEO-chair link in providing a confidential channel of communication between administrative and governance subsystems. Above all, both chairs and directors agreed that the working relationship between them was crucial. As one director explained, "We fully realize that we need each other."

The relationships studied here were not hierarchical. Chairs and directors provided leadership for the subsystems—administrative and governance—for which each was responsible, but they freely discussed concerns and issues affecting each subsystem and the organization as a whole, giving and seeking advice from one another. This reinforces Carver's (1991) view that because the CEO is accountable only to the full board, the relationship between the CEO and any individual trustee, particularly the chair, can only be that of "supportive peers" (p.116): The director is the professional expert, but the chair represents the employing board and the client public. This study has demonstrated, however, that the relationship between the director and the chair is quite different from the director's relationship with any other trustee. Because the director and chair spend so much time together, share so many confidences, and occupy such strategically important positions, their relationship is both unique and vital.

CONCLUSIONS

The reputationally effective directors who formed the sample for this study all reported good working relationships with their chairs. A good relationship appears to be characterized by mutual respect, openness and honesty, a mutual understanding of respective roles and responsibilities, and clear, frequent communication. Because the chairs differed in many ways (though they all felt included, involved, and important), we conclude that the effective director is able to establish and maintain good working relationships with a succession of chairs, making the most of that person's strengths and special abilities. As Stewart (1991) observed, "Part of the skills of being a good Chief executive is establishing a complementary relationship with a chairman" (p. 525). The reputationally effective directors in this study all appeared sufficiently flexible to accommodate their chairs' preferences and personalities in seeking to establish such a relationship. This, together with a religious adherence to Isherwood and Osgoode's (1986) theme of "No surprises," contributed significantly to the establishment and maintenance of good working relationships.

The major differences between the relationships established in small systems and those in larger systems seem to reside not in the relationship itself but in the role of the chair. Larger systems were more complex, and imposed more formal, public duties on their chairs, than did smaller boards. But while chairs in larger systems reported spending more time attending to their duties, they argued against the advisability of making the role into a full-time position, on the grounds that this would encourage chairs to meddle in administrative matters. Even so, three chairs of larger systems reported spending an average of forty hours a week—the equivalent of a full time job—attending to their duties.

Nonetheless, the relationships described in these pages were characterized as successful because the participants themselves thought they were. Moreover, it is reasonable to expect that reputationally effective chief administrators would be adroit at creating and sustaining good working relationships with the chairpersons of their governing boards, or at least in creating the impression of such. In the absence of more objective criteria, however, it is impossible either to accurately describe and compare specific behaviors and expectations that directly contribute to, or impede, effective working relationships, or to judge whether actual working relationships are, in fact, effective. Future research might attempt to identify and apply specific criteria to more accurately describe, compare, and evaluate CEO-chair working relationships. Moreover, future work in this area should sample a much wider, more representative range of working relationships. The approach taken in this study allowed us to focus on characteristics of assumedly good working relationships, but the selection of reputationally effective directors imposed a major limitation. If the relationships described here are indeed characteristic of good Chief-chair working relationships, then mutual respect, trust, and frank communication appear to be important elements. Chiefs and chairs are, in a manner of speaking, thrust together in a close relationship with the task of working together on an enterprise that is very important to both of them. Obviously, being reasonable adults who have sought to be in these positions, it is in their mutual interest to cooperate, regardless of any minor personal and/or philosophical incompatibilities; but at what point might this break down? This study did not address questions of congruence in philosophy, nor did it ask pointed questions about personal compatibility. It did not look at poor relationships or ineffective chiefs. What we did find, however, has provided us with a starting point in the study of this most crucial administrative relationship.

REFERENCES

Allison, D. J. (1980). *An analysis of the congruency between a model of public schools and Max Weber's model of bureaucracy.* Unpublished doctoral dissertation, University of Alberta, Edmonton.

Allison, D. J. (1983). Toward an improved understanding of the organizational nature of schools. *Educational Administration Quarterly, 19*(4), 7–34.

Allison, D. J. (1991a). Pride and privilege: The development of the school superintendency in the United States and Canada. In K. Leithwood & D. Musella (Eds.), *Understanding school system administration* (pp. 209–38). London: Falmer Press.

Allison, D. J. (1991b). Setting, size and sectors in the work environment of chief education officers. In K. Leithwood & D. Musella (Eds.), *Understanding school system administration* (pp. 23–41). London: Falmer Press.

Allison, D. J., & Allison, P. A. (1988, June). Discovering the Ontario school chief: Insights from the Fullan, Park and Williams study of supervisory officers. In *Proceedings of the conference "The Chief School Officer,"* D. Musella (Ed.) (pp. 73–132). Toronto: Department of Educational Administration, Centre for Executive Studies. Ontario Institute for Studies in Education.

Blumberg, A. (1985). *The school superintendent: Living with conflict.* New York: Teachers College Press.

Brown, C. (1976). *Putting the corporate board to work.* New York: Macmillan.

Callahan, R. E. (1962). *Education and the cult of efficiency.* Chicago: University of Chicago Press.

Carlson, R. O. (1972). *School superintendents: Careers and performance.* Columbus, OH: Charles E. Merrill.

Carver, J. (1991). *Boards that make a difference: A new design for leadership in non-profit and public organizations.* San Francisco: Jossey-Bass.

Chitayat, G. (1985). Working relationships between the chairman of the board of directors and the CEO. *Management International Review, 25*(3), 65–70.

Fullan, M. G., Park, P. B., & Williams, T. R. (1987). *The supervisory officer in Ontario: Current practice and recommendations for the future.* Ontario: Queen's Printer.

Hickcox, E., & Stapleton, W. H. (1970). *The chairman of the board: An examination of his role*. Toronto: Ontario Institute for Studies in Education (monograph series No. 8).

Isherwood, G. B., Falconer, K., Lavery, R., McConagy, G., & Klotz, M. P. (1984). The CEO speaks out: What makes a chief executive officer effective? Here's what top Canadian school board administrators think. *Education Canada, 24*(1), 16–27.

Isherwood, G. B., & Osgoode, N. D. (1986). What makes boards tick? *Education Canada, 26*(1), 4–11.

McLeod, G. T. (1984). The work of school board chief executive officers. *Canadian Journal of Education, 9*(2), 171–90.

Mintzberg, H. (1979). *The structuring of organizations*. Englewood Cliffs, NJ: Prentice Hall.

Parsons, T. (1960). *Structure and process in modern society*. New York: Free Press.

Puckey, W. (1968). *The board room*. London: Hutchinson.

Stewart, R. (1991). Chairmen and chief executives: An exploration of their relationship. *Journal of Management Studies, 28*(5), 511–27.

Thompson, J. D. (1967). *Organizations in action*. New York: McGraw-Hill.

Tyack, D. B. (1976). Pilgrim's progress: Toward a social history of the school superintendency, 1860–1960. *History of Education Quarterly, 16*, 257–99.

Tyack, D. B., & Hansot, E. (1982). *Managers of virtue: Public school leadership in America, 1820–1980*. New York: Basic Books.

Weber, M. (1978). *Economy and society: An outline of interpretive sociology* (Vol. 1) (G. Roth & C. Wittich, Eds. & Trans.). Berkeley: University of California Press. (Original work published 1922)

CHAPTER 4

Prospects for Organizational Learning in Expertly Managed Group Problem Solving

Kenneth Leithwood, Rosanne Steinbach, and Tiiu Raun

Peter Vaill (1989) claims that today's executives "live in a world of permanent white water" (p. 2)—a world in which few assumptions are beyond scrutiny and the environment sometimes appears chaotic. In such a "contingent" world, well-rehearsed, routine, managerial behaviors provide the solution to a rapidly decreasing proportion of the potential problems lurking in the choppy waters executives navigate daily. The prevalence of wicked or ill-structured problems, just below the surface of the water, explains why even a light breeze often results in whitecaps. And, sometimes, apparently benign problems turn out to be deceptively wicked. Such a perspective explains the need for executives to have a repertoire of general problem-solving skills along with a considerable store of knowledge about their specific businesses, to help cope with unpredictable and new problems.

The study of executives' problem-solving processes has been under way for some time in organizational settings outside of education (see, for example, Srivastva 1983; Schwenk 1988; Argyris 1982). But little systematic attention has been devoted to the thinking and problem solving of educators in formal leadership positions. The study described in this chapter was one in a series aimed at redressing this neglect. Prior studies in the series have focused on school principals (e.g., Leithwood, Begley, and Cousins 1992) as well as chief education officers (CEOs) (e.g., Leithwood and Steinbach 1991a).

Among the results of our prior studies is evidence that as educational leaders become more "expert," more experienced in their roles, and move to more senior positions, they rely more extensively on solving their problems in collaboration with groups of colleagues, rather than by themselves (Leithwood and Steinbach 1990). Indeed, some leaders are able to use the context of group problem solving not only for developing productive solutions to their problems and enhancing the subsequent implementation of those solutions, but also for fostering powerful forms of staff development (Leithwood and Steinbach 1991b). In addition, a growing body of evidence argues for much greater attention to the nature and role of values in executive problem solving; such values appear to be pervasive, and variations in their nature and use are closely related to variations in executive expertise (Begley and Leithwood 1989; Hambrick and Brandon 1988). To explore these tentative findings further, the study described here asked: How do CEOs solve problems in groups? And, in particular, what is the nature and role of CEOs' values in their group problem solving? What purposes are being served by CEOs when they engage in collaborative problem solving with their senior colleagues?

FRAMEWORK

A number of studies preceding the one described in this chapter have explored the problem-solving processes of CEOs (Leithwood and Steinbach 1991a; Leithwood 1988) and school-level administrators (e.g., Leithwood and Stager 1989; Leithwood and Steinbach 1990). Guided by information-processing theory, this research generated the multicomponent model of executive problem solving that served as a framework for data collection in the present study. The components of that model are interpretation, goals, principles/values, constraints, solution processes, and mood. This section briefly outlines several key features of an information-processing orientation to problem solving; it also identifies additional, selected features of such an orientation, in the context of describing the main elements of our problem-solving model. We assume very little prior knowledge about information-processing theory by the reader.

An Information-Processing Orientation to Problem Solving

Information-processing orientations to problem solving are embedded in a broader theory of how the mind works. This theory consists of hypothetical structures and relationships explaining why people attend to some aspects of the information available to them in their environments, how their knowledge is stored, retrieved, and further developed, and how it is used in solving problems (see, for example, Gagné 1985; Newell, Rosenblum, and Laird 1990; Rumelhart 1990). From this perspective, problems are defined as circumstances in which a gap is perceived between a current state and a more desirable state (Gagné 1985; Hayes 1981). When both states are clearly known and the procedures to follow (or operators) to get from one to the other are also known, a problem is considered routine or well structured. Lack of knowledge about any of these three elements in the "problem space" (Newell and Simon 1972) makes a problem more ill-structured. Hence both the objective complexity of the problem and the relevant knowledge possessed by the solver combine to determine the degree of novelty or structure of a problem.

Information-processing orientations to problem solving devote considerable attention to the concept of "expertise" and the patterns of thought that distinguish between those who possess expertise and those who do not. Expertise is associated with both effective and efficient problem solving within a particular domain of activity (like leading a school system). Research across many domains suggests, for example, that experts excel mainly in their own domains; perceive large meaningful patterns in their domains, solve problems quickly with few errors, and have superior short- and long-term memories. Experts also represent problems at deeper, more principled levels than novices do; they spend more time than novices do on interpreting (as distinct from solving) problems. And experts are able to monitor their own thinking much better than novices are (Glaser and Chi 1988). The amount of domain-specific knowledge possessed by experts and the way it is organized is offered as the primary explanation for these attributes (Van Lehn 1990; Nickerson 1988–89). General problem-solving processes or heuristics, in the absence of such knowledge, are not considered powerful tools for problem solving. Rather, such processes help people to gain access to useful knowledge and beliefs that they otherwise might have overlooked (Bransford in press).

Well-structured problems, usually those repeatedly encountered by expert executives, are solved with little conscious thought. The problem is recognized as an instance of a category of problems about which the executive already knows a great deal. As Herbert Simon (1993) argues:

> "Any expert can recognize the symptoms, the clues, to the bulk of the situations that are encountered in his or her everyday experience. The day would simply not be long enough to accomplish anything if cues didn't do a large part of the work for the expert."

Such recognition permits the executive access to all of the knowledge he or she has stored in long-term memory about how to solve that category of problem. But because no comparable store of knowledge is available for ill-structured problems, the executive needs to respond in a more deliberate, thoughtful manner. As executives face a greater proportion of ill-structured problems, better understanding of these deliberate, thoughtful processes becomes increasingly important (Day and Lord 1992; Schwenk 1988) as does enhancing the expertise with which they are carried out. Furthermore, the degree of discretion and the cognitive demands placed on executives appear to increase, the higher their position in the organization (Mumford and Connelly 1991; Hunter, Schmidt, and Judiesch 1990), in part because of the extended time horizons over which solutions to their problems must be planned and the accompanying abstractness of the thinking that this necessitates (Jaques 1986). This makes learning more about the problem solving of senior executives especially worthwhile.

Components of a Problem-Solving Model

There are two general categories of processes involved in problem solving: understanding and solving (Hayes 1981; Van Lehn 1990; Voss and Post 1988). Understanding processes serve the purpose of generating a CEO's internal representation of the problem—what she or he believes the problem to be. Solving processes aim to reduce the gap between current and desired states—how the executive will transform the current state into the more desirable goal state. Understanding and solving often interact during the course of problem solving as feedback from initial steps taken toward a solution builds a richer understanding of the problem. Both sets of processes require searching the contents of memory for existing knowledge helpful in either understanding or solving the problem.

The multicomponent model of executive problem solving that served as a framework for collecting data in this study includes two components that primarily address understanding: interpretation and goal setting. Two components are primarily concerned with solving: constraints and solution processes. The principles/ values and mood components seem equally relevant to both understanding and solving. This section provides an explanation of the cognitive processes encompassed by each component. In addition, characteristics of expertise in relation to each component are described, based on our own research with educational administrators. Those characteristics of expertise selected as a focus of attention in the present study are designated with an asterisk (*).

Processes Designed Primarily for Understanding Problems

Interpretation. Executives are bombarded with much more information from their environments than they can possibly think about (Simon 1993). Furthermore, because this information frequently presents itself as an untidy "mess," rather than a clearly labeled set of possibilities, there can be a host of potential problem formulations. Problem interpretation is an instance of giving meaning to and evaluating such information (Kelsey in press). Meaning is created as newly encountered information is compared with those "schemata"—organized contents of long-term memory—that the executive thinks might be relevant (Van Lehn 1990). Such schemata have two parts: one for describing the problem and the other for describing the solution. Nonroutine or ill-structured problems may be difficult to understand, for several reasons. For example, more than one schema could apply to the problem, sometimes giving rise to the need for a trial-and-error search for the most workable schema; two or more schemata might have to be combined in order to adequately cover the whole problem.

The complex process of understanding ill-structured problems is aided by the use of problem categories that are learned from experience. As Chi, Feltovich, and Glaser (1981) explain, " categorization of a problem as a type cue[s] associated information in [one's] knowledge base" (p. 22). The search for and combining of schemata can be limited to stored schemata considered relevant to the problem category. A series of studies by Cowan (1986, 1988, 1990, 1991) suggests, for example, that executives normally distinguish between strategic and operational problems, and between technical and human problems. Different processes seem to be used to solve problems in each of these categories.

Problem interpretation does not only involve making sense of information by comparing it to existing schemata. It also requires evaluation: the perception of a discrepancy between the executive's understanding of current reality and a more desirable reality. As Cowan (1990) points out:

> This dynamic highlights the importance of an evoked problem concept in directing attention . . . , in cuing related knowledge to assist interpretation . . . , and in constraining search and solution activity . . . Once executives categorize a situation as a particular problem, causes are related to the initial categorization . . . , as are reformulation, . . . [and] the search for solutions. (p. 366–67)

Our evidence from educational administrators suggests that, as compared with nonexperts, experts

- develop a relatively clearer understanding of the problem before attempting to solve it;
- devote more time and effort to the initial formulation of ill-structured problems; and
- are more inclined to view the immediate problem in its relationship to the broader mission and problems of the organization.*

Goals. Understanding an ill-structured problem sufficiently well to solve it usually requires decomposing it into pieces that are more manageable (Newell 1975; Hayes 1980). This begins to transform the often abstract, general interpretation of an ill-structured problem into a set of more-precise goals that can serve as targets for problem-solving activity (Voss and Post 1988).

Given these more-precise goals, the executive is better able to compare the current state with the goal at each stage of the process, as is normally possible with well-structured problems (Greeno 1978). Similar to what is accomplished through problem classification, such goals also provide relatively direct access to stored knowledge relevant to solving the problem without the need for more elaborate, time-consuming, and possibly inaccurate search processes necessitated by vague goals (Greeno 1980).

Expert, as compared with nonexpert, educational administrators

- adopt a broader range of goals for problem solving;*
- when solving problems in groups, have less personal stake in any preconceived solution, and aim instead to arrive at the best solution the group can produce;* and
- more often establish staff development as one explicit goal, among others, for solving problems in groups.*

Processes Designed Primarily for Solving Problems

Constraints. The distinction between well-structured and ill-structured problems is a matter of degree. How much an executive already knows that is relevant to solving a problem is one factor in determining the extent to which a problem is well structured. An equally important factor is the number of constraints that must be addressed in solving the problem (Reitman 1965; Voss and Post 1988). Once goals are set, much of problem solving involves recognizing and dealing with constraints to accomplishing those goals. Often constraints arise, or are encountered, only in the midst of solving a problem. These can be obstacles (the absence of things required in order to continue) or errors (actions taken that had inappropriate results); they can also be distractions (Shank and Abelson 1977)—for example, some other problem requiring immediate action comes to the executive's attention. And, in the case of multistep problem-solving processes, the actions taken at a prior step become constraints on possible actions at later steps. For example, to cope with the problem of a deficit budget, a CEO might request all central office unit heads to cut back 5 percent on their projected spending for the current year. A unit head who refuses to do so would be a constraint facing the CEO in solving the deficit problem. Threatening to fire the unit head unless he or she complies would make "voluntary restraint" among units an unlikely strategy for coping with the deficit problem in subsequent years.

Our prior research suggested that, as compared with nonexperts, expert educational administrators

- more adequately anticipate many of the constraints likely to arise during problem solving;

- show a greater tendency to plan, in advance, for how to address anticipated constraints;

- respond more adaptively and flexibly to constraints that arise unexpectedly;* and

- do not view constraints as major impediments to problem solving.

Solution Processes. Solution processes are the overt or covert steps or actions taken to achieve goals for problem solving. Such actions or steps result from a deliberate search through memory for relevant procedural schemata. These are structures in the mind about how to perform certain actions, that is, a set of instructions for action—how to develop a budget, how to resolve a conflict with a trustee, how to ensure that one's position is made clear in a two-minute radio interview, and so on.

Procedural schemata take several forms, each more or less appropriate to different problem conditions. One set of conditions occurs in the face of problems or subproblems that are relatively well structured. Under this set of conditions, procedural schemata of most use take the form of "scripts" (Shank and Abelson 1977). These are well-rehearsed sequences of actions leading to a desired goal. They may be quite elaborate, including long causal chains of actions and anticipated roles for many other people. But because they are so well rehearsed, they are also fairly rigid. Unanticipated deviations from the script (e.g., errors, distractions) require novel responses to be grafted onto the script. Such a response may be thought of as a microscript, a type of script that seems relevant, also, when solution processes are developed more spontaneously, during action. Reflection-in-action, to use Schön's (1983) term, involves intuitive and rapid search processes through memory for guides to short sequences of action or microscripts.

A second set of conditions occurs when the executive is faced with more ill-structured problems or subproblems. Under such conditions, searches through memory are unlikely to locate a script that will solve the problem. The more likely outcome of such a search will be a "plan" (Shank and Abelson 1977; Suchman 1987). A plan is

> the repository of general information that will connect events that cannot be connected by use of an available script. (Shank and Abelson 1977, p. 70)

It describes the choices available to the executive as she attempts to accomplish a goal. A plan can include a number of scripts connected in novel ways (Van Lehn 1990).

For a plan to be developed by an executive as a guide to solving an ill-structured problem, the executive must still possess considerable problem-relevant knowledge, although that knowledge initially is not organized as efficiently as a script for solving the problem. Under a third set of problem-solving conditions, executives might not possess even this initially inefficiently organized knowledge. When existing stores of problem-relevant procedural knowledge are not available, executives must rely on a third type of structure called general "heuristics." These include such content-free procedures as brainstorming, means-end analysis, use of analogies and metaphors, collecting more information about possible steps, and trial and error (Rubinstein 1975; Brightman 1988; Hayes 1981; Newell and Simon 1972).

Our previous study of school principals solving problems in groups (Leithwood and Steinbach 1991b) found that, as compared with nonexperts, experts

- had well-developed plans for collaborative problem solving (e.g., a meeting);*
- provided a clear, detailed introduction to the problem and its background to collaborators;*
- outlined clearly the process for problem solving (e.g., how the meeting will be conducted);*
- carefully checked collaborators' interpretations of the problem and their own assumptions;*

- without intimidating or restraining others, clearly indicated their own view of the problem and its relationship with larger problems;*
- remained open to new information and changed views, if warranted;*
- assisted collaborative problem solving by synthesizing, summarizing, and clarifying as needed;*
- had strategies for balancing the need to keep the group on track (focused) and allowing discussion;*
- ensured that follow-up was planned.*

Processes for Understanding as well as Solving: Values and Mood

Values. A value is an enduring belief about the desirability of some means or action. Once internalized, a value also becomes a standard for guiding one's actions and thoughts, for influencing the actions and thoughts of others, and for morally judging oneself and others.[1] Conceptualized in this way, values have a pervasive role in problem solving. They shape one's view of the current and desired goal state and figure centrally in the choice of actions to reduce the perceived gap.

To explain how values play such a role, it is necessary to situate them within two structures in the mind. One structure acts as a repository of one's goals and aspirations, as well as at least some of one's values. The purpose of this structure is to evaluate perceived information from the senses, deciding which to ignore and which to process further because of its potential relevance to one's goals, aspirations, and values. Such a structure is sometimes referred to as the "executive"; in Anderson's (1983) Act* theory, the function is performed by a "working-memory." Situating values in an executive or working memory structure helps explain the pervasive but indirect effects that CEOs' values have on their actions; they provide perceptual screens that, as Hambrick and Brandon (1988) explain, allow the CEO to "see what he wants to see" and "hear what he wants to hear."

Values also seem likely to exist, in two forms, in long-term memory. In one form, they are embedded as integral parts of CEOs' organized knowledge structures (schemata) about their organizational worlds, including procedures for how to solve known problems in that world. This is their implicit form. While values in this form are an important part of CEOs' domain-specific knowledge, CEOs often might not be consciously aware of such values and the strength of influence of their implicit values on their actions. Values also might be stored as independent structures in the mind—their explicit form. CEOs are likely to be consciously aware of their values in this form and, hence, to have more control over the influence of such values. Whether in their implicit or explicit forms, values stored in long-term memory have direct effects on CEOs' thoughts about what actions to take—a "behavior channeling" effect (Hambrick and Brandon 1988). Nevertheless, even when values are in explicit form, their effects on a CEO's actions are mediated by the amount of discretion the CEO possesses. CEOs' actions are formed from thoughts about many matters in addition to their explicit values. But it is difficult for CEOs to escape from the influence of their implicit values and the values that act as perceptual screens.

Our own research with educational administrators concerning the nature and role of their values in professional problem solving (Begley and Leithwood 1989; Campbell-Evans 1988; Leithwood and Steinbach 1991a) suggests that experts in comparison with nonexperts,

- are more aware of their values;
- use their values more regularly in solving problems; and
- use values as substitutes for knowledge in solving ill-structured problems.

This research has also resulted in a classification of values used by educational administrators. Incorporating elements of Hodgkinson (1978), Beck (1984), and Hambrick and Brandon (1988), these value categories are described later in the chapter.

Mood. Knowledge is stored in the mind in several forms—as words and pictures, for example. Furthermore, what is meant by "knowledge" goes considerably beyond the purely cognitive content implied by the term. In addition to values, as discussed above, other affective states or feelings will also be integrated as part of knowledge structures. A CEO not only has stored in mind a procedure for facilitating the decision making of trustees; she also has associated (and therefore unavoidable) feelings about carrying out the procedure—despair, elation, fear, boredom, and the like. Both the nature and the strength of their feelings shape the moods experienced by CEOs during problem solving. Additional feelings, such as pressure and uncertainty coming from the context in which problem solving occurs, also contribute to the CEO's mood. Research on social cognition suggests that, along with personal goals and the knowledge one possesses, mood has an important influence on the degree of cognitive flexibility the CEO is able to exercise during problem solving. Showers and Cantor (1985) explain flexibility as

(a) adjusting interpretations in response to situational features; (b) taking control of [one's] thoughts and plans; (c) seeing multiple alternatives for interpreting the same event or outcome; and (d) changing [one's] own knowledge repertoire by adding new experiences and by reworking cherished beliefs, values, and goals. (p. 277)

Intense moods reduce such flexibility, thereby limiting problem-solving effectiveness. Consistent with this explanation, our research with educational administrators has demonstrated that, in contrast with nonexperts, experts

are better able to control intense moods and remain calm during problem solving;

are more self-confident about their ability to solve ill-structured problems;* and

treat staff with respect and courtesy during the meeting and the interview, that is, show consistent and genuine respect.*

METHOD

Data for the study were collected through stimulated recall interviews conducted with seven "reputationally effective" CEOs [this is the same group of CEOs used in the study reported by Allison, Allison and McHenry in chapter 3—Editor]. A letter was sent to every CEO (director) in Ontario requesting them to nominate five CEOs who they believed had reputations with their peers as being particularly effective on the job. They were advised to use whatever criteria they considered relevant. One hundred and eleven ballots were sent out, and seventy-four were returned. The eleven top-ranking nominees were then invited to participate in the research. Ten of those eleven agreed. Subsequently, three others dropped out for a variety of reasons (health, time, change of heart), resulting in a sample size of seven CEOs.

Data Collection

Participants were asked to audiotape a portion of a regular meeting with their senior administrative colleagues, usually six to eight people, which would be dealing with a problem the CEO expected to be particularly controversial or "swampy." They were asked to select a nonroutine or complex problem because expert practitioners tend to deal with routine problems in a somewhat automatic fashion that makes it difficult to discern their thought processes.

Following the meeting, the CEOs were interviewed. Using the tape of the meeting to "stimulate recall," CEOs were asked to comment on what they were thinking at various points. Both the CEO and the interviewer stopped the tape frequently to ask questions or to offer information about intentions and thought processes. This discussion was recorded on a separate tape, which was subsequently transcribed carefully to eliminate all identifying characteristics. These transcripts provided the data for the present study.

Data Analysis

Elements of expertise identified with an asterisk in the previous section served as a focus for coding interview data collected from the CEOs included in the study. These elements emphasize the solution processes component within our model, because of expectations created by our prior research about the more-critical aspects of group problem solving. Also examined were CEOs' uses of problem-relevant knowledge, degree and quality of self-reflection, and the goal of staff development. In all, 18 codes were used to analyze the interview data.

For this study, each transcript was divided into relevant statements made by the CEO. Two researchers (neither of whom was the interviewer, to maintain objectivity) worked together to code the interviews according to the 18 elements. Researchers initially coded each protocol independently and then discussed and resolved any discrepancies.

RESULTS

The study was intended to address two questions: How do CEOs solve problems in groups, and What purposes are being served by such problem solving? Results of our data analysis are reported as a response to each of these questions. Where possible, we point out similarities and differences with the results of our other recent research.

How Do CEOs Solve Problems in Groups?

Table 4–1 reports the number of statements found in the verbal protocols of CEOs, which were coded according to each of the 18 components selected from our problem-solving model. Statements reflecting CEOs' values are reported separately (table 4–2).

A CEO's response for each component potentially might vary widely in its level of expertise, judged in comparison with the results of our previous research. However, the seven CEOs included in the study were selected because they had reputations, among other CEOs in the province, for being effective, and in fact all CEOs in our sample exhibited the kinds of thinking attributed to the expert problem solvers in our previous work. With the exception of one item (which will be addressed later), the CEOs displayed expertlike processes in relation to each component of our problem-solving model (table 4–1 does not speak to this).

Given such uniformly expert processes, evidence in table 4–1 clarifies which components of problem solving received most and least attention (number of statements made) by CEOs in their thinking aloud about their conduct of the meetings with their senior staffs.

More than half the responses (58 percent) are accounted for by just 6 of the 18 problem-solving elements; one of these elements was part of problem interpretation:

• Views immediate problem in relation to the larger mission and problems of the school system (rank 4: item 1.1).

Examples of CEOs' talk illustrating this process include these:

And that's what was going through my mind. Here was an opportunity to again reference that second strategic direction. I

Table 4–1
Statements in Protocols Coded as Different
Components of Problem Solving
(values omitted)

Problem-Solving Components	Total Frequency	Mean	Percentage of Total	Rank
1. Interpretation				
1.1 Immediate problem viewed in broader context	32	4.6	7	4
2. Goals				
2.1 Less of a personal stake in preconceived solution	9	1.3	2	16
2.2 Broad range of goals	29	4.1	6	7
2.3 Staff development an explicit goal	16	2.3	4	12
3. Constraints				
3.1 Responds flexibly to unanticipated obstacles	32	4.6	7	5
4. Solution processes				
4.1 Has well-developed plan	14	2.0	3	13
4.2 Provides clear introduction	12	1.7	3	14
4.3 Outlines the process for problem solving	7	1.0	2	17
4.4 Indicates own point of view without intimidating others	32	4.6	7	6
4.5 Remains open to new information	12	1.7	3	15
4.6 Summarizes, synthesizes, clarifies, etc.	56	8.0	12	2

Table 4–1 (continued)

Problem-Solving Components	Total Frequency	Mean	Percentage of Total	Rank
4.7 Balances need to keep group focused and need for open discussion	21	3.0	5	10
4.8 Checks for consensus, agreement, understanding	27	3.9	6	8
4.9 Ensures that follow-up is planned	19	2.7	4	11
5. Affect/mood				
5.1 Always appears calm and confident	3	0.4	.01	18
5.2 Genuine respect and courtesy shown to staff	54	7.7	12	3
6. Other				
6.1 Use of problem-relevant knowledge	22	3.1	5	9
6.2 Self-reflection	58	8.3	13	1

point to an area [school-based decision making] where we can start to move.

We have as part of our philosophy "people before things," involvement in decision making, and yet here we are still solving the problem.

A second, frequently coded element concerned constraints:

• Anticipates obstacles, responds flexibly to unanticipated obstacles which arise, and does not view obstacles as major impediments to problem solving (rank 5: item 3.1)

CEOs commented, for example:

There may be some awkward silences as we sort of look around and [think] what do you want us to say today? But really we have to be able to make a move somehow.

Now there's a conflict between S and S and they will go after each other. His question is unclear and sounds like he's setting him up. So I now start to focus on whether there's a set-up and whether I need to do anything.

Two frequently coded elements were part of solution processes. One of the elements involved CEOs assisting collaborative problem solving by synthesizing, summarizing, and clarifying as needed (rank 2: item 4.6); for example:

Your words reflect the need for some inservice, even for them.

As part of their frequently mentioned solution processes, without intimidating or restraining others, CEOs clearly indicated their own view of the problem or opinion about the issue (rank 6: item 4,4). As one CEO said:

D: You've said that it's the responsibility of the EA from time to time to demand a right guaranteed by the contract.
S: That's right.
D: Would you agree that we have some responsibility to create a climate in which (a) it's not particularly difficult to do that [demand own rights] and (b) it's improbable that you have to in the majority of the cases demand your rights? One of the real underlying issues is, who decides what the responsibility of the EA should be? And they seem to be saying overtime is better than lieu time because [then] we know that we are needed. And that seems to be a question of, you know, who defines when and where they're needed. Is it the teacher, the principal, or them? I think the principal. Am I making sense in that analysis?

CEOs consistently showed respect and courtesy toward their senior colleagues, not only during the meetings but in our interviews with them after (rank 3: item 5.2). For example:

I really appreciate all the backup. It really helps me.

. . . right, this is exactly what should happen. That superintendent should be speaking up and raising that question and that's what the group will expect to have happen.

I cheer him on. This is the superintendent of program. This chap has come a long way.

While we coded such respect as part of mood or affect, it reflects a strongly held value (respect for others) and also seems integral to a solution process designed to foster collaboration.

Finally, the most frequently coded elements of CEOs' problem solving were indications of self-reflection and self-evaluation (rank 1: item 6.2). For example:

> And I'm asking myself, while I hear that, whether our current organization and structure is adequate.

> So while he was saying, "Here's the problem as I see it," I've identified another problem that I want to raise with him in terms of how we get secondary school programs written, rewritten, refined and perhaps it's time to reconceptualize.

> What goes on in my head is, wow, conceptually we've got a difficulty here which won't affect the memo but is something I have to store for future reference.

CEOs planned extensively for their meetings. Nevertheless, the extent of mention of these self-reflective processes suggests that a high level of effort on their part is invested in the meeting: these meetings seemed to be crucial to them. They also worked hard at learning as much as possible from the meetings.

A disproportionate amount of attention was focused on solution processes in our coding because we believed this might constitute the focus of attention for the CEOs with their groups. This belief appeared to be unwarranted from the frequency count alone, however. Two of the 9 possible solution process items were ranked in the top 6. But the remaining 7 together accounted for only 24 percent of overall responses. Taking into account the third ranking of the interpretation item, these data are consistent with previous evidence suggesting that experts devote considerably greater attention than nonexperts to problem interpretation, thereby reducing the demands placed on solution processes. Nonexperts attempt (in vain) to compensate for inadequate attention to problem interpretation, by devoting substantially more effort to solution processes (Glaser and Chi 1988; Reynolds 1992; Leithwood and Steinbach 1993).

How, then, do CEOs solve problems in groups? Our evidence suggests, in sum, that superintendents' problem-solving processes appeared to be highly expert in comparison with those of principals, for example. Especially attended to were efforts to help their colleagues to place the immediate problem they were addressing in a broader context and to anticipate and address constraints. They also conducted the meetings so as to ensure the contribution of most in attendance, planning carefully in advance for how the meeting would be conducted. Furthermore, they were especially reflective about the meetings, both during the meetings and after the meetings were finished; they monitored progress in the meetings very closely but only intervened personally when the process began to stall or no one else was willing or able to further the group's progress. The superintendents were explicit about their own efforts to learn as much as possible from the meeting.

The Nature and Role of CEOs' Values

Table 4–2 reports the frequency of occurrence, in the protocols, of statements coded according to the four categories of specific values: basic human values, general moral values, professional values, and social and political values. Values were ranked according to how frequently they were used. The three right-hand columns provide comparable data on the ranking of values from our previous studies of expert principals (Leithwood and Steinbach 1991a) and CEOs (Raun and Leithwood 1993; Leithwood and Steinbach 1991b) using the same values framework.

Forty-two percent of all values statements were coded as professional values. Almost as many (40 percent) were coded as basic human values. Relatively little use was made of either social and political values (11 percent) or general moral values (5 percent). Such extensive reliance on professional values and little reliance on general moral values is consistent with trends evident in the three previous studies, noted in table 4–2. Discrepancies across studies are apparent, however, with respect to basic human values and social and political values. In both cases, the present study and Study 3 share similar findings, as do Studies 1 and 2. While there may be several other explanations for these similarities and differences, it is noteworthy that both the present study and Study 3 were carried out with "expert" administrators, although from different roles; Studies 1 and 2 included samples selected without reference to expertise, but from the same role.

Table 4–2 also shows the ranking of specific values associated with each of the four categories for the present study, as well as the three previous studies. Role responsibility and respect for others are among the most frequently cited values in the present study, as well as in two of the three remaining studies. Knowledge, ranked second in the present study, was also a prevalent value in

Study 1, although this is not evident in the data used for table 4–2. Finally, consequences (for immediate clients and/or the system at large) and participation are additional specific values ranked relatively highly in the present study as well as in several of the previous studies.

Raun and Leithwood (1993) concluded that pragmatism (consequences), participation, and duty (role responsibility) were prevalent value themes in their data. The present study provides additional support for the prevalence of these themes.

What Purposes Are Served by CEOs' Group Problem Solving?

To determine how CEOs solved problems in groups (above), we relied on a "microanalysis" of their verbal protocols using codes explicitly derived from our problem-solving model. To address the question of purposes, we offer a more holistic and more speculative interpretation of the data, based less directly on our model and its related coding system. Instead of the frequency of mention of brief, coded statements, our focus was on the meaning of (often) larger units of CEO talk. We searched for the explicit or apparent purposes CEOs attached to their problem solving with groups. We also searched for patterns of thought not likely to be evident in a component-by-component analysis of that problem solving.

The impression of purposes being pursued by CEOs, created by our holistic analysis of their group problem solving, was unexpected. Based on a previous study of expert principals solving problems in staff meetings (Leithwood and Steinbach 1991b), we anticipated that CEOs would be attempting to find better solutions to their problems than would be likely were individuals to solve the problems by themselves. Instead, CEOs in this study usually brought to their meetings a well-worked-out solution to the problem on the agenda. As one CEO explained:

> I'm very pleased because it's going exactly where I wanted it to go and it's coming from them. I'm not telling them what we're going to do; they are telling me what I'm going to do, but they are telling me what I want to hear.

This is the anomaly found in our coding (item 2.1). Like our typical principals (but unlike our expert principals), CEOs had a preconceived solution in mind, and the few statements coded as

2.1 reflected flexibility around how the solution would be played out. So, we wondered, why have the meeting? Was it only to serve the purpose, usually shunned by experts, of manipulating the group into agreeing on a predetermined solution so that members of the group would be motivated to implement it?

Based on both explicit talk and inferences about likely effects of their processes, we concluded that CEOs were attempting to accomplish two purposes. Their immediate purpose was to "transform ideas into organizational reality" (Daniels 1990, p. i); their long-term purpose was organizational learning (e.g., Senge 1990).

Transforming Ideas into Organizational Reality

The problems CEOs were solving with their colleagues in our study were primarily operational or maintenance problems (vs. strategic problems), and the context for solving these problems was usually a regularly scheduled meeting. Daniels (1990) claims that "what effective [leaders] are doing in regular meetings is exercising the organization's formal power" (p. iii). Such meetings, according to Daniels, are not intended for solving problems. They are a step beyond that. Their purpose is to ensure that those responsible for putting solutions into practice understand and agree with the solution: This is "the step by which the organization's intelligence gets integrated into its operations" (Daniels 1990, p. iii). In this respect, it is not so much that leaders are not solving problems, but that the nature of the problems they are solving has shifted. In regular meetings, then, at least part of the problem is how to ensure that everyone responsible for implementing the solution knows, in general, what is to be done and, in particular, what that means for their own practices.

Our evidence suggests that CEOs incorporated into their solution processes four strategies to ensure that ideas were transformed into practice:

1. Deciding on the specific nature of the action to be taken: Most CEOs used several strategies to help ensure complete agreement around the solution. Reflecting the value "solidarity," it was important to them that everyone in the group "speak with the same voice" or carry the same message to the people with whom they worked. One way

Table 4-2
Statements In Protocols Coded As Different Types Of Values: Current vs. Previous Studies

Categories of Values	Present Study				Rank in Previous Studies		
	# CEOs (N = 7)	Frequency	%	Rank	Study 1[a]	Study 2[b]	Study 3[c]
1. Basic Human Values							
TOTAL	7	189	40	(2)	(4)	(4)	(2)
1.1 Freedom					14	7	11
1.2 Happiness					11	13	
1.3 Knowledge	7	95	20	2	10	6	5
1.4 Respect for others	7	94	20	2	1	7	2
1.5 Survival					17	13	
2. General moral values							
TOTAL	5	23	5	(4)	(3)	(3)	(4)
2.1 Carefulness	4	13	3	6	5	9	9
2.2 Fairness	5	10	2	7	3	2	9
2.3 Courage					18	13	
2.4 Honesty					9		

| | Present Study | | | | Rank in Previous Studies | | |
Categories of Values	# CEOs (N = 7)	Frequency	%	Rank	Study 1[a]	Study 2[b]	Study 3[c]
3. Professional values							
TOTAL	7	193	42	(1)	(2)	(1)	(1)
3.1 General responsibility as an educator	1	1	1	9	7	9	6
3.2 Role Responsibility	7	127	27	1	16	1	1
3.3 Consequences for immediate clients	7				7	3	4
3.4 Consequences for others in the system	7	65	14	4	3	13	
4. Social and political values							
TOTAL	7	49	11	(3)	(1)	(2)	(3)
4.1 Participation	7	33	7	5	13	3	3
4.2 Sharing	2	4	1	9	12	9	6
4.3 Loyalty, solidarity, commitment	5	11	2	7	2	3	8
4.4 Helping others	1	1	1	9	5	7	

[a] A survey of values carried out with 53 Ontario CEOs (Raun and Leithwood 1993)
[b] Values evident in the individual problem solving of 8 CEOs selected without reference to expertise (Leithwood and Steinbach 1991a)
[c] Values evident in the group problem-solving processes of four expert elementary school principals (Leithwood and Steinbach, 1991b)

this happened was to ensure agreement on the details of the overall actions to be taken. For example:

> I'm information gathering. I want to have a clear picture from the players so that everybody is talking the same language. That was really what I was after.

> What I'm trying to do . . . I need my team with me so that we're going in [to the meeting] with a common understanding of what the outcome is to be and how we're going to do it.

> The problem here was to make sure that everybody understood those items and gave them appropriate weight.

> And thirdly, I wanted to be sure we all understood and agreed with the final position that I was articulating, making sure we all had a common understanding of what had been agreed to.

2. Being clear about the nature of the CEOs' actions for implementation. Another way of ensuring that everyone spoke with the same voice was to develop, with the group, those specific actions the CEO would initiate to implement the solution. For example, one CEO explained:

> The point there was to engage them in planning how I would respond to the people who had initially brought the concern [educational assistants]. And that's how the rest of the meeting is cast. Its in terms of their helping me plan what I'm going to say when I go back to them. Writing a script for me.

Another asked his colleagues:

> Do I make it a quiet presentation? Do I make it a passionate presentation?

3. Being clear about the nature of the actions to be carried out by other members of the group. Speaking with one voice was also fostered by explicitly working with the group on the actions other members of the group would take. For example:

> Okay, as a summary then, you're going to do some editing. This will go to the next principals' meetings—both of them. The superintendents will follow up with one-on-

one kind of interview with them and give them the support as we outlined in five.

4. Developing a viable implementation plan but remaining
flexible in the face of alternative proposals offered by others. As a kind of fail-safe mechanism, CEOs usually had
thought through the implementation problem and identified, in their minds, a viable course of action. Such mental
rehearsal seems likely to have prepared the CEOs for a
role in the meeting of ensuring that the group did not fail
to anticipate important obstacles and/or was able to generate useful implementation steps. However, possibly
reflecting their valuing of participation, CEOs did not rig-
idly adhere to their own preconceived plans in the face of
other good suggestions. For example:

> I never have a clear idea what to expect exactly. I've got
> a general framework for what I anticipate happening in
> the meeting. But if the meeting is working well, there is a
> lot of spontaneous stuff going on. It's not like the thing is
> well planned out like a play or something like that. So
> there is lots of good discussion. But yes, overall, we
> accomplished what I hoped would be accomplished.

Previous evidence (Leithwood and Steinbach 1991b) concerning
the group problem solving of expert principals demonstrated
efforts by them (unlike their nonexpert colleagues) to ensure that
follow-up to group problem solving was planned. The present
study, however, suggests much greater attention by CEOs to this
aspect of the problem, perhaps reflecting the swampier nature of
the implementation problem at the district or system level than the
school level.

Fostering Organizational Learning

Peter Senge (1990) conceives of learning organizations as

> organizations where people continually expand their capacity to
> create the results they truly desire, where new and expansive pat-
> terns of thinking are nurtured, where collective aspiration is set
> free, and where people are continually learning how to learn
> together. (p. 3)

Most CEOs made explicit statements about their long-term purposes that reflected the aim of organizational learning. One said, for example:

> We want to confirm leadership in the school and we want to clearly signal that things are under control, that problems are getting solved appropriately. We want to set the stage for addressing the longer term problems in the future, getting to the long term sorts of solutions.

Beyond such talk about their purposes, processes used by CEOs to solve problems in groups addressed conditions necessary for group learning. What is required to foster group learning, and how did the CEOs manage it? Senge (1990) views group (or team) learning as "the process of aligning and developing the capacity of a group to create the results its members truly desire" (p. 236). This happens when the group is able to think insightfully about complex issues by tapping the resources of many minds. There is also a need for innovative and coordinated action: Senge speaks of 'operational trust' . . . each group member remains conscious of other group members and can be counted on to act in ways that complement each others' actions" (p. 236). Learning teams also foster other learning teams "through inculcating the practices and skills of team learning more broadly" (p. 237).

There is evidence in the verbal protocols of CEOs attempting to meet Senge's three conditions for group learning in several ways. Two CEOs' reveal how they tap the mental resources of those in their groups in these comments:

> [S] is sometimes intimidated by program and instructional intellect and I . . . wanted to indicate to [him] that what he had to say was extremely valuable at that stage. If I allowed it to happen, we would wait until the end and that's becoming a pattern of his.

> . . . reacting to your body language, your facial expression . . . so that we can make sure that people don't miss an opportunity to meaningfully communicate. I watch that fairly carefully.

> Can we just hold off on the strategies. I haven't heard from Margaret. She's indicated she wants [to speak]. Then we'll come to that.

Examples of how CEOs encourage innovative and coordinated action are provided by these comments:

The role I play frequently is making sure that we get all the data out on the table and listened to before we go ahead and make a decision.

I see my role then as prodding, prompting, facilitating, encouraging . . . causing people maybe to stretch themselves a little bit further than where they were.

Let me explain a little bit about this. My way of operating is that I very much trust the ability of a group if it is functioning well to make really good decisions. So I leave a lot of power with the group and really pick my spots very carefully on something that I would try to impose on the group without getting their consensus or approval on it.

CEOs showed little evidence, however, of fostering other learning teams. Only one CEO alluded to this:

My role is to make them as effective as possible. Therefore I feel that I have to do that in every respect, not only as they conduct their daily work, or entertain all their leadership assignments, but also as individuals.

Group learning requires both dialogue and discussion. Dialogue, "the free and creative exploration of complex and subtle issues" (Senge 1990, p. 237), requires participants to suspend assumptions and to regard one another as colleagues. It also requires a facilitator who helps maintain the dialogue. The verbal protocols of CEOs show them thinking about providing such facilitation:

If I can't read the group and work for them to keep contributing, then I shouldn't be in the role.

. . . right, this is exactly what should happen. That superintendent should be speaking up and raising that question and that's what the group will expect to have happen.

In addition to dialogue, Senge claims that "discussion"—the presentation and defense of different views and a search for the best view to help solve the problem—is a condition for group learning. The intent of discussion is not to win, not to have your views prevail. Rather it is to clarify the meaning and consequences of the available alternatives to assist the group in finding the best solution to its problem. CEOs encourage such discussion in several ways. For example:

And I want to hear . . . just some opinions this morning about how you feel about the situation and what kinds of moves we're really going to have to take.

I went through all the items and paused long enough on each one to give people a chance [to talk].

One of my theories of a meeting is that you have to let the talk go on long enough to get everything that wants discussing out on the table. You make everything discussable by allowing somebody to introduce it.

SUMMARY AND CONCLUSION

The study asked three questions: How do CEOs solve problems in groups? What are the nature and role of values used by CEOs in their problem solving? And what purposes are CEOs attempting to serve through solving problems in groups? Verbal protocols collected using stimulated recall techniques with seven reputationally effective Ontario CEOs, each solving problems with a group of their senior colleagues, provided data for the study. Using evidence from principals as a basis for comparison, the CEOs' problem-solving processes appeared to be highly expert. CEOs helped their colleagues to place the immediate problem they were addressing in a broader context and to anticipate constraints. The CEOs also conducted the meetings so as to ensure the contribution of most in attendance. Furthermore, they were especially reflective about the meetings, both during and after they were finished; they monitored progress in the meetings very closely but intervened personally only when no one else was willing or able to further the group's progress. The CEOs were explicit about their own efforts to learn as much as possible from the meeting.

As expected, values were pervasive in the problem-solving processes of CEOs. In support of earlier studies, CEOs appeared to be largely influenced by the consequences that their problem solving would have on stakeholders in their organizations (pragmatism). Participation and their own sense of role responsibility (duty) were the other two values most evident in CEOs' problem solving.

CEOs appeared to be using their group problem-solving processes for two purposes. The short-term purpose, using Daniels's (1990) phrase, was to transform ideas into organizational reality.

This means ensuring that the solution to a problem was systematically reflected in the subsequent practices of the CEOs' senior colleagues, as well as in their own practices. A second, longer-term purpose was organizational learning, especially fostering the learning of the groups. Some of the conditions for organizational learning offered by Senge (1990) were used as a basis for capturing those processes used by CEOs likely to serve this purpose.

Processes used by CEOs to solve problems in groups serve a number of leadership functions, some of which have been made clearer by this study. To the extent that educational systems continue to restructure in ways similar to other large organizations, it seems especially important to continue the effort to better understand group problem-solving processes. To meet the demands for change and to respond opportunistically to unanticipated events, organizations are becoming structurally flatter (Naisbitt and Aburdene 1987; Toffler 1990). Much of the work of these organizations is being done in teams, with organizational learning as an explicit goal to help ensure their survival. These restructured organizations demand new forms of leadership based on collegial and expert sources of power. Referred to as "transformational", such leadership will often be expressed through the exchange of ideas in groups. As Bill O'Brien claims:

> Being a visionary leader is not about giving speeches and inspiring the troops. [It] is about solving day-to-day problems with my vision in mind. (quoted in Senge 1990, p. 217)

NOTES

A version of this paper with a somewhat different focus was published in the *Educational Administration Quarterly*, 1993, 28(3), 364–91.

1. Elements of the definition can be found in the work of Hodgkinson (1978), Rokeach (1975), Kluckhon (1951) and Williams (1968).

REFERENCES

Anderson, J. R. (1983). *The architecture of cognition.* Cambridge: Harvard University Press.

Argyris, C. (1982). *Reasoning, learning and action.* San Francisco: Jossey-Bass.

Beck, C. (1984). *The nature of values and implications for values education*. Unpublished manuscript, OISE, Toronto.

Begley, P., & Leithwood, K. A. (1989). The influence of values on school administrator practices. *Journal of Educational Administration and Foundations, 4*(2), 26–39.

Bransford, J. (in press). Who ya gonna call? Thoughts about teaching problem solving. In P. Hallinger, K. A. Leithwood, & J. Murphy (Eds.), *Cognitive perspectives on educational leadership*. New York: Teachers College Press.

Brightman, H. J. (1988). *Group problem solving: An improved managerial approach*. Atlanta: Georgia State University, Business Publishing Division.

Campbell-Evans, G. (1988). *The relationship between principals' values and their decision-making processes*. Unpublished doctoral dissertation, OISE, Toronto.

Chi, M. T. H., Feltovich, P. J., & Glaser, R. (1981). Categorization and representation of physics problems by experts and novices. *Cognitive Science, 5*(2), 121–52.

Cowan, D. A. (1986). Developing a process model of problem recognition. *Academy of Management Review, 11*(4), 763–76.

Cowan, D. A. (1988). Executives' knowledge of organizational problem types: Applying a contingency perspective. *Journal of Management, 14*(4), 513–27.

Cowan, D. A. (1990). Developing a classification structure of organizational problems: An empirical investigation. *Academy of Management Journal, 33*(2), 366–90.

Cowan, D. A. (1991). The effect of decision-making styles and contextual experience on executives' descriptions of organizational problem formulation. *Journal of Management Studies, 28*(5), 465–83.

Daniels, W. R. (1990). *Group power II: A manager's guide to conducting regular meetings*. San Diego: University Associated.

Day, D., & Lord, R. (1992). Expertise and problem categorization: The role of expert processing in organizational sense making. *Journal of Management Studies, 29*(1), 35–48.

Gagné, E. D. (1985). *The cognitive psychology of school learning*. Boston: Little, Brown.

Glaser, R., & Chi, M. (1988). Overview. In M. Chi, R. Glaser, & M. Farr (Eds.), *The nature of expertise* (pp. xv–xxviii). Hillsdale, NJ: Erlbaum.

Greeno, J. G. (1978). A study of problem solving. In R. Glaser (Ed.), *Advances in instructional psychology*. Hillsdale, NJ: Erlbaum.

Greeno, J. G. (1980). Trends in the theory of knowledge for problem solving. In D. Tuma & R. Fief (Eds.), *Problem solving and education* (pp. 9–24). New York: Wiley.

Hambrick, D. C., & Brandon, G. L. (1988). Executive values. In D. Hambrick (Ed.), *The executive effect: Concepts and methods for studying top managers* (pp. 3–34). London: JAI Press.

Hayes, J. R. (1980). Teaching problem-solving mechanisms. In D. Tuma & R. Feif (Eds.), *Problem solving and education* (pp. 141–50). New York: Wiley.

Hayes, J. R. (1981). *The complete problem solver.* Philadelphia: Franklin Institute Press.

Hodgkinson, C. (1978). *Towards a philosophy of administration.* Oxford: Basil Blackwell.

Hunter, J. E., Schmidt, F. L., & Judiesch, M. K. (1990). Individual differences in output variability as a function of job complexity. *Journal of Applied Psychology, 75,* 28–42.

Jaques, E. 1986. The development of intellectual capability: A discussion of stratified systems theory. *The Journal of Applied Behavioral Science, 22*(4), 361–383.

Kelsey, J. G. T. (in press). Learning from teaching: Problems, problem formulation, and the enhancement of problem-solving capability. In P. Hallinger, K. Leithwood, & J. Murphy (Eds.), *Cognitive perspectives on school leadership.* New York: Teachers College Press.

Kluckhon, C. (1951). Values and value orientations in the theory of action: An exploration in definition and classification. In T. Parsons & E. Shills (Eds.), *Toward a general theory of action* (pp. 398–433). Cambridge: Harvard University Press.

Leithwood, K. A. (1988). *How chief school officers classify and manage their problems.* Unpublished manuscript, Ontario Institute for Studies in Education, Totonto.

Leithwood, K. A., Begley, P., & Cousins, B. (1992). *Developing expert leadership for future schools.* New York: Falmer Press.

Leithwood, K. A., & Stager, M. (1989). Expertise in principals' problem solving. *Educational Administration Quarterly, 25*(2), 126–61.

Leithwood, K. A., & Steinbach, R. (1990). Characteristics of effective secondary school principals' problem solving. *Educational Administration and Foundations, 5*(1), 24–42.

Leithwood, K. A., & Steinbach, R. (1991a). Components of chief education officers' problem solving. In K. A. Leithwood & D. Musella (Eds.), *Understanding school system administration* (pp. 127–53). New York: Falmer Press.

Leithwood, K. A., & Steinbach, R. (1991b). Indicators of transformational leadership in the everyday problem solving of school administrators. *Journal of Personnel Evaluation in Education, 4*(3), 221–44.

Leithwood, K. A., & Steinbach, R. (1993). The relationship between variations in patterns of school leadership and group problem-solving processes. In P. Hallinger, K. A. Leithwood, & J. Murphy (Eds.), *Cog-*

nitive perspectives in educational leadership (pp. 103–29). New York: Teachers College Press.

Mumford, M. D., & Connelly, M. S. (1991). Leaders as creators: Leader performance and problem solving in ill-defined domains. *Leadership Quarterly, 2*(4), 289–315.

Naisbitt, J., & Aburdene, P. (1987). *Re-inventing the corporation.* New York: Warner Books.

Newell, A. (1975). Discussion of papers by Robert M. Gagné and John R. Hayes. In B. Kleinmuntz (Ed.), *Problem solving: Research, method and theory* (pp. 171–82). Huntington, NY: Robert E. Kreiger.

Newell, A., Rosenblum, P., & Laird, J. (1990). Symbolic architectures for cognition. In M. Posner (Ed.), *Foundations of cognitive science* (pp. 133–60). Cambridge: MIT Press.

Newell, A., & Simon, H. (1972). *Human problem solving.* Englewood Cliffs, NJ: Prentice Hall.

Nickerson, R. S. (1988–89). On improving thinking. In E. Z. Rotherkopf (Ed.), *Review of research in education* (Vol. 15, pp. 3–57). Washington, DC: American Educational Research Association.

Raun, T., & Leithwood, K. A. (1993). Pragmatism, participation and duty: Values used by chief education officers in their problem solving. In P. Hallinger, K. A. Leithwood, & J. Murphy (Eds.), *Cognitive perspectives on educational leadership and administration* (pp. 54–74). New York: Teachers College Press.

Reitman, W. (1965). *Cognition and thought.* New York: Wiley.

Reynolds, A. (1992). What is competent beginning teaching: A review of the literature. *Review of Educational Research, 62*(1), 1–35.

Rokeach, M. (1975). *Beliefs, attitudes and values.* San Francisco: Jossey-Bass.

Rubinstein, M. F. (1975). *Patterns of problem solving.* Englewood Cliffs, NJ: Prentice Hall.

Rumelhart, D. E. 1990. The architecture of mind: A connectionist approach. In M. Posner (Ed.) *Foundations of cognitive science* (pp. 93–132). Cambridge, MA: The MIT Press.

Schön, D. (1983). *The reflective practitioner.* San Francisco: Jossey-Bass.

Schwenk, C. R. (1988). The cognitive perspective on strategic decision-making. *Journal of Management Studies, 25*(1), 41–56.

Senge, P. (1990). *The fifth discipline.* New York: Doubleday.

Shank, R., & Abelson, R. (1977). *Scripts, plans, goals and understanding.* Hillsdale, NJ: Erlbaum.

Showers, C., & Cantor, N. (1985). Social cognition: A look at motivated strategies. *Annual Review of Psychology, 36,* 275–305.

Simon, H. (1993). Decision making: Rational, nonrational and irrational. *Educational Administration Quarterly, 29*(3), 392–411.

Srivastva, S. (Ed.). (1983). *The executive mind*. San Francisco: Jossey-Bass.

Suchman, L. (1987). *Plans and situated actions: The problem of human/machine communication*. Cambridge: Cambridge University Press.

Toffler, A. (1990). *Powershift*. New York: Bantam Books.

Vaill, P. (1989). *Managing as a performing art*. San Francisco: Jossey-Bass.

Van Lehn, K. (1990). Problem solving and cognitive skill acquisition. In M. I. Posner (Ed.), *Foundations of cognitive science* (pp. 527–79). Cambridge: The MIT Press.

Voss, J. F., & Post, T. A. (1988). On the solving of ill-structured problems. In M. T. H. Chi, R. Glaser & M.J. Farr (Eds.), *The nature of expertise* (pp. 261–85). Hillsdale, NJ: Erlbaum.

Williams, R. M. (1968). *Values*. International Encyclopedia of the Social Sciences. New York: MacMillan.

CHAPTER 5

Superintendents' Management of State-Initiated Reform: A Matter of Interpretation

Fran Wills and Kent Peterson

The current emphasis in the United States on national goals for education (Cuban 1990) and systemic reform (Smith and O'Day 1990) intensifies the need to understand the forces shaping implementation of policy directives at the district level. Firestone's recent work (1989) suggests that perceptions of the "regulatee" as well as those of the "regulator" are important in determining whether reforms are viewed as constraints or incentives. As Firestone (1989) explains, important insights into the successful implementation of reforms can be discovered by examining district leadership strategies to identify how districts respond differently to reforms. Such responses may range from mere "compliance" to "opportunistic use." The analysis of superintendents' responses to reforms suggests a new approach to understanding why districts implement reforms (Wills 1990).

As current demands for school improvement increase while available funds decrease, the varying responses of local districts to the external pressures for reform from state legislatures, regulatory agencies, and local constituencies offer a key to understanding outcomes. These responses result from district leaders' interpretations of the environments of reform and are the focus of this study.

How a leader responds to the local district is an important feature of the superintendency. In fact, the work of superintendents remains critical in transforming educational reform legislation into change, improvement, or ample "workshelf" compliance (Cuban 1984; Firestone 1989; Floden et al. 1988; Odden 1986; Timar and Kirp 1987).

The source of demands on school districts to change recently has shifted from change initiated within the organization and focused on individual schools to change imposed by state departments of education (Firestone, Fuhrman, and Kirst 1989; Odden 1986; Odden and Dougherty 1982). To better understand this phenomenon, our study investigated specific strategies superintendents developed as they implemented school improvement plans in response to state mandates. Thirty superintendents and assistant superintendents of large, midsize, and small districts in Maine were interviewed about their responses to the state's mandates. Clear relationships emerged linking superintendents' perceptions of their environments to their strategy decisions in response to the mandates.

The research, then, explored superintendents' perceptions (interpretations) of external demands and their implementation of state mandates. In this case, a legislative mandate to develop and implement a school improvement plan occurred in the context of environmental uncertainty. This study examined the ways superintendents interpreted their environments and how those interpretations shaped their decisions to implement change. The study also looked at the relationship between patterns of superintendent strategy formation and district size.

FRAMEWORK

Organizational Environments

Much has been written about how and why organizations respond differently to environmental pressure (Aldrich and Pfeffer 1976; Pfeffer 1982; Thompson 1967). Child (1972), Weick (1969), and others (Aguilar 1967; Aldrich and Pfeffer 1976; Miles and Snow 1978; Pfeffer 1982; Tung 1979) have identified as important factors (a) the properties of the environment, (b) the ways the environment shapes organizational structure, and (c) the ways organizations strategically respond to environmental demands.

Similarly, organizational size has been identified as a salient factor in strategy development and variation (Child,1972; Kasarda

1974; Meyer 1972). By stratifying selection of the superintendent sample by size of district, the study explored the relationship of that feature to superintendent perceptions of the environment and strategy implementation. Important influences of size on strategy formation include the increased reliance on "impersonal mechanisms" and formalization as organizations expand. The influence of increased size implies less personal control by administrators over their work and the standardization of procedure. Other findings indicate increasing structural differentiation and decentralization as organizations grow (Pfeffer 1982). Kasarda's (1974) study of the effects of school-district size suggests an inverse relationship between district size and the managerial component, adding specialized support of guidance counselors, librarians, and other specialists: More personnel, positions, and strategy alternatives are linked to greater access to specialists in larger districts.

The existence of fewer administrators in smaller districts, as found in Kasarda's (1974) study, also was linked to a more decentralized strategic response. More emphasis on decentralized site management and control appeared to affect strategy decisions. Nonetheless, the relationship of district size to interpretations of environmental uncertainty remained unclear in Kasarda's study. Only tentative propositions about this relationship emerged.

Responses to Organizational Environments

Managers must respond to the environment when it makes focused demands. It seems reasonable to assume that the "effects of environments are mediated through the filter of managerial perceptions" (Weick 1969) and that perceptions are both learned responses and strong, socially constructed reality. Daft and Weick's (1984) model of organizations as interpretation systems provided a template for examining the relationship between managers' perceptions of the environment and the strategies that they develop (see table 5–1). Applied to superintendents, variability in their response to state-initiated reforms may be explained as a product of varying superintendent perceptions of environmental uncertainty. Understanding the outcomes of educational reform may be enhanced by using the model to examine superintendents' strategies as they are mediated by these perceptions. Indeed, the success or failure of state-initiated reform might be inextricably tied to such perceptions.

The Daft and Weick model delineates the relationships among (a) modes of interpretation, (b) perceptions of the environment, and (c) specific management behavior. Organizations are considered to be "open social systems that process information from the environment" (Daft and Weick 1984, p. 285), and managerial cognitive maps are developed through information sharing. Interpretation of this information results in environmentally directed organizational behaviors and activities. The authors note that "strategic-level managers formulate the organization's interpretation" (p. 285) and then either control or manage internal behavioral responses to the environment based on their interpretations. Thus, interpretations of reforms shape superintendents' responses and the implementation processes that they initiate.

Finally, managers differ in their modes of interpretation and in the ways they "know their environment." Managerial scanning of the environment and the choosing or rejecting of information sources form a critical function of knowing the environment and acting upon it (Aguilar 1967; Bartunek 1984; Daft and Weick 1984; Duncan 1972; Hedberg 1981). Superintendents are key environmental scanners, interpreters, and reactors in the face of state-initiated reform. How these behaviors and interpretive schemata shape superintendents' responses to reform is a key to understanding policy implementation.

Table 5–1 also suggests that superintendents who view organizations as rational and the environment as analyzable will respond predictably. A substantially different decision-making process may be used by superintendents who believe that the environment is chaotic, unanalyzable, and uncertain. Such a process would likely include more informal trial and error. This is referred to by Daft and Weick (1984) as "conditioned viewing" (e.g., passive, programmed, defensive organizational decision making) and more active analyzing, or systems analysis. Both strategies assume that the organizational leader can make sense of the environment. For those superintendents who assume that the environment is not amenable to rational analysis, a passive approach would foster much reacting and little attempt at making proactive decisions. In contrast, the "enactor" would depend on "prospecting" through continual trial-and-error behaviors.

Daft and Weick's model of the "prospector" resembles work by physicists attempting to learn more about chaos and uncertainty. An example is Lorenz's work on weather prediction, which

Table 5-1
Relationship between Interpretative Modes
and Organizational Processes

Organizational Intrusiveness

	Passive	Active
Unanalyzable	UNDIRECTED VIEWING *Scanning characteristics:* Data sources: External, personal Acquisition: No scanning department, irregular contacts and reports, casual information *Interpretation process:* Much equivocality reduction Few rules, many cycles *Strategy and decision making:* Strategy: Reactor Decision process: Coalition building	ENACTING *Scanning characteristics:* Data sources: External, personal Acquisition: No department, irregular reports and feedback from environment, selective information *Interpretation process:* Some equivocality reduction Moderate rules and cycles *Strategy and decision making:* Strategy: Prospector Decision process: Incremental trial and error
Analyzable	CONDITIONED VIEWING *Scanning characteristics:* Data sources: Internal, impersonal Acquisition: No department, although regular record keeping and information systems, routine information *Interpretation process:* Little equivocality reduction Many rules, few cycles. *Strategy and decision making:* Strategy: Defender Decision process: Programmed, problemistic search	DISCOVERING *Scanning characteristics:* Data sources: Internal, impersonal Acquisition: Separate departments, special studies and reports, extensive information *Interpretation process:* Little equivocality reduction Many rules, moderate cycles *Strategy and decision making:* Strategy: Analyzer Decision process: Systems analysis, computation

Assumptions about Environment labels the two rows: Unanalyzable and Analyzable.

From "Toward a Model of Organizations as Interpretation Systems," by R. L. Daft and K. E. Weick, 1984, *Academy of Management Review, 9,* 291.

argued that "sensitive dependence on initial conditions" was an inescapable consequence "of the way small scales intertwined with large" (Gleick 1987, p. 23). In terms of organizational change and policy making, this view reinforces the notion that all situations are indeed unique, shaped by varying "initial conditions," and that predictability depends on a highly improbable congruence or consistency of these initial conditions. The variability of local district conditions suggests that prescriptive formulas for change, such as the intervention of a state-mandated improvement process, might result in varied and even unpredictable outcomes due to varying initial conditions.

It may be inferred, then, that effective organizational learning and decision making by leaders would have to respond to this less "analyzable" environment. Indeed, while studies on organizations imply that "points of crisis magnify small changes," the chaos principle suggests that such points are everywhere (Gleick 1987, p. 23), especially for leaders.

Multiplying demands and *points of crisis* are phrases that capture much of the world of school superintendents. The chaos principle suggests that the environment in which the district leader operates is turbulent, complex, and thus subject to considerable uncertainty. The state's demands for a school improvement plan provide a "point of crisis" through which to examine how uncertainty is dealt with by superintendents. This parallels recent work by Peters (1988), examining effective management in similarly "chaotic" or turbulent modern business environments. Such studies of district leaders are rare, however.

State-Initiated Reform

The reform used as the context for this study was a districtwide improvement planning process mandated by the Maine legislature in the School Reform Act of 1984. Representing one example of legislation adopted by states in response to concerns about education, this legislation designated the superintendent as being in "charge of the ongoing improvement process in each school unit" (State of Maine Department of Educational and Cultural Services 1985). The intent of this state reform was to promote more uniformly effective and excellent schools in response to the uneven, inconsistent quality of education in a geographically dispersed state with pockets of rural poverty. It was expected to improve educational outcomes and programming. The urgency to involve the state department more intensely at the district level was enhanced by the accelerated development of the "two Maines": Immigration and development in the coastal and southern sections of the state, and continuing economic decay in traditional areas of commerce, poultry, and shoe and paper manufacturing. The disparity in economic conditions appeared to act as a driving force in defining an education policy to support more-consistent economic growth and a more unified economic condition.

Detailed instructions accompanied state regulations, with special emphasis on the process of improvement planning, which included monitoring of outcomes. Detailed directions also were given for working through a planning cycle of determining goals, developing action strategies, evaluation, and assessment. A review mechanism for the planning process was implemented by sending to the district a "school improvement team," an arm of the state department's division of curriculum. The school improvement plans themselves were to address five general categories of goals: (a) leadership/management, (b) curriculum, (c) instruction, (d) staff development, and (e) facilities. The state department developed a database that coded the goals and analyzed individual district plans. Plans considered effective by the evaluating "approval teams" were those based on a planning process that emphasized the concepts and goals reported in the effective-schools research as essential to a successful change process (Purkey and Smith 1983). The goals included collaborative planning, community involvement, clear goals and expectations, responsibility of management for improvement efforts, and a focus on instructional leadership. Specific planning criteria were (a) a documented needs-assessment process; (b) a planning committee representative of community and district; (c) a readable planning document; (d) the assignment of implementation responsibility; and (e) an established process for monitoring the plan.

It is important to note that these reforms are primarily procedural. For example, they do not focus on the implementation of specific state curriculum frameworks or new forms of student assessment. The data suggest patterns of response to these procedural reforms, but it is not possible to extrapolate these findings to state mandates of substantive changes. Such changes can evoke strongly different responses due to the degree of uncertainty superintendents perceive or due to other factors fostered particularly by substantive reform efforts.

METHOD

This was an exploratory study (Guba and Lincoln 1981) using qualitative methods to examine how superintendents' interpretive schemata affect their reform responses. Data were collected through interviews with 30 Maine superintendents and assistant superintendents. These administrators worked in districts varying widely in size. District size was defined as small, midsize, or large, based on classification of the district's high school population by the Maine Secondary School Principals' Association. Districts without a high school were classified as small. Student population fell into the following categories: up to 1,000, small; 1,000 to 2,000, midsize; above 2,500, large. In this study, the sample included 10 administrators of small districts, 11 administrators of 9 midsize districts, and 9 administrators of 8 large districts.

While these districts fall within the range of smaller districts nationwide, most states have substantial numbers of such districts, making these findings useful to policymakers. Additionally, we found, even in the larger districts in the sample, increasing differentiation and specialization of staff, features that will continue to confound policy implementation in districts with many more students. Though it seems reasonable to assume that, in much larger districts, superintendents may also delegate responsibility to other central office staff (similar to what is found in this study), further research on districts larger than this sample will be needed to verify these possibilities.

Districts were identified by the state "school approval" team as having successfully developed districtwide improvement plans. Superintendents were interviewed using open-ended and structured formats, such as card-sort and ranking. Through this method, respondents reconstructed, in narrative, the process used by their districts to develop strategies in response to state mandates. Structured questions were asked also to validate the narratives. These data were content-analyzed to discover patterns of perceptions of the environment and strategic responses. Districts' written plans were also examined to confirm interview responses.

A systematic approach to content analysis was guided by the principles proposed by Mostyn (1985):

> The analyst must let the data "do" the work for him/her. That is, the proof . . . must arise out of the data, and it must guide that analyst to revise ideas or discover new hypothesis. The data must also be used to support any conclusions drawn in the form of questions. (p. 132)

Using this approach implies that (a) categories of analysis must emerge from the interview account itself; (b) redundancy of response, language, and imagery improves the validity of the approach and categories drawn from the data; and (c) the qualitative analyst must continually analyze the data. In addition, the reliability of the protocol is enhanced with the repetition of emergent categories found in the data.

This study focused on districts designated as having "good planning processes" by the department of education. By limiting the sample in this way, the study was able to examine the strategies of superintendents who actively responded to the mandate. It was assumed that the characteristics of this more active group could shed light on the range of actions, on implemented responses, and on conformity to mandates. Also, less-successful superintendents might have been unwilling to participate. Because the sample focused on "successful" responses, it is possible that superintendents reacted differently in unsuccessful districts, but we do not know. Data for this study were analyzed, categories were developed, and biases were examined and limited through expert assessments (Murphy 1980). Data categories were submitted to qualified researchers for review.

FINDINGS

Sources of Uncertainty

Using Daft and Weick's (1984) model, this study identified categories of uncertainty and described connections between district leaders' beliefs about uncertainty and strategies for change. Six categories of uncertainty emerged from the data analysis:

1. Career line, related to superintendents' beliefs about their own futures

2. Organizational structure, related to resource inadequacy or complexity of the organization

3. Accountability, related to formal responsibility and participation in decision making

4. Linkages in school improvement, related to beliefs about instrumentality

5. The economic environment, related to perceptions of the influence of economic and social change in the community

6. Intent, related to interpretation of state motivation in mandating the school improvement plan

Identified through textual analysis of the responses of district leaders, the six themes may be conceptualized as originating with superintendents' internal environments—ambivalence about career path—and moving outward to the ambiguities of the economic environment.

Analysis of these categories revealed varying patterns related to the size of the district in which superintendents work. District size appears to influence the superintendent's role in the improvement process as well as the strategies used in response to state mandates. In the larger district, several factors led to uncertainty—including the number of staff members, the organizational complexity created by numerous committees, inadequate communication, and the size of school boards. These factors affected superintendent responses differently in small districts: Without additional staff and resources, the superintendent of the small district was forced to "go it alone."

Strategies utilized by superintendents were found to be directed toward reducing equivocality or uncertainty (Daft and Weick 1984; Thompson 1967) arising from perceptions of the six environmental dimensions or themes. Indeed, the contextual uncertainty might be conceptualized as providing a moving frame or structure for situations that required responses.

The nature of superintendents' responses to uncertainty appeared to depend on their interpretations of contextual factors. In this respect, the study reinforced the findings reflected in the Daft and Weick (1984) model. Managers' strategic responses were often a corollary of varying patterns of information retrieval. Sources of information contributed to the reduction of perceived uncertainty or equivocality in the environment (Daft and Weick

1984, p. 291). For example, 70 percent of the superintendents interviewed indicated a preference for external and personal sources of information. Only one superintendent relied upon an internal, "impersonal" database for information relating to school improvement. After Daft and Weick, the majority of the superintendents used "reacting" or "prospecting" strategies in responding to the state reform demands. Reactors tended to "build coalitions" through a strong participatory process.

Size of district was related to variation in choice of strategies. In midsize and large districts, in which many of the school-reform strategies had already been introduced, the school improvement plan was primarily an opportunity for increased involvement and stronger linkages. The focus for improvement tended to be facility expansion and increased personnel. On the other hand, many of the leaders of small districts, the "prospectors" (superintendents who scanned the environment), used the school improvement plan as a lever for change and increased spending. More than 50 percent of the small districts responded to state demands by implementing nine of the strategies listed in the survey. They developed board-approved mission and goal statements, a districtwide process to develop consensus, an articulated written curriculum, teacher training in effective schools research, training in observation and peer supervision, long-range strategic planning, expanded programming (gifted and talented, fine arts, library), and increased guidance, support, and clerical staff to relieve teaching staff of nonteaching duties.

Essentially, the external personal scanning behavior of the superintendents promoted responses to the school improvement mandate matching their unique district conditions. Their behavior assumed an "unanalyzable" environment that did not behave predictably—it needed to be continually tested through frequent informal, external, and personal contacts so that adjustments could be made quickly and decisively.

Relations between Strategies and Perceptions of Uncertainty

A close examination of each of the contextual factors that emerged from the interviews revealed additional associations between the superintendents' perceptions and strategy formation. These varied by district size.

Superintendents' Beliefs about Their Own Future. Superintendents' beliefs about their future, especially what their careers held for them, led to feelings of uncertainty. Eighteen of the 30 district leaders (60 percent), 5 of the superintendents in small districts (50 percent), 7 of the superintendents in midsize districts (63 percent), and 6 of the district leaders (assistants and superintendents) in large districts (75 percent) expressed uncertainty about their future career paths and were reluctant to affirm any concrete alternative for future work, even after probing from the researcher. Eleven of the 30 district leaders (36 percent) sug-gested alternative possibilities after probing by the researcher. Five of the superintendents in smaller districts (50 percent) indicated possible movement to a larger district (1 super-intendent), to higher education (3), or other (1); 4 of the superintendents in midsize districts (37 percent) suggested movement to a larger district (1), higher education (1), retirement (1), or remaining in the district (1).

Ambivalence regarding their future was reflected in strategic behavior that ensured control over the improvement process and its outcomes or, alternately, provided a particular avenue for specialized expertise, such as facilities improvement or expansion. The most prevalent strategy was an immersion in the immediate situation. Time spent in reflection was limited to reacting to political realities of the present. This came from all directions through frequent impersonal contact rather than in personal reflection on future planning or self-study. The reduction of uncertainty in future planning and the effect of environmental demands on career security were facilitated through increasing opportunities for control and influence in the present. Superintendents sought such opportunities within the organizational structure and, in many cases, the surrounding community and social environment. The school improvement mandate appeared to provide such an opportunity for immersion.

Especially superintendents in small districts exerted effort in many directions. The phrase *jack-of-all-trades* was used to identify the generalist role of the superintendent in the small district:

> In a small district you do everything. . . . In a larger district you have help; I'm not sure if it would be easier for me, but if you cut your teeth. . . . Here I'm jack-of-all-trades.

Also, more superintendents in smaller districts imagined themselves moving to a larger district, a move viewed as an opportunity to specialize and delegate. At the same time, these superintendents expressed ambivalence about losing control of the entire leadership process as district size increased.

In midsize districts superintendents searched for internal supports and resources to bolster change efforts. Administrative team and staff development were pursued in an attempt to derive mutual interpretations and common beliefs and norms to secure the superintendent's position. Superintendents used delegating and participatory strategies that most effectively deployed limited personnel; the superintendents relied upon shared belief systems to maintain influence over organizational direction. More than 50 percent of the leaders in midsize districts indicated strategies for planning that involved community groups and school-based site management. Midsize district leaders, while ambivalent about their career directions, were more apt to see the state-mandated improvement plan as a possible fulcrum for change in the district and as an opportunity to enhance their own leadership role.

In contrast, superintendents in large districts developed opportunities to specialize and to focus on an area of expertise (e.g., facilities, policymaking at the state level) that would serve them in their future careers. They sought concrete demonstrations of improvement and planning as a point of departure for career development. Superintendents in larger districts often focused on facilities plans and construction projects as major goals of their improvement plans. Larger staffs could provide greater flexibility in task performance. Superintendents appeared to have access to greater versatility of responses as well as more diverse internal and external resources to maintain control of strategy formation and interpretation of environmental information. However, a common experience of superintendents in districts of varying sizes is illustrated by one superintendent in a large district:

> I take it a day at a time. I don't really anticipate any other positions in education, but I just don't know. I take it a day at a time ... especially in the superintendency, because you don't know what's going to happen in this job.

Uncertainty Related to Resources or Complexity of the Organization. In small districts the scarcity of human and fiscal resources increased demands on district leaders and threatened stability of the organization. While human and fiscal resources were more abundant as district size increased, the complexity of the larger organization presented other types of challenges. One superintendent in a small district noted the dilemma of maintaining an image of self-sufficiency while struggling to meet all the demands of the job:

> It's easier to see now that the district organization was an obstacle . . . the central office staff consisted of just a special educational director who left because of the amount of work expected to do . . . I never asked for more help . . . which I think now I should have . . . for the sake of the system . . . superintendents are slow to ask for help for themselves . . . people are skeptical of increasing administrative costs. As a group they want to be seen as people who can do it all by themselves.

Small district superintendents expanded and multiplied their roles as fiscal agent, construction and facility manager, curriculum coordinator, and staff developer to cope with inadequate structure and sparse administrative staff. In one case the superintendent was also the principal of the school. Smaller district organizations also varied in design and structure. Some were K–8, others K–12. Others consisted of a variety of units of governance: school administrative districts, unions, and community school districts. Superintendents of school unions, for example, administered multiple school boards, budgets, and improvement plans.

The complexity of organizational relationships also increased uncertainty. Strategies ranged from political activities, such as increasing influence on the receiving high school and representation on the board of directors of the receiving institution, in order to organize such restructuring initiatives as decentralized or site-based planning. Other strategies included participation in a comprehensive staff-retraining program, investment in a systems-analysis approach utilizing computer technology, and a complex monitoring program to track goals and objectives.

Superintendents in midsize districts felt pressure to grow with inadequate resources. Midsize districts were too small to acquire additional resources and too large to rely on internal personal contact for strategy formation and monitoring. These superintendents used the state's school improvement legislation as a lever to increase staffing, to add additional programming, and to improve facilities. They placed heavy emphasis on staff development and differentiated staffing. Several superintendents of midsize districts identified comprehensive visions for change and the development of teachers as leaders within a controlled process of staff training and development.

An issue for leaders was the complexity of governance and political structure in midsize and some larger districts. The number of board members in school districts increased with the number of towns served, with as many as twenty-three board members in one large district. In addition, the number of school boards ranged from three to five in some "union" districts. Each of these boards often had five members and separate budgets and facilities. For each board a different agenda for improvement emerged. Resources varied in each "union" town, based on property wealth, thus fiscal problems varied.

Superintendents of midsize districts frequently attempted to control the improvement process and reduce uncertainty through a steering-committee structure. They would attempt to enact control over process through controlling structure, frequency of meetings, and administrative team leadership. However, the school union organizational structure consisting of individual town school committees and budgets stymied a systemwide organizational change process. The need to satisfy individual constituencies encouraged a site-based approach to school improvement based on unique community needs and expectations. In such instances, the administrative role was moderated to elicit input within acceptable parameters. Superintendents tried to influence through information rather than direct control over outcomes.

> I wanted a school improvement plan that wasn't so comfort oriented, but I stayed out of it, because I knew people had to deal with comfort first though. . . . I didn't want to let them go wild. . . . The coordinating committee connects. . . . I purposely kept influence away from control. My input was: Here's some other information you really have to consider or we might be off base. I influence only if they are off base . . . it's inefficient, but gives ownership. . . . For example, people felt they lost out when we combined words, changed their words.

For superintendents of large districts, several factors contributed to the complexity and uncertainty of organizational structure and strategy formation. The larger school boards in these districts produced highly complex committee structures. In municipal districts, tenuous relationships among city councils, the board, and the superintendent increased the monitoring of budget implications of planned improvements. Elections for both city council and school committee provided additional uncertainty of response to improvement proposals. A shrinking arena for district leadership evolved as administrative intensity increased and improvement activities were decentralized.

One superintendent in a large district reflected on the issue of delegating tasks and relying on monitoring and setting of "parameters":

> I am a forward-moving person ahead of trouble. When the state plan came, however, it created a period of confusion, frustration and losing control, because I'm a very control-oriented guy. And I can remember we unraveled it coming back from a superintendents' convention downstate, and I said to my assistant, "I guess I'm not just going to delegate this to you, not because I don't trust you . . . and so I'm going to provide parameters in which you can operate, still giving me the veto power in terms of the recommendations, pros and cons.

In response to the complexity of large district organizations, superintendents developed a variety of strategies designed to reduce unintended outcomes. These strategies included (a) strong administrative control on steering committees; (b) delegation of supervision of process to the assistant superintendent with frequent interaction between superintendent and assistant; (c) frequent committee meetings at the board level; (d) review procedures for the school-based improvement process; (e) strong administrative team process and frequent meetings; and (f) increase in external environment interaction, including frequent contacts with city council, influential community members, and elected board members.

These measures attempted to reduce uncertainty and "chaos."

Responsibility and Involvement in Decision Making. As districts increased in size, the number of committees and levels of responsibility increased. The development of a strong administrative team was an attempt to reduce the uncertainty that grew with increased distances among the district leader, planners, and implementors. The basic paradox, accepted by the majority of the superintendents, was the need to expand their involvement at the same time as they struggled to maintain management control and sources of information.

In smaller districts the history of the planning process, including the level of involvement of the superintendent and participation by other personnel, affected the acceptance of change. When all levels were involved in planning, deviations from the decisions of planners by the district leader created underlying conflict, resentment, and resistance. Involvement of staff was an essential strategy for increasing resources, maintaining support, ensuring implementation, reducing uncertainty, and expanding influence. The process in one small district was especially painful for the superintendent, who entered the district after the planning process and did not anticipate the significance of the ownership in even small changes recommended by teacher-planners. For example, plans to renovate a teachers' room and purchase new drapes for the library played a larger role in one district and affected the superintendent's ability to gain support and influence. The school improvement effort in some cases seemed to be reduced to "comfort items," such as a window in a teacher's room. Such cosmetic changes discouraged examination of more-profound deficits in district performance.

Further, superintendents in small districts lacked personnel to include in committee structures. A heavier burden of participation, as a consequence, was placed on individual staff members. However, ownership in implementation and the emphasis on personal and community-based issues were greater. This ownership lessened uncertainty.

With increasing district size, issues of ownership appeared to dissipate somewhat. Instead, in larger districts, issues surfaced that related more to monitoring of implementation, consistency of participation, and coordination of improvement strategies. In midsize districts a similar strain was placed on personnel to meet legislative requirements. Frequently, the superintendent, not able to participate in all committee efforts, delegated leadership to building or community representatives. Superintendents were then frequently surprised by the emergence of specific and less predictable agendas and expectations. Some of the issues that emerged were particularly disconcerting as some school improvement teams jumped normal hierarchical lines of communication. Unexpected issues, such as long-smoldering dissatisfactions with a principal, surfaced at school improvement committee meetings.

This type of unintended outcome resulted in personnel changes that often led to deeper and more lasting levels of improvement and satisfied long-standing concerns.

Often, for superintendents in larger districts, the structure for change and improvement was already in place. Uncertainty was less of an issue. Sufficient staff existed to take on leadership roles and form a strong administrative team. In one district, reliance on decentralized decision making and a teacher-led staff development process co-opted the legislative mandates. Otherwise, reliance on buffers, such as strong steering committees, reduced surprise recommendations and outcomes in other districts.

Beliefs about Instrumentality. Leaders have differing beliefs about instrumentality; that is, whether plans, actions, and outcomes are linked. Although largely a matter of individual interpretation by superintendents, the response to uncertainty about linkages between school improvement planning and expected outcomes varied somewhat according to the district size or the availability of resources to apply to the problem. The prevalent strategies in small districts were focused on seeking resources, maximizing scarce resources, and building on the strength of a few bureaucratic layers. Discrepancies between teachers' and administrators' perceptions of improvement needs were more apparent in smaller districts, less veiled by administrative layers. On the other hand, communication was more direct among administrators, staff, and board members in small districts.

In many cases, the state mandate was seen as a lever for deeper levels of change. This was obvious from the number and types of strategic changes that took place in smaller and midsize districts in response to the school reform legislation. An aggregated total of 139 strategy changes were identified by the 10 superintendents of small districts. The 11 midsize district leaders identified 14 strategies that were enacted, and the 9 leaders of large districts identified 102.

Leaders of small districts more frequently included in their improvement plans long-range planning, teacher training, and staff development than did the leaders of midsize and large districts, who in many cases had initiated these programs prior to the reform legislation. This suggests stronger beliefs in instrumentality. Thus, while personnel and programs were also added, there was also an emphasis on developing personnel and clarifying the technology around instruction and outcomes.

Additionally, in some small districts, leaders attempted to link program change with effectiveness and achievement through instructional and supervisory skill development. Monitoring and evaluation of this process were facilitated by the smaller number of staff members and the ease of identifying performance or implementation deviations. All staff members could be trained at once, observed, and involved in a process of remediation when necessary. Size, then, may have influenced the development of instrumentality beliefs.

Effective superintendents of smaller districts tended to engage in training and supervisory roles, acting as curriculum- and staff-development coordinators while maintaining their credibility and influence on the implementation phase. Linkages were tightened to validate and to evaluate change through revised staff evaluation procedures.

With increased district size came superintendents' perceptions of having less control over outcomes. As a result, more technical approaches were used to tighten linkages. Strategies included (a) adding program and personnel, (b) increasing professional development opportunities, (c) increasing staff responsibility, (d) coping with diversity of input with program additions and alternative programs, and (e) focusing on the immediacy of the issue of achievement.

The focus on concrete and structural changes demonstrates the kinds of issues that emerge in the planning process. These are issues such as windows in a faculty room, which might be labeled by March and Cohen (1986) as "garbage-can" agendas through which more-telling concerns are disguised or identified. As one leader stated:

> [Our district] had a well-established planning, not hit-or-miss, system. The SIP [School Improvement Plan] just added unnecessary paperwork. This is the form you have to use. This is crazy. We would have been better off if the state sat down with us saying, "What are you folks planning to do in the next 5 years? Where is [the district] going?" We could have told them . . .
> Critical issues emerged at the elementary school [regarding a principal]. Main issues emerged: no windows in a faculty room. That went to the school committee. We got windows. Different islands of influence emerged. The SIP became a catalyst

for advocacy of certain issues. The staff came out to vocalize issues, like certification, [a] lost opportunity; they [the state] blew that one. It was dumped on us. W had to shift gears.

By addressing such items as windows in the teachers' room, the superintendent was also able to connect to deeper concerns of staff. The school improvement team offered a credible voice and agenda to constituents. The fact that the plan forced the district to develop a written curriculum did not obscure the concerns that developed when the team became "the place to take all complaints," Unforeseen and possibly unwanted issues rose to the surface, increasing uncertainty. The strategy for many of these superintendents was to fashion a technical response made visible and concrete: Put new windows in the faculty room, write a curriculum, or add new positions. As one said, "We added a full-time computer teacher, full-time art. The SIP was the lever for getting some of these." This shaped beliefs about instrumentality by demonstrating direct causal changes.

However, two superintendents of midsize districts described a thorough and comprehensive process for change that made the most of resources at hand while attempting more-profound changes at the level of instructional exchange in the classroom. Both of these superintendents were willing to address "less measurable things" rather than collecting only test results. One superintendent imposed a thorough reorganization of administration and a teacher-training process utilizing a penetrating needs assessment; the second superintendent worked from the inside, providing opportunities for teachers and administrators to reassess their own performance and obstacles to effectiveness. The dialogue on instructional change emphasized a personal and reflective approach to individual change in the classroom.

In most large districts, superintendents viewed the school improvement plan as a "touchstone" or symbol of program effectiveness. As one district leader stated, the parts were lying about and simply needed to be put together. The state mandate was frequently described as redundant and intrusive in larger districts that had already engaged in strategic planning. But nevertheless an effort was made to rewrite district plans to comply with state demands.

Issues for superintendents in larger districts appeared to include rising expectations implied by the state demands and internal pressures for concrete improvements. The complexity of the larger organization intensified the difficulty in clarifying linkages and securing implementation of strategic changes. Translating curriculum into classroom instructional practices became more problematic. In these cases, beliefs about instrumentality were more uncertain.

The pitfalls in decentralized implementation were a concern. These pitfalls included distorted interpretation of improvement objectives and uneven levels of communication to staff members in schools. Investment in the process depended upon agendas of principals and agreement by administrative staff on the value and interpretation of the program. Leaders' beliefs about instrumentality were weakened by these features of large districts.

Interaction of Organizational Factors: An Example from a Large District. The process of developing the school improvement plan in one large district was described by the assistant superintendent in charge of the planning process. His narrative of one district's response to the mandate demonstrated issues of uncertainty related to organizational structure, responsibility and involvement, and beliefs around instrumentality.

The assistant made it clear that the responsibility for the plan came to him via the "hole in the wall" (door of his office) from the superintendent. He reported that the state mandate did not change the district's approach to planning. "I'm the person in the system who deals with committees," he said.

> The committees are representative, but if you ask them what aspect of the SIP [it was] they were working on they would look bewildered . . . [it] looks like people are involved. . . . I did the whole thing here at my desk . . . that became the plan. . . . I wouldn't have cared if they'd thrown it out. . . . This is not a ship being built. . . . Parts were lying around the shore waiting to be put together. . . . We shook up the apple cart . . . apples will land with a few bruises here and there . . . there were some . . . piled a little differently; it's still an apple cart . . . I work in the most promising arena . . . you can't change anything if you get killed in the process. But you don't want to get "gawmy" with the state.

This rather metaphorical commentary by the assistant superintendent continued with further remarks on the concept of participation:

> Participatory decision making is widely misunderstood. . . .
> [You] don't have to have everyone involved in everything . . .
> but I believe in the principle. . . . I orchestrated it all. . . . [It]
> doesn't mean I dictated it . . . "how does it look—does it have
> what they want?" . . . The state is interested in the process only
> in that people get involved. . . . If you ask them [the teachers] if
> it's real they won't know what you are talking about. In fact
> they are doing it. . . . Certain groups in the system get savvy . . .
> get an agenda through the SIP, such as a media center or middle
> school.

The imagery of the "shipwreck" on the beach and the spilled apple cart evoke the kind of scattered and "loosely coupled" (Weick 1976), uncertain, chaotic aspects of larger districts. The organizational structure is composed of necessary tools and resources, but putting them together to work in an organized, predictable, instrumental manner is another matter altogether.

The assistant writing the plan at his desk is emblematic of an attempt to appear to "tighten" the coupling. However, as he implied in his discussion of the level of real knowledge of the plan by staff members, the "tight" elements were more metaphor than substance. This assistant remarked on the fact that teachers were not aware of their participation on the school improvement process as such. At the same time, he admitted that by opening up some opportunities for involvement, certain staff members developed a forum and recognized a chance to advance their cause.

Contextual themes of organizational complexity in the large district, represented by the superintendent's delegating the planning process to an assistant, are found in this example. The dilemma of involvement is shown by the emergence of interest groups and causes. A strategic response to uncertain beliefs about instrumentality by leaders was demonstrated in the assistant's unilateral development of the plan utilizing already implemented programs. Lack of staff awareness was mitigated by the fact that they were already participating in the programs outlined in the plan (uncertainty over future outcomes is greatly reduced when those outcomes have already been achieved or are close to being realized).

Beliefs about Economic Uncertainty. Four primary factors concerning economic and social change contributed to uncertainty about the *external environment* for districts of all sizes:

(a) fluctuating enrollments, (b) rising property valuations, (c) threats of decreasing state subsidies, and (d) threatened caps on property taxes.

Leaders' strategic responses to economic and social changes varied with the interpretation that district leaders constructed from observed trends. Increased involvement with legislative representatives, increased concern with community reaction to budget figures, and increasing caution about program growth and costs associated with improvement affected school improvement strategies. Concrete returns or symbols of improvement were preferred. The addition of personnel, facilities, and program were preferred to expenditures for less visible improvements, such as staff development and time for staff interaction. Negative community responses to release time and to the use of substitute teachers to replace teachers who were working on district planning or attending conferences may have inhibited alternative approaches.

Superintendents did not emphasize problems affecting decision making from special interest community groups. Nor were problems with the board of directors representing separate constituencies or individual agendas a common concern. More prominent were issues of economic variability and concern for future support by the state legislature for local improvement.

Beliefs about Intention. Superintendents' interpretations of the state's motivation for initiating the school improvement planning process ranged from (a) a purely political reaction, (b) a response to pressures emanating from the federal government, (c) a sincere effort to promote academic excellence, to (d) an effort to equalize educational opportunity throughout the state. Several superintendents perceived pressures for accountability at the state and local level and a dissatisfaction at the state level with local efforts, specifically in small rural districts.

Superintendents were uncertain about the state's motivation for mandating the improvement process. Also, the possibility of losing the state's support for the improvement process may have resulted in more efforts toward documentation of compliance and less risk taking with regard to strategic decision making. Most of the strategies employed by district leaders were focused on meeting minimum school-approval requirements, rather than assessing specific local needs and organizational deficits. Small districts were able to use the process to "catch up" with programming, personnel, and training. Thus, uncertainty over continued state support may have been linked to less-comprehensive planning and doing the minimum.

Over 50 percent of leaders of small, midsize, and large districts reported expanded programming, including programs for the gifted and talented, programs in the fine arts, increased guidance and support staff, and increased clerical staff to relieve teaching staff of nonteaching duties. However, the majority of superintendents of small districts interviewed in the study (and therefore identified by the state department as having developed an effective improvement plan) also reported the implementation of a more comprehensive districtwide improvement process that included staff development, curriculum revision, and training in effective-schools research.

Leaders in midsize and large districts for the most part reported having implemented these strategies prior to the school improvement effort. The focus of leaders in midsize and large districts was primarily on increasing staff and programming, refining already initiated programs, and documenting compliance to the state department.

Differences between state and local goals for the improvement process was identified by eight (27 percent) of the respondents. The issue of accountability was often raised in a tone of exasperation with the state's advocacy of uniform assessment. Such assessment often was not viewed as congruent with local planning goals or processes nor necessarily with the state's expressed interest in the school improvement plan: "I wish the state would come out and standardize the curriculum because that's what they are going to do . . . I think they ought to be more upfront about it."

Strategy Formation and District Size

Findings in this study suggest that superintendent interpretations and strategies vary with district size, but a direct relationship cannot be inferred. However, district size appears to be linked indirectly to the environmental perceptions and strategic decision making of superintendents. This study does not presume to predict a direct relationship between size of the district and the superintendent's perception of equivocality or the potential for reducing uncertainty. Indeed, issues of inadequacy of resources and personnel appeared in some cases to increase uncertainty of outcome in smaller districts and to reduce superintendents' consideration of strategic options.

In the ten small districts, small size also necessitated administrators' taking on multiple roles. Thus, state mandates increased and expanded role demands, in a few cases threatening the stability of the organization. In addition, smaller districts varied considerably in organizational structure. This often meant that their connections with other districts and administrative units were complex and varied by their degree of dependency on other organizations.

Rather than district size itself affecting superintendents' perceptions of uncertainty, it might be that the six contextual themes identified in the study interact with the size of the district to intensify or dilute the way superintendents interpret the environment. Within the context of these interactions, strategic decision making takes place in response to external demands. Superintendents' strategies appear to depend on variation in the superintendent's need to reduce contextual uncertainty and the intensity of his or her concern or interest in the state mandate. Thus, some superintendents chose to buffer or defend, while others fought the uncertainty as a bullfighter engages the unpredictable yet existentially present adversary.

Strategy Formation and Levels of Engagement

Superintendents engaged in legitimating activities (Cuban 1984; Thompson 1967), such as extensive documentation, to buffer the organization from increased monitoring by the department of education. In fact, the documentation and satisfaction of legislated requirements, as revealed by monitoring visits, resulted in the identification of district leaders to be included in this study. However, in several instances the range of strategies exceeded the demands of the state and were integrated into superintendents' larger visions for change (Bennis and Nanus 1985; Firestone 1989).

Although evidence suggested that increased personnel and expanded programming were the most frequent responses of superintendents to state demands, there were examples of mutual adaptation or co-opting of mandates to gain community support for needed improvements (Selznick 1948; Thompson 1967). For example, construction of library facilities in three midsize districts required not only funding for personnel and materials in a budget process but also a special referendum to construct facilities, surpassing the minimal requirement of the mandate for access to a library program. In some districts, superintendents went farther to articulate deeper levels of change through staff development, peer coaching, and efforts at engaging staff in rethinking teacher roles and instructional decision making. In these ways, superintendents used the state mandate to enact programs to reduce internal uncertainty.

How the superintendent perceived the mandate—narrowly or broadly, as a threat to be parried or an opportunity for articulating a vision for the district—seemed to be a key factor in structuring the situation and defining the response. This matches the work of Child (1972) and Weick (1969) and augments Firestone's (1989) discussion of the influence of a "dominant coalition" in determining the use of reform. Further, structuring responses through adopting either a defensive posture or a trial-and-error mode were congruent with the unpredictable behavior of the internal and external environments.

Although increased staff and programming might appear to be concrete, defensive strategies focused on compliance with state demands, these changes were the result of incremental actions, testing outcomes and responses and garnering support through informal and formal interactions with affected groups. This is a response to high perceived uncertainty. For example, in one large district, the school improvement process was "integrated into the system." The district was already engaged in a decentralized, teacher-led staff development and goal-setting process. The assistant superintendents asserted that the school improvement plan "doesn't run the system as I gather it does in some places." He described a system in which committees work autonomously. His role was to facilitate communication:

> They understand their role and how they fit together. So they do a good job. I know the superintendent's priorities. . . . I make him aware of the feeling of the committee. We don't turn to conflict. Not more than two proposals were rejected by the superintendent in the last 5 years.

In another midsize district the superintendent focused on the articulation between the initiation of change and effective implementation. This person directly tried to reshape both the way shared meaning was constructed by teachers and traditional beliefs about how students learn:

I make the assumption that they [teachers] can think and will think and I set an expectation level because I believe they can. . . . I'm interested in making incremental changes. I felt substantial pressure in that direction. We all discovered a lot; trying to understand what people have in their heads is a definition of curriculum and it's a massive task.

In sum, these responses suggest that superintendents' strategies are linked to their perceptions of environmental uncertainty.

SUMMARY

District leaders interviewed in this study appeared to make decisions and design reform strategies within a context of uncertainties regarding (a) their own career line, (b) the inherent qualities of the district organizational structure, (c) issues of accountability and responsibility in decision making, (d) beliefs about instrumentality or efficacy of improvement measures, (e) perceptions of economic and social change in the community, and (f) their assessment of the motivation or intent of state reform directives.

District size appeared to be related to superintendents' strategies. Effectiveness of the school improvement plans, though, was related to the way superintendents coped with uncertainties that they identified as critical.

Utilizing the Daft and Weick (1984) model to identify the way superintendents coped with uncertainties, we might characterize many of the superintendents interviewed in this study as *prospectors*: Their preferred sources of information were both external and personal. Their interpretation mode was "enacting," with active dialogue and engagement of their environment. They acted on the assumption that the environment was unanalyzable and relied primarily upon an "incremental trial-and-error" decision process. This mode of interpretation, according to Daft and Weick (1984), results in "some equivocality reduction." Behaviors and strategies of leaders are adjusted based on reactions from environmental factors, while the prospector actively probes the environment for responses, revising and modifying. Effective strategies adjust to uncertainty by allowing for unpredictable responses and further testing. As one superintendent framed this approach:

It's a question of building myths of credibility, accountability with the plan. . . . The state motive is accountability. It would be nice to say it is improving the quality of education. The SIP is the scapegoat to do educationally what I wanted to do anyway, a good catalyst, especially in a small rural community where people have low educational goals, trying to do it all at once.

It is significant as well to note that while superintendents in large districts could rely on a more sophisticated central office staff, none of the districts contained a research, development, or systems-analysis unit. Only one superintendent in a midsize district used a computerized goal-setting and measurement system. The superintendents' responses appeared consistent with the Daft and Weick (1984) profile of superintendents leading organizations with "irregular reports and feedback from the environment" as well as "selective information."

Given the interpretation of an "unanalyzable" school district environment, superintendents who were selected for having responded successfully to a demand from the external environment appeared to have managed the uncertainty by synchronizing their own strategic behavior to the unpredictable nature of their environment. That is, the strategies selected by the superintendents were, for the most part, supportive of practices already in existence or involved changes in visible areas such as personnel or facilities. These strategies could be rewritten, reshaped, or reframed to meet new demands.

For most, the *process* of school improvement was the critical event; those who appeared to be most effective placed their emphasis on process rather than outcome in improving schools. Superintendents viewed their influence on the process of reform as significantly greater than their influence on outcomes of the planning. Paradoxically, the process seemed to engender uncertainty; outcomes suggested concrete and visible effects. However, given the complexity of identifying clear and measurable outcomes in education, the improvement process may indeed appear to be more tangible and measurable than the results. One superintendent in a midsize district, after developing a sophisticated comprehensive view of planning, suggested that the school improvement plan was capturing "what was going on." He assumed a wider vision of the community and its interaction with the learning process by "seeing the whole community learning." Going beyond a technical response to the improvement process, the superintendent was able to engage a larger constituency and to meet deeper levels of need in the community.

CONCLUSION

As states impose more constraints on local attempts to meet the educational needs of diverse constituents, the process of implementation increasingly becomes a key issue (Cuban 1984; Firestone 1989; Floden et al. 1988). Findings point to ways policymakers might recognize the diversity of leaders' interpretations, incorporate this knowledge into more sensitive-regulatory processes, and thereby encourage effective implementation.

The study presents substantial evidence that the imposition of state standards or assessment criteria may ignore superintendents' interpretations; these interpretations shape the approach taken to meeting the standards or criteria. The distance "twixt cup and lip" needs to be understood in order to increase the probability that local outcomes are congruent with a realistic state view of meaningful improvement.

One focus of attention for state policymakers may be the knowledge that flexibility in reaching a common set of outcomes is preferable to a rigid program that does not take into account the variability in district resources and responses by district leaders. A clearly defined set of outcomes would allow for unique approaches by districts of different sizes and resource capabilities. It seems axiomatic that the development of the improvement plan and the plan itself are less important than the outcomes for students. Requiring all districts to provide documentation of process might lead to redundancy and to legitimating behaviors rather than a search for improvement strategies that are workable and effective within a particular district. Standard operating procedures have not necessarily been successful in providing quality education; accepting the "uncertainty" principle as it relates to generating strategies to attain agreed-upon outcomes might make for greater reliability in policy design.

In a recent review of reform, Firestone, Fuhrman, and Kirst (1989) suggested that districts that were committed to the reform agenda "exceeded state requirements" and initiated restructuring programs utilizing state grants to assist their unique experiments. Thus, state policy may be directed toward nurturing district efforts through defining outcomes and providing resources to assist district ventures toward attainment of defined goals. Outcomes should be concerned less with lists of course requirements or programs and more with legitimate expectations for what students should know and be able to do.

Clearly, superintendents in this study viewed the school improvement legislation as a useful lever for change in their districts, especially in the smaller districts. However, unless a set of clearly defined outcomes for strategic change is provided, differing interpretations, comfort issues, local political interests, or other more "manageable" strategies may lead to a detour around improvement efforts.

Moving from an emphasis on process, in state mandates, to a clearer definition of outcome will also mean addressing district context, including superintendents' perceptions of uncertainty, district size, resources, and community composition. Outcomes that require additional funding, such as the teaching of a foreign language at the elementary level, should be treated differently than expectations of improved levels of reading comprehension. Funding for a specialized program that demands additional personnel needs to be targeted to the less affluent and smaller districts.

Current policy and accompanying regulations often ignore the complexity of superintendent interpretation systems. By providing fewer barriers to funding and by focusing more on outcomes, policymakers may reap more effective implementation from the diversity of superintendents' resulting strategies.

NOTES

We would like to thank Lorraine McDonnell and the anonymous reviewers for their useful suggestions. In addition, we would like to acknowledge the careful editorial points made by Corinne Solsrud, as well as the many Maine educators who gave of their time and energy.

REFERENCES

Aguilar, F. J. (1967). *Scanning the business environment*. New York: Macmillan.
Aldrich, H. E., & Pfeffer, J. (1976). Environments of organizations. *Annual Review of Sociology, 2*, 79–105.

Bartunek, J. M. (1984). Changing interpretive schemes and organizational restructuring: The example of a religious order. *Administrative Science Quarterly, 29*, 355–72.

Bennis, W., & Nanus, B. (1985). *Leaders: The strategies for taking charge.* New York: Harper & Row.

Child, J. (1972). Organizational structure, environment and performance: The role of strategic choice. *Sociology, 6*, 1–22.

Cuban, L. (1984). Transforming the frog into a prince: Effective school research, policy and practice at the district level. *Harvard Educational Review, 54*(2), 129–51.

Cuban, L. (1990). Reforming again, again, again. *Educational Researcher, 19*(1), 3–14.

Daft, R. L., & Weick, K.E. (1984). Toward a model of organizations as interpretation systems. *Academy of Management Review, 9*, 284–95.

Duncan, R. B. (1972). Characteristics of organizational environments and perceived environmental uncertainty. *Administrative Science Quarterly, 17*, 313–27.

Firestone, W. A. (1989). Using reform: Conceptualizing district initiative. *Educational Evaluation and Policy Analysis, 11*, 151–64.

Firestone, W. A., Fuhrman, S. H., & Kirst, M. W. (1989). *The progress of reform: An appraisal of state education initiatives.* New Brunswick, NJ: Rutgers University, Center for Policy Research in Education (CPRE).

Floden, R. E., Porter, A. C., Alford, I. E., Freeman, D. J., Irwin, S., Schmidt, W. H., & Schwille, J. R. (1988). Instructional leadership at the district level: A closer look at autonomy and control. *Educational Administration Quarterly, 27*(2), 96–125.

Gleick, J. (1987). *Chaos: Making a new science.* New York: Viking.

Guba, E. G., & Lincoln, Y. S. (1981). *Effective evaluation.* San Francisco: Jossey-Bass.

Hedberg, B. (1981). How organizations learn and unlearn. In P. Nystrom & W. Starbuck (Eds.), *Organizational Design, 1*, 3–27. Oxford: Oxford University Press.

Kasarda, J. D. (1974). The structural implications of social system size: A three-level analysis. *American Sociological Review, 39*, 19–28.

March, J. G., & Cohen, M. D. (1986). Leadership and ambiguity: *The American college president* (2d ed.). Boston: Harvard Business School Press.

Meyer, M. W. (1972). Size and structure of organizations: A causal analysis. *American Sociological Review, 37*, 434–41.

Miles, R. E., & Snow, C. E. (1978). *Organizational strategy, structure and process.* New York: McGraw-Hill.

Mostyn, B. (1985). The content analysis of qualitative research data: A dynamic approach. In M. Brenner, J. Brown, & D. Canter (Eds.), *The research interview: Uses and approaches.* New York: Academic Press.

Murphy, J. T. (1980). *Getting the facts: A field work guide for evaluators and policy analysis*. Glenview, IL: Scott, Foresman.
Odden, A. (1986). School effectiveness, backward mapping, and state education policies. In J. J. Lane & H. J. Walberg (Eds.), *Effective school leadership*. Berkeley: McCutchan.
Odden, A., & Dougherty, V. (1982). *State programs of school improvement: A 50-state survey* (Report No.182-3). Denver: Education Commission of the States.
Peters, T. (1988). *Thriving on chaos*. New York: Knopf.
Pfeffer, J. (1982). *Organizations and organization theory*. Boston: Pitman.
Purkey, S. G., & Smith, M.S. (1983). Effective schools: A review. *Elementary School Journal, 83*, 427–52.
Selznick, P. (1948). Foundations of the theory of organization. *American Sociological Review, 13*, 25–35.
Smith, M. S., & O'Day, J. (1990). *Systemic school reform*. Palo Alto: Stanford University Center for Policy Research in Education.
State of Maine Department of Educational and Cultural Services. (1985). *Manual for school improvement plan process*. Augusta: Author.
Thompson, J. (1967). *Organizations in action*. New York: McGraw-Hill.
Timar, T. B., & Kirp, D. L. (1987). Educational reform and institutional competence. *Harvard Educational Review, 57*(3), 308–31.
Tung, R. L. (1979). Dimensions of organizational environment: An exploratory study of their impact on organizational structure. *Academy of Management Journal, 22*, 672–93.
Weick, K. E. (1969). *The social psychology of organizing*. Reading, MA: Addison-Wesley.
Weick, K. E. (1976). Educational organizations as loosely-coupled systems. *Administrative Science Quarterly, 21*, 1–19.
Wills, F. G. (1990). *Organizational responses to external demands: Strategies employed by district level administrators in developing and implementing state mandated improvement plans*. (Doctoral dissertation, University of Wisconsin–Madison, 1990). (University Microfilm International #9106710)

CHAPTER 6

Restructuring in Kentucky: The Changing Role of the Superintendent and the District Office

Joseph Murphy

The current wave of school reform has left few traditional roles unchallenged. At the district level, school critics and reform advocates have called for drastic restructuring of the educational systems as they have been historically configured. (Clear 1990, p. 1)

During the mid to late 1980s, the educational reform movement that had commenced around 1980 began to change form and texture. Up to that time, reform initiatives were informed by the belief that schooling could be improved if standards were raised, more effective prescriptions and regulations written, and educators, from the boardroom to the classroom, asked to do more. As the prevailing assumptions underlying the excellence movement came under attack (Cuban 1984; Sedlak et al. 1986), a new belief system began to take root—one that would grow to support what has become known as the "restructuring movement." Central to this perspective on school improvement are the following assumptions about reform: Educational problems are attributable more to the failure of the system of schooling than to the shortcomings of individual educators; empowerment (of students, teachers, and parents) is a more effective tool than prescription; and bottom-up, school-based solution strategies will lead to more satisfying results than will top-down, mandated ones (Murphy 1990).

While subject to criticism for a perceived lack of conceptual clarity and definitional specificity (Tyack 1990), the school-restructuring movement nonetheless—or perhaps because of this very ambiguity (see Mitchell and Beach 1991; Rowley 1992)—began to flourish, becoming a clearinghouse for a wide assortment of improvement initiatives. Chief among these are (1) choice and voice for parents; (2) deregulation of decision making from the state and district to the school community; (3) professionalization of teachers; (4) privatization of schooling; and (5) teaching for meaningful understanding, or the infusion of constructivist views of learning and teaching into the classroom (Murphy 1993a). Cutting across these strategies is the emergence of new roles and responsibilities for the various educational stakeholders. Conceptually, and to a lesser extent empirically, our understanding of what these changing roles mean for students, teachers, parents, and principals is becoming firmer (see Murphy 1991), but our knowledge of how the role of educators in the central office is being transformed through restructuring initiatives is considerably less robust. Particularly troubling in this regard is the conspicuous absence of an empirical grounding.

In this article, we begin to address the need for a deeper understanding of the ways in which the roles of superintendents in particular, and central office staff in general, are changing in response to the school-restructuring movement in Kentucky. After a description of the procedures employed in the study, we discuss the findings as they relate first to central office staff and then to superintendents. We conclude with some suggestions about how to facilitate the transformation of district roles so that they will be consistent with the underlying philosophy of the restructuring movement.

PROCEDURES

Sample

Our first task was to select school districts that were involved in serious transformational reform efforts. Given the slowness of the restructuring movement to affect central office operations in the United States (Murphy 1991), we decided to focus on a state in which considerable legal, political, and community pressure had been brought to bear to radically overhaul schooling, from the classroom to the statehouse. Because it is generally acknowledged that Kentucky represents the best example of statewide systemic reform of the restructuring variety, districts in that state were targeted.

At the time of this investigation, there were 176 school districts in Kentucky. The group selected for this study is comprised of the 48 Kentucky school districts that belong to the Kentucky Educational Development Corporation (KEDC)—a consortium that is organized to provide superintendents and other central office staff with an assortment of support functions, including professional development opportunities. These districts are representative of others throughout Kentucky in terms of size and type—city, suburban, rural. This study focuses upon the superintendents of these 48 districts.

Data Collection Methods

Because we were interested in generating potential hypotheses and other insights of an exploratory nature, a qualitative methodological approach was deemed to be most appropriate.

Focus Group. In order to have superintendents hear from each other and stimulate each other's thinking, a focus group interview was held with 24 members of the KEDC. Morgan (1988) defines focus groups as follows:

> [F]ocus groups are basically group interviews, although not in the sense of alternation between researcher's questions and the participants' responses. Instead the reliance is on the interaction with the group, based on topics that are supplied by the researcher, who typically takes the role of moderator. (pp. 9–10)

Accordingly,

> The hallmark of focus groups is *the explicit use of the group interaction to produce data and insights that would be less accessible without the interaction found in a group.* (p. 12; emphasis in the original)

The role of the researcher in the focus group is twofold: to provide the stimulus material for the discussion, and to facilitate the interactions. In this study, three broad stimulus questions—set against the Kentucky Education Reform Act of 1990 (KERA)—formed the basis for discussion: What are your thoughts about the effects of the KERA in general? How are the KERA and subsequent restructuring efforts affecting the superintendency (i.e., your role)? And how is this reform activity affecting district office operations?

Questionnaire. A questionnaire was developed to tap into five broad topics—the three areas discussed in the focus group, as well as superintendents' perceptions about the major purposes of restructuring and their insights about "the good, the bad, and the bothersome" in Kentucky's transformational reform efforts. Eleven open-ended questions focused on these five topics. Questionnaires were returned by 35 of the 48 superintendents (73 percent) in the sample.

Data Analysis Methods

For purposes of this paper, data from the focus group notes and questionnaire protocols were analyzed to discern superintendents' perceptions of changes occurring in district offices and in the role of the superintendency. Procedures described by Miles and Huberman (1984) were followed. The questionnaire data—comprised of phrases, sentences, and paragraphs in response to the 11 open-ended probes—were coded like interview transcriptions. Pattern coding and the construction of conceptually clustered matrices formed the heart of the analyses. A discussion of the findings follows.

FINDINGS

Everything is different at the current time. [30][1]

Changes in District Office Operations

Central office structures and routines must change—but it is occurring slowly. Old opinions and attitudes go away begrudgingly. [13]

The data in this study provide some useful insights about both the process and the types of change in the central offices of districts involved in transformational reform efforts.

Process of Change.

We struggle somewhat on how much to relinquish to the schools, because of a fear to not have continuity and consistency throughout the district. (Is it really needed?) [7]

For a few of these districts, the reform process to date had not been particularly traumatic—operations were "still quite similar to how [they were] prior to the restructuring" [26]. In a couple of these cases, this was true because, while "massive changes are in the making" [24], they had not yet begun to wash over the system. In other cases, however, this sense of equanimity resulted from the fact that the districts were already operating in line with the basic tenets of restructuring: "Not a lot—our office was never run as a dictatorial office" [8]; "thus far there has not been much change— we always believed that decisions should be made at the lowest level of the organization" [31]; "have always tried to have central office personnel see themselves as supporting principals; we're well positioned in this regard" [21].

Most districts, however, were experiencing noticeable pains in their efforts to overhaul central office operations in response to such initiatives as school-based management and enhanced parental participation. They "continue[d] to reorganize and redefine their roles" [11], but there was a clear sense that they were "in a transitional stage" [6]. The superintendents in this study talked about district office staff who were "still feeling their way." They identified the "need for training relative to the new programs, their implementation and management" [34] as their colleagues strove to master their "new leadership and training roles" [16].

References to two types of growing pains are evident in the responses of these superintendents. First, they believed that the KERA was "overburdening" [5] their staffs, that "the work demands [were] tremendous" [12]: "Up to this point KERA has almost broken the backs of central office staff. In some areas, demands are coming so quickly I have deep concerns about quality work and programs being developed simply because of lack of time" [19]. References to "increased work load" [7], "more questions and more paperwork" [30], "more meetings for central office staff to attend" [14], "the addition of many more tasks . . . and responsibilities" [26], and "too many questions as to what their role might be" [29] peppered both the questionnaires and the focus group discussion. All in all, these superintendents felt that there were "too many programs and too little staff" [12]. They reported that their staffs were under considerable stress: "Everyone's hours have increased and there is a good deal more stress evident in the faces of my staff" [31]; "restructuring seems to place more strain on the time of central office staff" [34]. Given these perceptions, it is not surprising, though certainly contrary to the intention of the KERA, that many of these district leaders expressed "the need for more central office people to handle the paperwork" [23], "some studies indicate less central office staff needed—I disagree" [34]; "KERA has effected a complete restructuring of the central office. A great amount of daily operations are being shared by more than one person, which has increased the amount of work performed by each individual. . . . Out of necessity, restructuring has and may continue to create the need for additional staff at the district office." [33]

At the same time, the remarks of these superintendents convey a sense of loss among central office staff—loss that appears to be accompanying their efforts to decentralize decision making to the school level and their "struggle [about] how much to relinquish to the school level" [7]. On the one hand, "district office staff [felt] the loss of district-wide policy making and leadership from their departments" [6]. Superintendents also perceived "more apprehension [among staff] as schools assume[d] more responsibility" [15]. On the other hand, there was a sense of loss resulting from a perceived "distancing of the relationship between central office and the schools" [23] as new working arrangements were being forged. This phenomenon of "schools reducing contact" with the district office [15] and central office staff "hav[ing] much less time to be involved in daily school activities" [7] seemed to undermine the sense of purpose of some district office personnel.

Types of Change.

> Central office staff are taking on new roles—sharing with building level personnel in a more cooperative manner. [1]

At least from the perspective of the superintendency, the district offices in this study were undergoing a fairly radical transformation in the way that they work with schools. The superintendents saw district office staff abandoning their traditional bureaucratic, control mind-set in favor of a "service orientation" [4]—there had been "a complete shift from top-down directives" [27]. The themes of "support rather than directing" [18] and "facilitation rather than leadership" [17] are at the heart of this new way of doing business.

Superintendents offered several clues about how district offices provide support and service as "facilitators rather than [as] initiators" [34]. Because they believed that the KERA dictated "more and better cooperation if restructuring is to be successful" [19] and "created a need for greater communication between the district office and the schools of the district" [33], they observed that their district-level employees were "working more closely with the schools" and developing more "cooperative working relationships" [28]. They acknowledged that "more responsibility had been given to schools" [25]—that "the Board [of Education] doesn't have the power it once had" [32]—and that schools would "be making decisions that once were done at the central office and mandated to the schools" [30].

As a consequence, superintendents reported more "services being designed by schools" [10], and they saw their district office colleagues "trying hard to support and assist the schools in *their* lead to offer changes and improvements" [7, emphasis added]: "School-based councils have changed the role of elementary and secondary supervisors. The personnel now go where they are asked" [20]; "central office has to wait to be *asked* before being included" [15, emphasis in the original]; "we do get more direction from the building principal or school-based council for services and needs rather than coming from the central office" [18].

For these school district leaders, "central office as support" [9] and "facilitator" [6] translated like this: "less emphasis on telling, more on selling" [15]; being "more advisory-consulting" [16]; "not offering as many directives" [11]; "broker[ing] services to schools" [27]; "becom[ing] more active in securing requested information for the schools" [35]; moving toward a focus on "information dissemination" [33]; and "becoming more of a transmitter of information rather than a developer of strategies" [35].

The study also provides some insights concerning the areas that district offices were emphasizing in these emerging collaborative relationships with schools. According to the superintendents, "teacher empowerment [and] community involvement" [1] were often the foci of district activities. Providing "professional development activities" [7] "to prepare/train school-based decision making councils and school personnel" [15] also took on added significance in these districts, as did activities that helped local sites maintain their "focus on KERA strands" [16]. Assisting school staff in developing "new programs and meeting [KERA] guidelines" [8] were other tasks on which central office staff were spending additional time and energy.

Changes in the Role of Superintendent

> KERA has forced or mandated a new way of operation. Has led to learning the job over. [19]

> I have spent more time trying to develop a "system of schools" rather than "a school system." [13]

> I think my position will evolve into something like the university president—public relations, fund raiser, counselor, but actual work is carried forward by chairmen and deans—hiring, curriculum development. Will still be a powerful position, but not in the line authority way of thinking. [21]

Woven throughout the responses of these superintendents are three themes that capture the evolution in their roles since the passage of the KERA: orchestrating from the background, enhancing participation, and managing reform.

Orchestrating from the Background.

> I am spending more time maximizing input and shared decision making rather than trying to sell others on centrally generated directions. [4]

These superintendents reported that "restructuring has caused [them] to rethink [their] idea of what the role of the superintendent is" [33], to "rethink their jobs" [31]. Most centrally, they were learning to lead from the background rather than from the apex of the organization. They saw themselves as managing more by consensus than by command and as facilitating rather than controlling. They reported "adjusting [their] management style to accommodate site-based decision making" [16], a situation in which they no longer "had the final say" [31]: "As a result of restructuring, I perceive myself to be more open to input from staff, parents, and the community" [35]; "I have also adjusted my management style to share decision making in our district" [34]. Management by consensus required "less arbitrary decisions [and] more negotiations" [15]; "more open, inclusive, cooperative relationships with others" [3, 4]; "working through different organizations" (e.g. school site councils) [9]; a "decision making process [that] is more open" [33]; and an increased time commitment to "collaboration/group problem solving" [27]. One superintendent summarized his new role as follows:

I find that I must work harder to not enforce my opinions on others. I must see that I am not perceived as "the superintendent" who demands but who works with "you" to get "it" done. [8]

For most of the respondents, "rethinking [the] role to become more of a facilitator/enabler" [31] accompanied efforts at more democratic management. Facilitative leadership was consistent with the philosophy of administration of a few superintendents: "my leadership style has always been democratic. I believe strongly in using committees and implementing their recommendations. This style goes right along with KERA and site-based decision making" [2]; "the reform emphasizes many of the philosophies that I have believed in for years and have struggled to implement" [7]. Others, however, were less sanguine about having to spend "more time as a facilitator rather than a manager or leader" [3]. Members of this group viewed facilitation as a reduction in the importance of the superintendent's role: "KERA has reduced the superintendent to being a facilitator in many areas . . . I feel more like a paper shuffler than an educational leader" [6]; "I am no longer supposed to be an instructional leader" [24].

Most superintendents concluded that the "move to [an] enabler-facilitator" [16] role was inevitable: "position leadership has been helpful [in the past]; may not be in the future" [21]; "others' perceptions of me are moving toward 'technical assistance advisor'" [27]; "for my district to be successful I must by persuasion convince teachers and principals to change" [31]. Although many acknowledged struggling to move from "the past [when] superintendents were expected to be the source of knowledge" [4], they did not lose sight of the fact that "the methods used previously [had] been altered [and with them had come] a change from a role as 'boss' to a role as 'leader'" [28]—from the fount of knowledge to the "organizer and facilitator of innovation" [4]. "Serving more as a facilitator" [10] meant specific things to this group. Most importantly, it indicated the ability to "lead, not drive" [15], to "motivate by leading" [9] rather than by directing. Facilitating meant "more explaining, selling, and convincing" [15] rather than telling; shaping "instead of final decision making" [8]—"overseeing the operations with less decisions" [23]; "modeling appropriate activity" [10]; "thinking consistently of the development of others" [27]; and, as discussed throughout this article, "broadening the base of participation in management" [16], and "involving others in helping achieve goals" [28].

Enhancing Participation.

> The role of the superintendent, I think, has changed. Superintendents must now take the time to inform as many people as possible and to involve as many people as possible. [33]

Another function that has moved to center stage for these administrators, and one that is tightly linked with their orchestrating role, is that of enhancing the participation of all stakeholders in the educational enterprise. There was consensus among the superintendents in this study that the KERA "created an open door for involvement of parents and teachers to be a part of solutions rather than problems" [4], that "restructuring has served to involve more people in the decision making process than ever before" [33]. At the most basic level, expanded stakeholder involvement was seen to require increased consensual management: "the way I think about my role involves more people in more ways; more of a team approach than ever before" [1]; "all activities now require more involvement" [10]; I "have to include more players (*more inclusive*) . . . more people activities [and] more people discussions with more groups" [15]; "you must involve others in decision making" [28].

Developing "more interactive relationships with others" [3] and opening decision-making processes widely within the community had begun to find expression in the work schedules of these district leaders. References to "more meetings" [14, 23], more "consulting" [8] "with countless administrators, publics, etc." [19], "more time spent involving others" [3], "more time with community awareness" [13], and "more time talking to people [citizens] and employees" [23] peppered the focus group discussion and questionnaire responses. It is safe to conclude that, for nearly all of these leaders, "restructuring has required more meeting time and communication with all members of the faculty and the staff, as well as community and board members" [33].

One topic that received considerable attention in these discussions was the amount of time devoted to "community awareness" [13] and "public relations" [27]. Regardless of their own concerns and doubts, the leaders reflected a commitment to "present a positive image about [the] mandated changes" [31]. The statements of the following two superintendents nicely represent the feelings of the group:

> I have become a salesman for KERA. One of the most important aspects of my job has suddenly developed from the need to convince district personnel, parents, and the community that reform is necessary and essential. [34]

> I have found it necessary to become more of a salesman, coordinator of groups and an agent of change. [35]

This enhanced public relations function also requires keeping the community informed about restructuring activity: "my role has become more complex, especially in communicating information about reform to all elements of the community" [11]; "I have had to place a greater emphasis on public relations. This has been necessary to keep district personnel and our community informed of the changes taking place" [34]. Yet another component of the public relations function is coalition building, "coalescing interest groups around a particular focus . . . gaining support of the various constituency groups (i.e. teachers' union, administrators, Board, School-Based Council, students, and community at-large)" [27]. "Creating a visible image" [9] seemed to be an important aspect of all three public relations functions—selling, informing, and coalition building. Meeting with "individual school councils" [13, 15], in turn, was viewed as a key strategy for enhancing visibility.

Managing Reform.

> I can see the important role I must play during the first few years of implementation of the reform efforts in Kentucky. [11]

Although it might come as a surprise to the legislature, these leaders generally shared the belief that the role of the superintendent in Kentucky "has become more complex" [11] because of the restructuring initiatives of 1990, and that they had "more responsibility" [3], not less. Of particular importance was the "added responsibility to see that KERA [was] on track" [25]. These superintendents reported making heavy investments of energy in overseeing or managing the KERA. At the most basic level, because of the heightened "concern for legislative and State Department of Education mandates" [17] throughout the state, superintendents were committing large amounts of "time trying to understand the requirements of KERA" [12], "keeping up to date with KERA initiatives" [24], and "trying to keep informed of the many new programs and how to implement them" [34]. Considerable time was also being allocated to "training meetings" [20], "training sessions, updates, etc." [22]. One superintendent seemed to speak for all when he said "time is spent meeting, meeting, meeting—I am trying to find answers" [32].

As noted earlier, much effort was also being invested in selling the KERA to the community and in "trying to answer questions about restructuring" [30], especially from external constituents, and in meeting with stakeholders to make restructuring a reality. A common lament was that "much more paper work" [29, 35] was now required at the district level: the KERA "requires more time and more paperwork" [22]; "I fill out countless forms, reports, 5 year plans, etc." [31]; "too much time is still being spent keeping track of the paperwork involved with this effort" [11].

The policy, financial, and monitoring dimensions of the superintendent's role were all enhanced by the restructuring measures in Kentucky. These superintendents believed that they were doing more "policy work" [8], that a considerable amount of "time [was being] spent on policy development and how it relates to reform and restructuring" [33]: "I have become more of a policy maker for the district" [25]. In particular, the "need to plan more" [15] was heavily stressed: "I spend a great deal of my time planning how all these programs can be *effectively* implemented" [12]; "restructuring eliminates several day-to-day operational concerns but [requires] more long range goal setting policy (as it relates to KERA) development" [8].

The need to "deal with finance" [32] also increased; both "financial planning" [8, 25] requirements and "time on budgeting matters" [10] expanded: "restructuring . . . created the need for greater financial analysis of all areas of the budgetary process" [33]. Added monitoring responsibilities included "developing regulations in an attempt to meet mandates" [5] and "enforcing compliance" [16] with the KERA "statutes and regulations" [10] at the local level—including "keeping timelines on new programs" [25] and "seeing that [those] timelines are met" [8], creating "new record keeping systems" [25], "checking on [local] follow through" [11], and keeping personally "informed on all aspects of the restructuring process" [33].

One topic that received considerable attention, and on which there was a clear division of opinion, was that of the superintendent's role in the educational program. One group argued that they were being pushed farther away from the core technology of their business, from teaching and learning. They found themselves "spend[ing] more time with non-educational duties than before" [7]. They saw the KERA as "not allowing [them] to get into the schools" [14] as frequently as they had prior to 1990. They maintained that they were spending "much less time in the field visiting schools and talking to teachers" [29] and had "little time to really get into classrooms" [25]. Members of this group felt that they were "no longer supposed to be . . . instructional leader[s]" [24]. A second group arrived at a totally different conclusion. They viewed the KERA as an "impetus [for] instructional leader[ship]" [16]. They saw the "need for superintendents to educate others—educators, community, students—as to education itself" [21]. Consequently, they claimed that "more time was spent on the instructional program than the support areas" [18]. They believed that "getting into classrooms would be more important" [and that there was] "more need for management by wandering around" [21].

CONCLUSION

A careful reading of the literature on school reform over the last decade reveals that thoughtful analyses of district office operations, especially of ways that the superintendency may change (or is changing) to support restructuring efforts, are conspicuous by their absence (Crowson 1988). This appears to be the case for at least two reasons. First, reform action under the restructuring agenda is focused elsewhere (Elmore n.d.; Murphy 1990). The local school community—teachers, students, principal, and parents—is one center of attention. State, and, to a lesser degree, federal initiatives generally consume the remainder of the reform energy. Thus it seems to be widely believed that the restructuring agenda can be pursued without concern for the role of district office personnel. Second, many reformers believe that district offices and their chief executive officers are a major cause of the problems with schooling and that they should therefore be relegated to the sidelines of the reform playing field. Strategists in this latter group generally argue that superintendents are (and will be) unwilling to make needed changes, because in so doing they will relinquish their entrenched control over education (see Chubb 1988). Thus superintendents are often consciously excluded from discussions of educational improvement via school restructuring.

Our work in Kentucky leads us to conclude that both of these lines of reasoning are flawed. In the first case, it is true that decentralization transfers influence from the district office to the school site, but evidence continues to accumulate that the superintendent is essential to successful implementation of nearly all widely discussed reform initiatives, including parental choice and site-based decision making (Carnoy and MacDonell 1990; Murphy and Hallinger 1993). Although we question the validity of the second perspective—that of the superintendent as the self-serving entrenched bureaucrat—for our purposes here the accuracy of these claims is not important. It is clear that the tactic of deliberately attempting to circumvent the superintendent and district office, and of focusing all hopes on state-shaped local initiatives, does not work very well, at least not in Kentucky. For a variety of historical, political, cultural, and social reasons, district stakeholders, especially superintendents, remain central figures in Kentucky's educational reform activities, despite concerted efforts to reduce their influence. As we have discussed elsewhere (Murphy 1993b), superintendents' willingness to wield their influence has been dampened by what they see as a pattern of being unfairly singled out as players who cannot be trusted to participate in the reform of Kentucky's public schools.

Where does this leave us? What are the options for the superintendency and district office in the future? There seem to be at least four distinct possible outcomes. First, central offices and their chief executive officers might become extinct, or, at the very least, put out to pasture. However, little empirical evidence exists that this scenario is either likely or possible. It is also conceptually flawed (Murphy 1989).

Second, district personnel—and central office operations—might ride out the current storm of reform efforts largely unscathed. Given the abilities of bureaucracies to deflect or absorb change (Downs 1967), and the track record of educational reform initiatives in the United States (Cohen 1988; Cuban 1990; Elmore 1987), this scenario should not be discarded lightly.

A third possibility is that the superintendency—and concomitantly other district office positions—will undergo a metamorphosis, a dynamic change in the nature and function of the role. Luvern Cunningham's (1989, 1990) thoughtful discussion about superintendents as commissioners of well-being is the best example of this option in the reform mix to date.

A final possibility is that the superintendency and other district roles will be overhauled consistent with the tenets of educational restructuring, especially those principles that are shaping the evolution of new roles for teachers, students, and principals.

Our own understanding of school reform and improvement convinces us that options 1 and 2 are not to be embraced. On purely pragmatic grounds, attempting to neuter one or more stakeholders in a culture of empowerment—option 1—undermines the spirit and purpose of the entire reform agenda, in addition to the fact that such an approach is ethically bankrupt. Option 2 is not appealing for obvious reasons: It is impossible to improve if people do not change. Option 3—at least Cunningham's version of it—is, in many ways, very attractive. A broader conceptual and more socially and morally grounded view of the superintendency is a worthy objective. On the other hand, change of this magnitude in education is rare. At the very least, it would take some time to materialize. This brings us to option 4, a restructuring of district office roles consistent with the principles of transformational reform.

Restructuring the roles of district office personnel to support school improvement efforts offers the most promise of success in advancing the quality, equity, and choice values of transformational reform initiatives such as those contained in the Kentucky Educational Reform Act. The insights from the 35 superintendents in this study provide some initial clues about how district offices are restructing their own operations in order to facilitate better education. They provide guidance to policymakers and educators who are interested in pursuing option 4—nurturing the transformation of central office operations and the role of the superintendent to promote restructuring of education at the school site.

NOTES

Support for this research was provided by the National Center for Educational Leadership (NCEL) under U.S. Department of Education

Contract No. R 117C8005. The views in this report are those of the authors and do not necessarily represent those of the sponsoring institution or the universities of the NCEL consortium—the University of Chicago, Harvard University, and Vanderbilt University.

1. The numbers [refer] to the 35 superintendents who completed the questionnaire.

REFERENCES

Carnoy, M., & Macdonell, J. (1990). School district restructuring in Santa Fe, New Mexico. *Educational Policy, 4*(1), 49–64.

Chubb, J. E. (1988). Why the current wave of school reform will fail. *Public Interest, (90),* 28–49.

Clear, D. K. (1990, October). *Changes in roles and responsibilities of central office supervisors: Organizational and functional outcomes.* Paper presented at the annual meeting of the University Council for Educational Administration, Pittsburgh.

Cohen, D. K. (1988, September). *Teaching practice: Plus ca change . . .* East Lansing: Michigan State University, National Center for Research on Teacher Education. (Issue paper no. 88-3)

Crowson, R. L. (1988). Editor's introduction. *Peabody Journal of Education, 65*(4), 1–8.

Cuban, L. (1984). School reform by remote control: SB813 in California. *Phi Delta Kappan, 66*(3), 213–15.

Cuban, L. (1990). Reforming again, again, and again. *Educational Researcher, 19*(1), 3-13.

Cunningham, L. L. (1989, May). Speech presented at a conference sponsored by the National Policy Board for Educational Administration, Charlottesville, VA.

Cunningham, L. L. (1990). Reconstituting local government for well-being and education. In B. Mitchell & L. L. Cunningham (Eds.), *Educational leadership and changing contexts of families, communities, and schools* (pp. 135–54). Chicago: University of Chicago Press.

Downs, A. (1967). *Inside bureaucracy.* Boston: Little, Brown.

Elmore, R. F. (1987). Reform and the culture of authority in schools. *Educational Administration Quarterly, 23*(4), 60–78.

Elmore, R. F. (n.d.). *The role of local school districts in instructional improvement.* Unpublished paper. Michigan State University, East Lansing.

Miles, M. B., & Huberman, A. M. (1984). *Qualitative data analysis: A sourcebook of methods.* Newbury Park, CA: Sage.

Mitchell, D. E., & Beach, S. A. (1991, March). *School restructuring: The superintendent's view*. Paper presented at the annual meeting of the American Educational Research Association, Chicago.

Morgan, D. L. (1988). *Focus groups as qualitative research*. Newbury Park, CA: Sage.

Murphy, J. (1990). The educational reform movement of the 1980s: A comprehensive analysis. In J. Murphy (Ed.), *The educational reform movement of the 1980s: Perspectives and cases* (pp. 3–55). Berkeley: McCutchan.

Murphy, J. (1991). *Restructuring schools: Capturing and assessing the phenomena*. New York: Teachers College Press.

Murphy, J. (1993a). Restructuring schooling: In search of a movement. In J. Murphy & P. Hallinger (Eds.), *Restructuring schooling: Learning from ongoing efforts* (pp. 1–31). Newbury Park, CA: Corwin/ Sage.

Murphy, J. (1993b). *Restructuring schools in Kentucky: Insights from superintendents*. Nashville: Peabody College at Vanderbilt University, National Center for Educational Leadership.

Murphy, J., & Hallinger, P. (1993). Restructuring schooling: Learning from ongoing efforts. In J. Murphy & P. Hallinger (Eds.), *Restructuring schooling: Learning from ongoing efforts* (pp. 251–71). Newbury Park, CA: Corwin/Sage.

Murphy, J. T. (1989). The paradox of decentralizing schools: Lessons from business, government, and the Catholic church. *Phi Delta Kappan, 70*(10), 808–12.

Rowley, S. R. (1992, April). *School district restructuring and the search for coherence: A case study of adoptive realignment and organizational change*. Paper presented at the annual meeting of the American Educational Research Association, San Francisco.

Sedlak, M. W., Wheeler, C. W., Pullin, D. C., & Cusick, P. A. (1986). *Selling students short: Classroom bargains and academic reform in the American high school*. New York: Teachers College Press.

Tyack, D. (1990). "Restructuring" in historical perspective: Tinkering toward utopia. *Teachers College Record, 92*(2), 170–91.

CHAPTER 7

How a Few Politicians and Managers of Education Find Policy Success and Happiness: Part I

Richard G. Townsend

> Success is getting what you want. Happiness is wanting what you get.
> —Educational policy maker, Maple

Politicians and administrators use language for three goings-on: (1) to speak their minds about policy *contents*, the courses of action taken by authorities for addressing felt problems in schools; (2) to talk about policy *processes*, that is, how the courses of action are formulated, implemented, and evaluated for schools; and (3) to describe *learning outcomes*, that is, the knowledge, culture, and skills that students master, achieved through the implementation of educational policies. Furthermore, policy people use three kinds of talk: of *symbols*, of *cause-and-effect* relationships, and of *stakes* in winning and losing.[1]

The language of symbols, cause-and-effect relationships, and stakes is not trivial if we want to get into the minds of politicians and administrators who work up policies for schools. Policy fights are conducted with words. Catch the linguistic threads, and we catch weapons of policy. We can see how people organize their experiences for themselves and others, how they try to affect information in their spheres, and how they promote self- and collective interests. To ignore the symbols that authorities articulate, the causes and effects they advance, and the stakes they count is to ignore certain rules of their road. These types of talk alert us to ideas through which those authorities understand and act within their worlds. In talk, they combine argument with persuasion.

The emphasis here is on the language and enactments of *groups* involved in policy implementation. The private ideas and behavior of individuals are not dismissed as unimportant—they just are not analyzed here. Yet it is individuals' words that I report. I assume that the pragmatic interests of their groups affect the information that these individuals pass on.

Let me say more about symbols. First, authorities tell *stories*, or, more accurately, they allude to *storylines* or they draw narrative threads from literature, popular culture, and professional lore. Second, authorities use *metaphors*, in the traditional sense of making substitutions or drawing comparisons between one thing and another. And, finally, authorities use *synecdoches*, figures of speech in which a part represents the whole, where typical cases are said to embody the comprehensive situation.

Below, when a symbol takes on an inflated status in interviewees' discourse, the first letters of the italicized words are capitalized. Every single one of those symbols could be put in quotes, but that would make for choppy reading. So, quotation marks are dispensed with, unless the symbol is part of a longer quote that is reproduced. So, steel yourself for storylines and typography like *We Dialogue, They Gave Us A Snow Job*, and *I'm Always Putting Out Fires*, phrases that a handful of my interviewees use to describe their policy experiences. The capitalizations and italics cannot obscure that these are overly familiar expressions. If you could listen, mole-like, sometime to the patter of politicians and administrators in education, then likely you too would notice that these people are indefatigable but unapologetic purveyors of clichés.

Certain symbols are favored, and so the same storyline appears in different dress. *Meeting Students' Needs* is perhaps the all-time favorite. The phrase is exploited to try to get others to see all sorts of situations as one thing and not another. Thus field trips, sex education, and fifteen percent of music students' time being spent in listening are justified as giving primacy to students' needs. This needs perspective is tapped to reject initiatives, too. Thus, as an organizing principle, mastery learning is said to not meet students' needs as well as age-appropriate grouping. Outcomes-based education is deemed problematic because of difficulties in defining a uniform set of outcomes that would meet all students' needs. Sometimes the needs are not represented as changing. Politicians who are interviewed seem to refer to society's needs somewhat more than the educators do.

Commonly the metaphor of *War*, which arises in conjunction with a war on drugs, surfaces in other situations, such as unionists saying, "That policy is indefensible," or, in more of a wipe-out mode, "We're targeting the province to emerge wounded and bleeding from this battle." This text avoids such redundancies. However, this account's sections are not built around forms of language with, say, one section built around stories, another section around metaphors, and a third around synecdoche. Such a treatment would subordinate what I want to accent, namely, the notions that interviewees have—behind their talk—about the dynamics of policy contents, processes, and outcomes. Talk will be presented, but in the service of meanings that policy people attach to events and behaviors.

My sense is that most of these people are not self-conscious about exploiting these symbols. An exception is the politician who smirks, "I avoid clichés—*Like The Plague.*" My sense also is that, to a degree, these symbols are constructs of faith, even more believed than superstitions.

Several sources here have a favorite single cause for the attacks they are receiving these days in the media and elsewhere: *We're Only Human.* Another shrugs, "That's the only thing we can be—human," as he gestures toward a statistical printout that earlier he characterized as "inept." With a nod at the poet Alfred, Lord Tennyson, a different executive describes a policy/program memorandum from her own bureaucracy: "Our reach exceeds our grasp, I almost said 'gasp.' That's normal. It couldn't be otherwise. We live with realities that don't have a natural history."

Threaded throughout this report are a number of other cause-and-effect linkages. Certain of these are direct and uncluttered, but often the links between cause and effect are obscure and strongly mediated by factors beyond the one(s) given.

Sometimes authorities refer implicitly to us and them, friends and enemies, reliefs and sufferings. A politician, an administrator, or an educator thus portrays a policy to attract the support of others who might let that particular portrait speak for themselves. In this spirit, when top administrators of local education commonly represent provincial policies as violating their autonomy, they try to spur others into thinking negatively about the effects of controls that are remote. Provincial authorities, on the other hand, generally depict those controls as protecting the stakes of important interests that local officials neglect. Because each level can be skeptical about others' intentions and motives, defining a situation means making a claim about what is at stake.

IMPLEMENTATION FRAMEWORK

The definitive account of a province's policymaking will never be compiled by one researcher. Even limiting the treatment to a twenty-year period, and to that province's relationship with local boards' administrators, does not allow for an inclusive description of scores of forces, such as how neighborhoods, principals, and teachers impinge on those administrators. It is necessary, therefore, to risk the charge of superficiality in taking a selective approach to the subject matter.

The theoretic claim I select is that educational politicians and top administrators link policy precision with policy monitoring (Thompson 1987).[2] This claim is that although every provincial policy and every local response is unique regarding programs, processes, and people, a pattern can be traced. Policy people at different levels might talk and act quite differently for assorted policies, but a pattern lurks: it reflects actions these people take en route to more or less consensual implementations.

One might well ask whether particular linkings of precision and monitoring represent a purposeful strategy of any of the interviewees in this study; the answer is no. I simply built fences around what I think authorities say. The elements in the figures are conceptual slots that I have filled with facts that interviewees gave me concerning attributes of their circumstances. These are my pivotal, but not my only, sortings-out. Through these terms, and through depictions later on, I am feeding back a global view pulled together from separate individuals.

The framework for this part of my analysis has two dimensions, as figure 7–1 makes clear:

1. *Precision*, the horizontal axis of figure 7–1, marks policies that move beyond banal generalities. Precision is the tightness or looseness of a policy that politicians pass on

to top administrators. Simply put, this refers to the *clarity of policy direction*.

By definition, "statutory precision" is great when a vision is backed by a set of formal directives that are rigorous, quantified, specifically defined in correct sequence, affixed with timetables and regulations, flagged with rank orderings where multiple priorities exist, and spelled out even to include administrative practices and incentives for implementing policy. In certain situations, policy people believe in a policy or backup regulation for every situation. They think decision making is simplified by documents that clearly eliminate alternative solutions.

On the other hand, precision is limited when a policy is flexible. Serving as organizing frameworks for complex webs of actions, policies may need to be ambiguous in their statements of purpose. *Loosey-Goosey* is what a portly interviewee calls one policy that mostly prescribes a desired future while leaving the means to it open to interpretation. This fuzziness points to an opposite kind of excellence. The less specific a policy is, the less its risk of being pinned down and, so, of contradicting other policies. So the more a policy vision and format is opaque, the more it can arouse effect, engender unity, and focus dramatic attention. A policy with limited precision also can let politicians hide behind a rhetorical facade and perhaps avoid public criticism for partisan decisions. Vagueness further can avoid the disagreement that clarity can bring, since diverse groups can intuit imprecise policies as having nuances that they like. As interviewees in this account argue, limited provincial discretion also yields a delectable plus for local officials: they gain leeway for their own visions for improving schools. Often, however, interviewees complain about this leeway. In a now-corrected situation, poor wording of a policy for vacation entitlement was blamed for having prevented support staff from taking parts of their vacations; managers were said to have been reluctant to interpret that vague policy in favor of employees.

2. *Monitoring*, along the vertical axis of figure 7–1, is the degree to which originating authorities enforce their policy. A gamut for monitoring, or *degree of control*, runs from great to limited. If great, enforcement is close by elected authorities, their appointed top executives, the judiciary, and their policy advisors at the provincial level, also known as "overhead actors." Along those lines, an

elderly interviewee pulls out a large, yellowing newspaper photo and article from the sixties about a panel of secondary teachers seconded by the province to mark "departmentals." The Department of Education never should have ceded that great monitoring of high school seniors' marks on exams, he declares. He seems unconcerned about the inequity of better-informed parents then making sure their children get the "better" teachers.

Alternatively, monitoring or enforcement review is limited when provincial politicians supervise lightly and show such confidence in local authorities that they devolve authority. Hence another interviewee, who caustically and metaphorically refers to the province as *Superparent,* means that central monitoring/ degree of control today is nowhere limited enough: his cause-effect link is that *if* the province would only devolve responsibility, *then* great energies at the local level would be released.

Consider the top right corner of figure 7–1. Controlled implementation represents the situation in a recent newspaper where the provincial cabinet is reported to be fussy about how to finance education. The newspaper does not use the term *monitoring*, but it might well have—the province is exercising careful monitoring by setting up formulas that cut back provincial dollars for local education.

Varied kinds of policies do not apportion themselves neatly into figure 7–2's cells. Curricular policies and purposes are scattered throughout all four cells. Policies affecting personnel and organization are scattered around too.

Figure 7.1
Thompson's Types of Implementation

		Limited	*Great*
Monitoring	Great	Up-for-grabs implementation	Controlled implementation
	Limited	Buffered implementation	Prophylactic or preventive implementation

Figure 7.2
Images of Educational Policies in Maple Province by
Approximate Type of Implementation

Precision

Limited	Great
Construction	Amalgamation of boards
Continuing education	Architectural standards
Detracking	Biology teaching
Higher-order thinking	Collective bargaining
Holistic grading	Cooperative education
Language across the	Denominational funding
curriculum	Drug education
Media literacy	Electoral distribution of trustees
Process writing	Entrepreneurial studies
Science fairs	French-language education
Special education	Grants for per-pupil enrollment
Staff development	Grants for pupils with special needs
	Junior kindergarten
Up-for-Grabs	Lord's Prayer
Implementation	Length of school day/year
	National indicators (testing)
	Patterns of course timing
	Pay equity
	Secondary reform
	Student admissions and expulsion
	Teacher certification
	Tendering and other "housekeeping"
	Technical equipment

Monitoring *Great* ... *Limited*

Controlled Implementation

Black (Afro-Canadian) history	AIDS education
Canada's multicultural studies	Antiracism
Cognate disciplines	Budget estimates
Elementary science	Computers and their funding
Endpoints evaluation	Core French
French immersion	Day-care facilities
Hands-on and family math	Deaf education
Music	Gender parity in administration
Play curriculum	Heritage languages
Small primary classes	Lunchroom supervision
Whole language and phonics	Partners in (library) action
	Teacher evaluation

Buffered Implememtation	**Prophylactic or Preventive Implementation**

Figure 7–2 treats learning outcomes as background because these days the language on outcomes is pervasive among policy people. That talk underlies all four types of implementation, the foreground to the figures.

The most complex part of the framework used in my analysis concerns the argument that the goings-on of educational governance to some extent hang on five *modes of being* (Thompson 1987). Those modes of being affect, or help to affect, the processes of provincial-local relations in implementation. These modes are presumed to *precede* rather than *follow* governments' selection of particular types of implementation, although during implementation those modes may become more pronounced—*A Vicious Circle,* in an interviewee's metaphor.

I have boiled down the 120 interviewees' comments about process to suggest that *if* such-and-such mix of dynamics of being apply, *then* such-and-such type of implementation would commend itself to governments. Probably the practitioner and the academic both long for simpler truths rather than these five stimulants to the processes of policy implementations, but these distinctions do reflect what people said was important:

1. *Certainty of technology of policy method and material.* A certain technology or method would be a curriculum that is teacher-proof and classroom-ready, with tasks specified in correct sequence. An uncertain method, without linking chains of action from conception to final result, might or might not work.

2. *Stability of a policy's environment of context,* mirrored in situation dynamics like economics, demography, culture, law, and other macroforces in a province, locality, or neighborhood;

3. *Level of commitment to a specific policy within the implementation agency*—that is, the resolve and norms of teachers to understand and absorb the policy. When the level of commitment is low, those within the agency have an attitude (as a local official tells me) that *Policy Sucks.*

4. Level of tension in the sociopolitical milieu or, put more familiarly, the amount of opposition and support from *pressure or interest groups and factions.* When the level of

tension in the milieu is high, interest groups try to reconstruct preferences of the authorities or the public.

5. *Capacity or ability of overhead actors or elected officials* and their political appointees to devise approaches to implementation. These legislators and partisan executives are the external controllers of, and ultimate implementors of, public agencies, but their criticism of policy is only intermittent (Vickers 1965). "Capacity" refers to their effectiveness and skills in correcting errors and so amending their policy in the face of learning by doing; that is, practice does not necessarily make perfect, but practice does make for good political adjustments in implementation's aims and means.

As I worked through data and conducted more interviews, complicating the story seemed an honorable, if unparsimonious, move. Hence I characterize how administrators at the provincial and local levels get on with the policies that provincial politicians hand to them for school sites. The cast of characters was expanded to include the following:

6. *Implementation activities of the province's top educational administrators,* including assistant deputy ministers and their ranking deputies, such as branch heads, and education officers, known below as "middle managers"; these are the internal controllers of the provincial department of education.

7. *Implementation activities of top administrators at the local level* (chief education or executive officers, hereafter CEOs) and their top associates within school systems. They are the internal controllers of local school systems.

In table 8–1 of chapter 8, these players' relations with each other are depicted. Suppose another researcher were to interview another 120 people or the very same 120 people a year or two later. Would that researcher analyze the 57 implementations the same as I did? I agree that today is quite different from the late eighties, when work for this report began. Probably any map of policy relationships should be redrawn almost monthly to keep up with sporadic and willful needs of participants. My hunch, however, is that many of these turns of speech are among those that other politicians and top administrators bring to the policy table. Admittedly, I want it both ways. I want to recognize the uniqueness of the 120 interviewees' talk about governmental goings-on, just as I want to offer something about policy that is faintly general. A great deal about policy is out of reach of even the most restless analysis. That world does not distill itself completely into the categories I have used. The researcher needs to look longer and breathe deeper of policy than this mole has been able to do.

To be scanned are 57 implementations that originate at the provincial level for local realization. Bold-faced within the text, they already have been introduced in the four quadrants of figure 7–2. Their contents, processes, and outcomes might not be the most important. They are, however, the policies that interviewees discuss most frequently. The 57 carry weight in terms of impact on school improvement and have been the object of politicking in varying degrees. The 57 are either expressions of need that society expects schools to attend to, or, in a less trusting storyline, they are policies that fulfill educators' need for activities to keep themselves gainfully employed.

A crucial part of the framework for this analysis is its quasi comprehensiveness. A policy's impacts are affected by other policies and their processes; a relevant frame for telling about provincial education is not a single, discrete implementation. The stand here is based on the premise that a variety of policy contents, processes, and outcomes spill over onto each other. Each policy is presumed to exist within an interactive web of other policies' dynamics. An example of such spillover: (1) The flow of joined-up writing helps (2) imprint spellings in the mind, where (1) is part of a handwriting policy to encourage correct and fluent letter formation, while (2) is part of a spelling policy that looks with sympathy and understanding at what pupils have written.

Rather than a thorough cultivation of a small patch of land such as a single policy, a panorama is offered here, a bird's-eye view of language in a large tract where bundles of policies are tilled. Consequently, this text will move quickly from policy to policy—much as a farmer, tending fields, might move from a row of green peppers to an adjacent row of chives, without elaborate transitions. Some policies are particularly interesting, however, and more text is devoted to them.

The report tarries over these courses of action, not for their controversies, but for the intensities with which these policies engaged residents. Their rough approximations in other provinces upset their residents, too. Their implementations are among the most widely redistributive in education of late, each shifting resources from one large group to another. Granted, some of these bracing visions for public action are decades old, therefore out of today's headlines and almost taken for granted. Yet these and other standing policies on the books decidedly are hardly, as an interviewee says, *Water Under The Bridge*. They bear testimony to past, deeply felt crises that even today shape how politicians and top administrators symbolize, envision cause and effects, and count stakes. Both as memories and as everyday guides, as an interviewee says by way policy-izing an old proverb, *Old Policies Run Deep*.

METHOD

Meet Those Interviewees and Their Backstairs Talk

I observed central office functionings, listened at closed and open meetings, read documents, and, most vitally, talked with 120 people.

These people have a reputation for being among the most important insiders of one province's education. The 120 interviewees have experience both as participants and as observers, formulators, and implementors in the unfolding of policies. Maybe it was self-confidence that prompted them to open up during generally long, in-depth, and confidential interviews. Or maybe it was because they had abandoned attempts to succeed in other roles that animated them: they had staked themselves as knowing about governance, and now they were going to talk about it. Whatever the motives of these provincial legislators, chairs of boards, heads of lobbies, supervisory officers, executives at several levels in the department of education, and top administrators of local boards, verbally they gave much, usually at their offices.[3]

Seven of my interviewees cast themselves as *Survivors*. A survivor might have only modest managerial skills and managerial gifts, yet these interviewees do not seem to be maligning themselves. What they seemed to be saying, laconically, is that they have conscientiously outlasted and outwitted others' manipulations, being especially open to what's essential.

What about the *Juicy Stuff*, so termed by an interviewee who looked forward to my accounts' inclusion of backstairs gossip? This informal juiciness may be off-putting to those for whom facade takes precedence over the expression of feelings. *"Don't Wash Dirty Linen In Public,"* a local administrator warns. So her profane interpretations of several provincial directives and authorities are not quoted. Exuberant others are.

Sources of Data

Information here comes from one Canadian jurisdiction,[4] disguised as "Maple Province" for three reasons.[4]

First, the report follows through on a promise to give interviewees and sites anonymity. To lessen interviewees' guardedness and inaccessibility, the pledge was made to omit descriptors that might compromise identities. Many then spoke in an unbuttoned mood.

A second reason for not divulging names and addresses is to honor my interviewees' humanness. The report thus has a resonance with that earlier-mentioned "We're only human" explanation of several interviewees that "no government could live up to all the outsized hopes out there for education." Since no human is ever fully known to another, this means honoring elements of the interviewees' greatest mystery, their personalities.

A third reason is that the features highlighted here might be more general than one jurisdiction's alone. This bow toward generality is not especially popular in research—more commonplace is the claim that every setting is unique and quite nonreproducible. All the same, among humans, nothing is totally provincial or limited in interest. All topics are universal. Authorities in Maple Province face the same tasks of growth and maintenance as other jurisdictions' leaders. This is why, after a time, public organizations and their members' talk begin to look and sound alike.

CONTROLLED'S PRECISION & MONITORING

Like its etymological cousin *police*, the word *policy* is freighted with images of coercion into patterns of submissive behavior. Local top administrators say they know much about the tight con-

trol and rigid clarity of direction that can go with this policy. For
instance:

> Teachers long to bring the resources they have to policy. . . .
> Department attitudes and *Hurdles* get in the way.

> Who has faith anymore in hierarchical command? In somebody
> in Capital City [pseudonym] knowing "the" best practice . . .
> *Lifting His Little Finger* and making education happen?

> Provincial policy means *Red Tape* and sanctions that force us to
> comply. Being *Boxed In*. If you don't fill out the forms for tech-
> nical renewal correctly, you don't get the money.

With different particulars, others recoil from the notion of policy
mechanically ordering people about. The very idea of provincial
politicians wielding the sovereign power of the state over local
education seems to violate what they know about the creativity of
individuals, organizations, and democratic societies.

Controls come when statutory precision is high, when the *I*'s
of policy execution are dotted and the *T*'s are crossed. Controlled
implementation's great monitoring further enables provincial
leaders to repudiate locals and to correct mistakes (outcomes different from what's been centrally planned). This type of implementation's monitoring leads locals to think of themselves as
responsible to, and as legislated *Creatures Of, The Province*. As
long as the province follows broad constitutional proprieties,
many interviewees recognize, albeit grouchily, this coercion as
legitimate.

Of course, people at the peak of the provincial bureaucracy
know that their control is not ironclad—one tells me so—for no
policy can ever cover every possibility. Yet by creating the illusion
of control, authorities warn locals and reassure the public that
presumably has "a desire to believe that someone is responsible."
In all this, Department of Education officials like to project themselves as reasonably allowing deviations from their controls. But
they insist that the burden of proof is upon boards to justify
exceptions.

Policies within sections are presented in the order of frequency
of mention. Sections on controlled implementation provide the
longest treatment—22 policies will parade past. This attests to
education in Maple Province and elsewhere operating substan-

tially through stories of policy clarity or precision and top-down control or monitoring.

Language about Firm Policy Methods (Technology)

For policy method, the first mode of being for a particular type of implementation, the intended meaning is the formal rules, roles, conventions, strategies, compliance procedures, and standard operating practices around which policies are constructed. Provincial and local authorities tell good stories about these methods— stories with a beginning, a middle, and an end.

An interviewee/reactor to a draft of this report says I'm *Missing The Boat* by the sequencing of policies here. She wants to read first about a policy oriented toward students, not **collective bargaining**. To be sure, that policy might not be what persuaded teachers to go into education, although Maple's wages are high enough for this consideration to be a lure. Taxpayers in Maple are *Rattling* for lower teachers salaries: thus, "Teachers didn't suffer the recession of the early eighties . . . and now it's their turn" and "*The Public Interest* would be better served by wage-comparability boards rather than collective bargaining." No policy is talked about more by my educational insiders than the precise, complex, thorough, and ultimately controlled-implementation arrangements for settling disputes by union bargaining. Firm methods of a provincial bargaining commission hold a grip on the psyches of educators: it is among their most sacred storylines that, no matter how fiscally strapped government might be, *Collectively Agreed-Upon Contracts Must Not In Any Circumstances Be Broken*.

In the seventies, Maple experienced *The Strike*, a memorable walkout, involving a cold picket line and almost all school teachers in the province; those who *Hit Those Bricks* are accorded semilegendary status in their unions today, or so a thin interviewee says. Maple politicians had been going through a *Rain Dance* soliciting opinions about what to do about teacher negotiations. "The politicians already had strong preferences, so their call for suggestions was a sham," is how a leader of a teachers' union recalls the birth of collective bargaining for Maple's teachers, a birth that was resisted by local school board trustees. They thought, some of their successors also think, that bargaining narrows trustees' abilities to make decisions.

Thereafter, union leaders regularly have negotiated binding labor-management agreements on such contract items as compensation, workload, staff development, fringe benefits, interpersonal disputes, and the size of all classes except for grades 1 and 2. When, however, bargaining has broken down between teachers and their trustees, the bargaining commission's fact finders, mediators, and arbitrators follow sharply defined limits of scope and timing. At hearings, for instance, a group of boards might appeal to shorten classes from 76 to 75 minutes, while unionists complain that a hundred of their teaching positions would be lost, in violation of their contract, by such a time shortening. Such differences are not necessarily settled to unions' complete satisfaction, yet a common story is that this precise method of dispute settlement, involving increasingly detailed contracts, has yielded good payoffs to teachers. "The seniority system is crazy," a politician differs, "it's *The Only Profession* [in which] you get paid for getting older." He "proves" his point by citing two examples.

Until recently, the procedure for teacher bargainers was to seek percentage increases. That was *The Name Of The Game.* "If the provincial average was 2.8 [percent], a local tried to get 3 or 3.2 [percent], that was it." Boards and teachers learned that each side could attest to moderate success. Now, however, with acute drops in provincial funds for the public sector and with a public perception, one interviewee says, that *Teachers' Snouts Are Too Firmly Planted In The Public Trough,* provincial legislation is tightening the bargaining process even further. "Teachers are into protecting jobs. . . . Skip the percentage increases. There's none to get. . . . We bargain with a *Gun at Our Head."* A provincial politician has an optimistic counter-story wherein authorities *Show Resolve* in meeting fiscal emergencies:

> *The Man In The Street* is short-tempered, and willing to make abrupt changes in governments. . . . In the last decade, you know, fiscal support for education rose over 75 percent, when school enrolment went up less than 2 percent. Many boards got used to *Living High On The Hog.* . . . No way that could continue. We have taken *Deep Political Hits* over our changes, but in the long run *Government Management of Spending* is going to help us adjust. We may not *Keep Teachers Happy,* there's sure a lot of grief . . . but we're counting on teachers' willingness *To Walk That Extra Mile.*

(This notion of keeping teachers happy also recurs, by the way, in administrators' conversations. The thought arises: Do judges talk of keeping lawyers happy? Do doctors speak of keeping nurses happy?)

To finance education, the richest board has access to 15 times the tax base per pupil available to the lowest. Some boards are small and isolated, unable to capture the economies of scale enjoyed by larger boards in urbanized areas. Since finance involves balancings of local property assessments with provincial grants to promote equality of student treatment, interviewees tell the story that newly elected formulators and implementors of department policy are "*At Sea* when it comes to working the dollar numbers." Yet because interest groups strenuously contest the fine details of general legislative grants, politicians are seen as willingly *Poring Over The Books* to master this arcane discourse involving "other people's money." To a degree, they count the political stakes of who wins from expenditures and who loses from cost controls. Thus, in an interviewee's metaphor of the Department of Education as *Banker,* provincial functionaries develop payout formulas for per-pupil enrollment, for grants supporting students with special needs, for all boards making the same tax effort to raise the local share of costs for base-level programs and services, and so forth. That "and so forth" is encompassing: in a causal story that is both melancholy and omnipresent, *Money, Or The Lack Thereof, Colors Everything.*

In all this, a must is *Value For Money,* a business storyline, sometimes broached in the same breath as audits and as trimming positions for consultants, custodians, and others. Although difficult to measure, policy success is being defined in the lean and crusading storyline of *Efficiency.* Thus, one politician urges locals to *Cut The Fat Out of Budgets* by cooperating on program, computers, and procurement with coterminus boards. He could have urged locals to improve efficiency by increasing output at little or no additional cost, but he does not so urge. Nor does he answer the common storyline from another interviewee that increases in efficiency can damage academic programs that are on *The Cutting Edge.*

In any event, for him locally incurred expenditures are not to become obligations of the provincial government. In defense of Maple's technique of funding below the inflation rate, the cabinet member quoted above spins out this explanation: "If there were provincial money for more grants, you can be sure this government would have many more priorities." Another politician defends a decision to reduce grants for computers by 50 percent: *"Get This Government Off Our Backs* is the message my constituents tell me." (The *This Government* phrase is one that those in power like to brandish.) Because voters are said to be finicky dollarwise, a governmental technique is to never even think of setting mill rates for taxes that are suicidally high. Meanwhile, the film playing in my interviewees' minds has the province feeling free to diminish its grants to boards almost by technical fiat, so great is the department's control over aspects of finance. In most cases, local officials do not have the *Political Will* themselves to raise taxes that would replace reductions of provincial funds.

At first, when an interviewee jokingly says that provincial top administrators use *Confusion Power*, that phrase is interpreted as a droll example of the speaker's drawing a comparison between any government's capacity to bewilder and other well-known types of force like coercive power, legitimate power, and referent power. But then, wanting a prototypic instance to represent a larger peril, this interviewee turns to synecdoche. He notes, "Since boards are beginning to understand the grant structure, it's time to change it again." Confusion in the grant structure exemplifies everything about a finance regime that, he says, is convoluted and turgid. His synecdoche about finance is contested, however, by another interviewee: "The department circulates its fiscal proposals. . . . When it consults on that, hell, it'll consult on anything."

Students of Maple's finances remark that over the years the Department of Education increasingly has funneled more money away from urban boards with strong tax and industrial bases. "We get *Negative Grants* from the department" is how interviewees from well-to-do boards technically portray their situation of not needing provincial subsidies. These rich boards bridle at almost any procedure to pool more of "their" money through the Department of Education to boards less able to meet expenses; one interviewee referred to this as the perceived *Robin Hood Effect* of school finance. Interviewees from Capital City argue— on cause-effect grounds—that, moreso than other boards, they have special problems that require expensive programs. In the name of equity, department officials unflinchingly match that cause-effect rationale with at least three metaphors of their own—

about *The Poor As Victims* and the need for the province's ineq-
uities to cease, about the need for *Level Playing Fields* achieved
through the well-to-do sharing their resources, and about *The
Canadian Way of Haves Helping The Have-Nots*, protecting
those least able to protect themselves, through monetary transfers.
To refute the department's claim, spokespersons for rich localities
use the wishful storyline that *Local Taxpayers Expect Their
Money To Be Used Locally.* Unheard from these interviewees is
the older, more emotive, and famous storyline about no taxation
without representation.

   Well-known is the firm technique that when local boards incur
deficits, or when the Department of Education auditors suggest that
local CEOs' requests are not justified, boards are brought up short.
"While *Money Can't Buy Dreams, It Does Talk,*" one interviewee
says, and so Maple's authorities indicate they hold back funding
until local administrators explain their anomalies or submit budgets that finally conform to provincial standards and reporting systems. This incites one local authority to say, bitterly, that *He Who
Has the Gold Makes The Rules.* At the same time, policy people
appreciate that the method of withholding cheques is not supposed
to affect student outcomes adversely, lest citizens perceive the provincial government to be a metaphorical and fiscal *Bully.*

   Through controlled implementation, the story is that tender-
ing and other potentially chaotic **"housekeeping"** aspects of board
operations are managed predictably. These operations include fees
that teachers pay to their union, in-school announcements of high
water levels (so students are forewarned to avoid overflowing
creeks and rivers), lengths of academic day and school year, patterns of course timing, procedures in buying educational supplies,
and **student admission and expulsion.** Water in the drinking fountains comprises a curiously oft-mentioned example of the level of
detail that local top administrators share with me, as if it were a
typical case that synecdochically defined the department's whole
approach to close housekeeping. These fountains need to be run
for five minutes each morning, expunging dangerous lead that
may have accumulated overnight.

   Many stories hinge upon time, as in *Timing Is Critical* in articulating solutions for problems, and as in one bureaucrat's comment about department strategy in housekeeping: *"Time Means
Change* and Time Lessens Local Resentment.*"* To illustrate, in the
wake of recent department counts of provincial disbursements

pegged to student attendance figures, the story is that teachers and boards are becoming more pristine about keeping accurate registers on student absences. An audit-minded department had seen local disregard of time spent in school as a cause of cost overruns.

Language about Moderately High Stability of Context

Controlled implementation thrives when economic, demographic, cultural, and intellectual conditions are stable. The presumption is that when everything is going smoothly, and nothing is rocking the sociopolitical boat, provincial forces can monitor precise policies closely.

Most talked about in this regard is a Maple initiative for junior kindergarten. Its major impetus dates back to its advocacy on an election campaign bus by the principal (political) advisor to a premier. It is amazing how many interviewees refer to that advocacy on that bus. The province was enjoying a boom economy, encouraging local educators and board members to savor this possibility of serving a new constituency by providing, symbolically anyway, what was called *An Even Start* for children from disadvantaged homes. Schools thereby could relate to their neighborhoods' demographic context while filling empty spaces and retaining teachers who might otherwise have been redundant.

Then questions arose over whether cost implications of this controlled implementation had been well honed. Local officials said the proposal was shifting *The Limited Pot* of provincial dollars away from education to preschool education. An interviewee who is a lobbyist repeated the storyline of *Things Going To the Dogs*: "After we laughed about it [junior kindergarten in all the schools], we wondered where the bucks were coming from. . . . Which important program would we have to cut to make way for this *Frill?*" The "frill" remark tends to mask or trivialize a legitimate conflict in priorities, but sometimes a metaphor politicizes a situation. Thus, "Publicly, in a gym full of parents yet!" one local administrator broke ranks with higher authorities to predict *Major Social Unrest* if the policy were soon implemented.

For a few years, given a downturn in the percentage of provincial revenues going into education and the policymakers' insistence that this controlled policy had to be implemented anyway, a *Tug-Of-War* is said to have occurred. Both sides saw themselves as caring about student outcomes, but a leading question became,

"Would recession-ridden local systems have to pay for those mandated new classes themselves?" Provincial authorities gradually evinced some flexibility—approving, for instance, a rural board's alternative to junior kindergarten—yet those politicians let it be known that other boards were moving at a *Snail's Pace,* a metaphor that in another context is hurled back, with gusto, at the Department of Education. When it became clear to those politicians that localities were not able or willing to serve up money for junior kindergarten, the province backtracked. The control initiative either was *Put On Hold,* which is the province's face-saving story, or the province *Threw In The Towel,* which is the locals' story. To defeat that initiative, local authorities had focused on factual assertions, hypothetical relationships, and value assertions that were fiscal, not moral, social, or cultural. That proved politically successful, at least for a while.

The story about **teacher certification,** also much bandied about, is one of a greatly specific, greatly monitored policy that has been implemented, until lately, as if the context were relatively stable. As elsewhere during the sixties, Maple had (1) a surplus of graduates from faculties of education and (2) intellectuals telling stories of decline unless programs for prospective teachers were enhanced. The department began requiring the boards' new staff to earn postbaccalaureate degrees in education, not really an unreasonable credential for Maple's postindustrial society. Then came the eighties, with staff shortages and much notice being given to global competitiveness and information revolutions; stories were told again of potential decline in a not-very-industrial society. Legislators were among those to question whether the policy for teacher postings was open enough in high-tech areas.

Eventually, the department took the cue and revised its certification regulations—but only slightly. Classifications were added for subjects such as transport technology and auto mechanics. Further exceptions were permitted for computer and other specialists to begin work while still completing teacher training. Today, a proposal to deepen skills and double the postbaccalaureate training for would-be teachers is said to be *In Limbo.* "It'll take ten or twenty years to get that proposal through," one official says, with exasperation. Wanting authorities to move faster in upgrading teacher education, the proponent of deeper skills for teachers values a context that is more volatile. Her explicit cause-effect relationship is that *Crises Are Mothers Of Invention.*

She is ambivalent, however, about the worth of the province's system for teachers' gaining additional qualifications by taking "easy," department-oriented courses. "It's good for the beginning teacher or those who after five or ten years want to change panels or subject matters." She thinks those department-controlled courses are good for somebody who has been teaching for twenty years—"They need livening up. . . . [But] has in-service in turn helped any children?" she asks, lifting her eyebrows. Her skepticism is shared by several politicians who plan to phase out the province's underwriting of in-service courses. One of these politicians is even more radical—he would free all schools of the provincial licensing requirement for teachers. That step would enable qualified professionals in other fields to work in schools, thus "enriching a system that's *Grown Inbred And Stale.*"

Interviewees say how Maple's politicians have accepted the story that the board staffs are *Too Lily White* and that minorities have been historically disadvantaged by past intentional prejudice. These politicians subscribe to the familiar cause-effect link that if more minority-group members were in teacher ranks, as role models, they could raise learning outcomes for now-unmotivated minority youth. Yet, and again to the dismay of some, authorities have not rushed ahead with *Crash Courses* for preparing ethnically diverse teachers. The notion of risk to contextual stability here enters into policymakers' talk. Interviewees tell me that, until recently, the department has been concerned that greater aggressiveness in affirmative action might have been divisive and therefore potentially destabilizing.

On the other hand, a degree of stability often is achieved by dawdling over an issue that might excite public resistance. Thus the government has dawdled in insisting on more minority teachers. Reportedly the department's cause-effect scenario has been that interracial tensions would mount if a large cohort of minority teachers were fast-tracked at a time when (1) budget shortages were throwing surplus white teachers out of work and (2) many graduates of faculties of education could not find work in Canada. Only in 1993, decades after heavy migrations into Maple and decades after similar initiatives in the United States, did a minister of education stop temporizing on this issue. He asked universities to encourage self-identified members of minorities to declare themselves when applying to faculties of education. In return for continued financial support, universities were to use special admission routes, provide support systems within education faculties, and otherwise recruit and reserve percentages in their teacher preservice programs for people from underrepresented groups.

Governments can craft stories of themselves as quelling forces that, if allowed to fester, would rip the social fabric. So it was that after the drowning of a Capital City adolescent on drugs, a cabinet speedily initiated a mandatory **drug education** program for grades 4 to 8. Synecdochically, the dead boy became the dominant image of the problem. Provincial budgets enabled new materials to be introduced to teachers, a step that let the provincial government answer those who might say it was shamefully blasé about that boy's death, drugs in the schools, and related societal issues. Purportedly this effort, even though taken in the context of a fairly stable and prosperous economy, was unpalatable for several local authorities. Advising the province that it had *Caved In* to community pressures, these board administrators added that the province's action symbolized precisely all that was wrong with *Political Influence* on academic focus. These local administrators agreed with the metaphor that drugs had indeed *Invaded* the schools. But instead of handing teachers yet another learning outcome to worry about, politicians should have blamed the boy's parents for not being watchful enough for substance abuse.

Biology teaching is a curricular as well as a social issue that boards' top administrators have yearned for politicians to step in and help resolve, in order to stabilize the beyond-schoolyard context. In contradiction to scientific theories of the origin of the species, religious fundamentalists regularly petition for biology textbooks and other pedagogical guides to include biblical assumptions regarding biology and spirituality. They question, "Why is evolution being taught as fact?" Their story that *Man* is created in the image of God is discrepant with progressive cause-effect postulations that human beings are a product of natural processes. Three interviewees who brought up this matter seem to introject themselves more into Clarence Darrow's modernist role than into William Jennings Bryan's die-hard one; an interviewee invokes this graphic symbol from the Scopes trial, or from a movie video he has seen about that trial. Local administrators are delineated as having sided with modernists in believing that all living things develop from simple to complex by means of natural processes.

Wishing to promote academic inquiry while avoiding antiscientific thinking in the curriculum, provincial politicians ultimately turned away from creationists' demands. Then, more on their own than by politicians' outright steering, local educators say they did subsequently respond to creationists. They responded to the extent that different versions of the truth about evolution have become vehicles for instruction. One interviewee volunteers that today's students are learning to recognize bias in both approaches and to examine presumptions underlying outlooks on evolution and other topics, thereby demonstrating facets of critical thinking. "No student is compelled to accept any theory presented in the curriculum," he says. Biblical creationists have won a learning outcome and the controlled implementation they wanted, as did evolutionists.

Words Relating to Educators' Slight Commitment

An old chestnut of a storyline among interviewees is that commitment from teachers is achieved by involving those teachers early in the policy process, rather than by authorities' flaunting their coercive powers. Not surprisingly, then, when it comes to controls initiated by politicians in Capital City, local administrators commonly picture themselves as low in commitment.

Occasionally, storylines for portraying such implementations seem like parables of the human adventure, of how gains in wisdom come through loss. Several storylines feature a top administrator at the local level with illusions that provincial mandates can truly be achieved. Perhaps by way of coping with his misplaced aspirations, one local administrator even compares himself— exaggeratively and a little weirdly—to *Adam In A Fallen State.* This decline storyline involves seed money introduced with sloganary language. In 1989, Maple's government earmarked millions for buying **technical equipment** for broad-based generic-skills courses, not for specialized-skills courses. "We didn't need machine shops anymore," he quotes Maple as decreeing. This self-proclaimed Adam remembers deferring other tasks to make budget submissions with the advice of the department's technical experts. He secures for his board the provincial grant and dutifully purchases the broad-based items—he bites into the provincial apple—although he sees a greater need for more specialized, more narrowly focused tools. Presently, however, with boxfuls of this equipment reputedly *Sitting Unused In Schools,* this uncommitted educator muses that getting a grant is not the be-all and end-all. Two other interviewees add that, in light of industrial standards, they are ashamed of the dated mechanical equipment they have to implement provincial mandates.

Pay equity activities in the eighties provide an alternative example, this time of the province bringing on side local administrators who were uncommitted. The latter feared sufficient money would not be available for equal compensation for men's and women's work of equal value. As one interviewee remembers, the province set deadlines for gender-neutral comparison systems and job descriptions to be developed. Having established a regulatory body for this thrust, the province adopted regulations for boards to put aside portions of their payrolls for this purpose. Implementors complied; they had little choice. Reportedly, however, some boards now get around the policy, which is for in-house staff: these boards contract out custodial work, for instance, at low wages.

Organizational aspects of curriculum—what should be taught, more than how subjects should be taught—are associated, too, with the Department of Education as *Tough Guy* and with local implementors as relatively uncommitted. The issue goes back several years, but passions still linger around one government's revision of curricula for secondary schools. A minority of interviewees thought the Secondary Schools' Reform was a *Scam* on the part of certain high school educators to keep their enrollments up—their courses were required. A more typical story is that department politicians bowed to back-to-basics pressures arising from the provinces' recessionary context, as filtered or fueled through a media with *An Axe To Grind.*

The **Secondary Reform** was a policy strong for traditional course sequences and science requirements. High on specifics and monitoring, the Secondary Reform was exactly what one would expect for a conservative government. This controledness, where high school departments lost students and positions, also was precisely what one would expect when scant commitment to the policy was evident among teachers. Among them, sway was held by course options, "soft" humanities, and progressivism (child-centered learning in contrast to teacher-directed instruction). Bill Spady, the famous proponent of planning for measurable learning outcomes, had not influenced Maple in this regard, yet.

Aware that policy metaphors can help define problems, provincial authorities portrayed the high school problem as one of *Cafeteria Selection*—for rigor's sake, students should not be able to choose courses as if they randomly were picking food. The problem was further portrayed as one of *Fixed Space*—the academic day, like a container with only about three-hundred minutes, was filled with too many choices. Among members of the public, this depiction is said to have succeeded. Teachers remained dubious, however. The minister of the day "would not have dared introduce these reforms" had political support been a prerequisite. Instead of bringing the Secondary Reform arrangements before the legislature for the usual sort of approval, that minister chose to *"Unveil* these changes by regulation and coercion." That unveiled metaphor implies, by the way, that the minister's changes had been kept a secret until the last minute. That implication is wrong. Before adoption, these ideas were long discussed by unions and in the press.

Interviewees' subsequent recollection is that while some principals tried to welcome the Secondary Reform, many local officials at board offices *Laid Low* for a while. They minimized the package as a *Passing Fad* (fads are always passing, never taking off): "We hoped it would go away." Eventually, however, recalcitrant board officials acceded to provincial authority, some announcing to teachers that "there'll be a review of your school and I'll be looking at Secondary Reform's courses of study."

From interviewees, it appears these declarations occasionally led to reconfigurations within a mere month or two—across a number of schools, central office visits about program are rare enough to become a stimulus for trying to finish up. In no mood, however, to approve the government's policy, many implementors tell a story of decline and havoc: Secondary Reform was narrowing knowledge, teachers were being deskilled, and learning opportunities were being diminished in home economics, shop, and other subjects that had lost out in student numbers. Among situations visited for this report, though, two counter-stories were passed around: (1) Secondary Reform mostly was reinterpreted to conform to what staffs already were doing, and (2) the legislatively required reports did not genuinely reflect what schools were doing.

Interest Groups in a Debilitating Sociopolitical Milieu

Aim a policy at a particular group, and conventional wisdom has that group's opposition frustrating policy execution. Presumably, the more contrary-minded an affected interest group is toward a policy, the more essential it is for politicians and top administrators to frame precise, clear-headed legislation. That, anyway, is the rationale of controlled implementation, a point evidently not lost on Maple's politicians for education. The point especially is not lost when clarity and precision help the pocketbook and boost citizen support.

Witness the issue of the **Lord's Prayer** in schools, decried by some minority groups who believe that a class recitation of a Christian prayer devalues, by comparison, non-Christian religions. The court's verdict, said by politicians to embody the highly ambiguous storylines of *Justice* and *Fairness*, required that the province specifically ban religious opening exercises in schools. The province's monitoring, through Department of Education officers and Christmastime reminders from the minister, had immediacy. Consequently, in most—but not all—boards, school days now convene with one minute of silence, giving no primacy to Christian values. Policy people smile knowingly, however, as trustees in several outlying homogeneous Anglo-Saxon communities continue, years later, to *Thumb Their Noses* at the government's ban. These boards seize the opportunity to open their nighttime business meetings, not explicitly covered by the ban, with that same Prayer. A lawyer-interviewee dramatically sees this episode as an instance of symbolic terms, as *Secular Power Losing Out To Sacred Power.*

The province further is seen as *Dividing And Conquering* interest groups to control their sociopolitical milieu. This storyline is that when they split off problems along interest group lines, Maple politicians defuse those groups' concerns and chase away issues that are in the queue jockeying for the legitimacy of government choice. Avowedly, provincial politicians point to conflicting demands from everyone: large boards versus small boards; French boards versus English boards; Capital City–area boards versus other boards; Catholic boards versus public boards; elementary versus secondary panels and unions; ratepayers versus private schools seeking public financing; ethnic or class groups versus groups with more-inclusive orientations; and so on.

Avowedly, too, the province is identified as regularly setting up a cause-effect dynamic that leaves its Department of Education free to put off unpopular decisions. The cause: "See, you groups can't get your act together." The effect: "So we don't have to deal with you. Come back and see us once all of you finally agree." In their defense, groups in that sociopolitical milieu have a testy response. The following is a composite from the words of six interviewees who would speak to the department:

> Hey look, we are together on important issues [such as the need for trustees, such as the need for school boards and having more seats on the Training and Adjustment Commission, and we are moving toward togetherness on other issues such as copyright]. *Don't Walk Away* from other issues we can't settle among ourselves. The cabinet should go ahead and *Bite The Bullet*. As a government, *Show Bold Leadership*.

Leadership in this instance may mean coming up with trade-offs that hold together and satisfy assorted constituencies. Arguably too, *leadership* is a code word for producing policies that benefit the interviewees' interests. In any event, the symbol of bold leadership seems fundamental to policy language. Frequently authorities and interest-group leaders, evidently believing the story that *Change Starts At The Top,* refer to it as seminal for effects they desire. A sometime-cited example of leadership occurred twenty-five years ago when Maple **amalgamated** hundreds of **school boards**. More recently, provincial authorities stepped forward to change provisions for the **electoral determination of trustees**. Such leadership also includes dominating **architectural standards** for erecting and repairing schools; of late, **cooperative education** has been tightly controlled too.

Language about Politicians in Touch and in Control

The allure of controlled implementation grows when political authorities, in and out of the Department of Education have the capacity to craft sound procedures and to rectify defects in operations. An oft-told storyline, though, is that "as the deputy minister goes, so goes the department." In interviews, Maple's deputy ministers loom—somewhat like Sir Humphrey in "Yes, Minister"—as political, not strictly as administrative, figures in all types of implementation, most especially those that are provincially controlled. Nothing goes to the minister until the deputy says so, and this *Gatekeeping* means the deputy politically affects the government's policy allocations of attention, resources, and the like. "A good deputy supplements the Minister's agenda with his own."

Moving within an ambigious domain where agreements of values have not been reached, deputies are a special breed; women have been ministers, but in education, until now, Maple's deputies have all been men. They differ from most other high-level officials and from middle-level bureaucrats who work within hierarchies considerably affected by the themes of their branches. Chosen by premiers and serving at their pleasure and even reporting directly to them, a deputy cannot help being beholden to politicians, as politicians are beholden to him for policy stories and advice. Educational critics in Parliament also turn to the deputy for guidance, although on occasion the deputy may tell the critic, "Ask the minister."

Supporting the tradition that the deputy is apolitical and strictly a civil servant are varied storylines, but these symbols of deputy as pure manager are fading fast. One is the rule of thumb that traditional school people *Rise Through Civil Service Ranks* at the Department of Education to deputyhood. In a familiar storyline, by beginning with a love for teaching, by working their ways up the *Educational Establishment's* ranks, by learning the range of educational and political behaviors expected in different roles, by logging their share of taking orders as well as giving them, by sharpening occupational proficiencies and social skills, deputies were said to learn about effectively promoting camaraderie among educators. They know *Which Buttons To Push,* what passions have to be quashed, and what has to be said to stir *The Troops* willingly to do what is required.

Over the last decade, however, as part of a government-wide push for aggressive and fast-moving generalists ahead of overly socialized professionals in this peak role, that taboo has been broken; the last four education deputies came to their office from other career paths. One now-local administrator complains about her former employer, "It's discouraging when your boss knows nothing about education." These deputies have been relied on to execute the government's toughest policy, even when that means being *A Slash-And-Burn Man,* going beyond trimming and tacking, cutting back everywhere.

Reinforcing the story of deputies as *Above Politics* is a spatial separation at the Department of Education headquarters. Space for the deputy and his assistants is on a different side of the building from the premier's two other appointees picked from the ruling party's elected members, the minister of education and a parliamentary assistant (or two). Symbolically to keep the bureaucracy *Pure,* these command posts are further separated by several potted plants and pieces of furniture. By and large, personnel in and around those offices do not talk regularly with each other, nor presumably do they often *Do Lunch* together, nor do they usually swap concerns around the reception area's coffee pot. At meetings with local administrators, for some issues the deputy might "stare at his shoes"—he is interpreted to thus be distancing himself; meanwhile the government's position may be presented by the minister and by articulate, quick, policy advisors. These policy advisors can be thirty-year-olds, or younger in many cases, who are patronage appointees. About her work, one says, "Politics is almost everything we do and everywhere we go."

When flashpoints arise, the spatial separation of minister and deputy offices continues, but the story is that these elite figures do interact. Thus they reach—out to the community at large, up to the cabinet, and down to educators and the media for odds and ends of ideas about who should get which stake. Generally thereafter, the deputy and the minister speak with one voice, announcing, for instance, that the province supports (1) **French-language education** for francophones in two localities that are *Up In Arms* against that program, (2) the **entrepreneurial studies** curriculum that business interests had lobbied for as a *Cure* for the school-workplace transition, and (3) a **national indicators** project that would measure learning outcomes.

This last issue of measurement brings out multiple storylines. From educator interviewees, one is that *Schools Cannot Control The Factors That Affect Student Achievement.* "Measuring results is like someone always *Looking Over Your Shoulder,*" a teacher lobbyist adds, "and unless tests are used in a positive way, results can put kids *Down The Dumpster.*" Two minutes into an interview, a politician revives the storyline that *Teachers' Observations Are Not Enough, Parents Should Know Precisely What Their Children Are Learning.*

Anyway, if decisions involve redistributions that ruffle political feathers, the deputy makes the announcement and hence, in an interviewee's metaphor, *Catches The Heat. The Minister Never Says No.* An effective minister of education is seen as pushing her

or his own platform on the press, on the civil service, on the sometimes solid fronts among advocacy groups. An interviewee calculated that the Department of Education in the eighties had 183
such potential blockers, more constituencies than the Departments of Health or Justice; the larger umbrella groups tend to be
the ones to get audiences with the minister. Also envisaged as necessary for an education minister are toughness, an ability to waffle
diplomatically at times, and a knack of staying out of headlines.
Valued too are *Antennae* for when to enlist expert or citizen opinions as a way of bringing pressure on locals, and a timeliness in
making strategic announcements.

"The job requires one of the best politicians in government,"
a local politician comments, saying that the quality of the minister
is probably *The Single Most Important Factor* determining the
success of the department. This "most important" storyline is told
at other levels too—for instance, that the quality of the board's
chief executive officer—or of the principal, the mathematics head,
or whoever—determines the success and happiness of the system,
the school, the mathematics staff, or whatever. This assertion is
ridiculed, though, by another observer who denies "powers of
clairvoyance to any minister. . . . He has little chance to fashion or
reverse the forces that control him." Other interviewees add that
new ministers either are fearful of the bureaucracy or are unable
to bring the bureaucrats into their confidence. As a result, ministers sometimes have important policies written by a politician as
policy advisor within the minister's office.

For control and precision, in others' glimpses of ministerial
affairs, moral support has to be identified and networked through
bureaucracies, interest groups, the cabinet's social-policy field
committee and management board, a planning and priorities unit,
ultimately the cabinet itself, where over a dozen other ministers vie
for air time, and the Parliament. Ministers can find that premiers
are hurdles, too, for they may *Tone Down* implementations that
vitiate reelection or commitments in other arenas. Small wonder
then that a recent premier retained the support of combative educators by scuttling the plan of his education minister, a family phy-
sician, for a college of teachers. Like a college of physicians, this
proposed agency was to be an monitoring body, closely evaluating
and disciplining members. On this count, that premier—"*Czar-
Like* with a benign presence"—was revered as the teachers' friend.

A controlled policy that interviewees are emotive about is **public funding for denominational education**. In contrast to other party leaders in a provincial election decades ago, a premier said his government would not support such financing for denominational schools. The nondenominational school system, tolerant of diverse points of view, was said to facilitate an increasingly heterogeneous society. Financing for the *Indoctrination* of denominational education allegedly would lead to a *Splintering Of Society*. Subsequently, however, that premier untimorously reversed himself, announcing, after "little or no consultation, except maybe with his wife," what public educators metaphorically call the denominationalists' "*Golden Egg.*"

"Buying Their Way Out"

Like counterparts elsewhere in the country, this premier had been celebrated for making issues nonthreatening by turning them into *Jellyrolls Of Blandness*. Still, that manner did not calm his cabinet or supporters of nondenominational schooling. Unlike the premier, they did not immediately see the situation as *The Correction Of A Long-Standing Inequity,* and they needed time *To Play Catch-Up*. An ordinary storyline is that this redistributive announcement belonged to the premier, de-czared and no longer the benign friend of all teachers. Talk commonly used with that funding announcement is that it *Cost* the premier's party the next election.

Now, some years afterward, three strikingly distinct storylines circulate about this policy's by-products:

1. Increasingly, the denominational high schools are resembling other publicly funded high schools, principals having lost their power to dominate.

2. At long last, denominational education is being strengthened by much stronger links among school, family, and church; moreso than nondenominational communities of interest, they make joint appeals to task forces and royal commissions, for instance.

3. The overall community continues to be fragmented, while the quality of nondenominational education falters; less money is coming into it.

Story 1, about the dwindling of distinctiveness and principals' power in denominational schools, clashes with Story 2, about values in school, family, and church now being congruent. Story 3's *Fragmentation* metaphor implies a narrative: what was once whole, now is shattered; parts that were once bound together, now tend toward mutual indifference. The metaphor implies a remedy: restore funding levels for nondenominational education.

Before his party's defeat, an education minister appointed a planning and implementation committee to monitor local plans for transferring students, staff, and facilities from nondenominational to denominational systems. Politicians initially had been imprecise and now was a time for that committee to proceed inductively, learning what was feasible and preferable on a community-by-community basis. Although the policy was the education minister's so-called *Main Tent,* not until another party took over the next government a year later did politicians assert control of the policy's implementation.

That new government's minister is remembered for having the bill's legislation to drive him and for *Breathing Energy* into the process. He *Sold* the policy and directly settled disputes that threatened to *Tear Communities Apart.* To diffuse rancor in the sociopolitical milieu, a legislative committee traveled the province for months, hearing public briefs. Several of the Department of Education's top administrators were in attendance, and pressures were incredible to integrate suggestions into the draft legislation from all sides.

Oft-told too was this story: the premier's decision to fund denominational education revealed how control had been in the hands of a few who used it to their benefit—to win votes from denominational supporters. That conspiracy story works like others of its ilk: control should be wrested from *The Few,* the offending policy should be terminated, the wish of *The Many* should flourish.

By referring this issue to the courts, the new minister forced opponents to wait out the judges' constitutional interpretation. That judgment was called the policy's *Acid Test.* Even after the courts' go-ahead, *Shoot-Outs* occurred, none more visible, more emotionally resisted, or more rancorous than that over transfers of schoolhouses. This was only one of the problems created by the new policy, but much ink was split about it in the press. For three interviewees, *The Great Land Grab* was symbolized by doings in Third City (pseud.) Since the denominational board there was growing faster, the crux was whether partially empty schools should be retained by Third City's nondenominational public board. Its stake was that public ratepayers had paid, or partially paid, for those buildings; why should they now lose them? Insisting, however, that they had greater needs for classroom space, Third City's denominationalists demanded the public board's "best" facility. In defiance and to attract reinforcements from alumni and neighborhoods, nondenominational students and staff rallied under the emotional storyline of *Save Our Schools*.

Cabinet members and their arbitrators then picked through ideas flowing to them from the Department of Education and local interviewees, ultimately establishing a precise resolution for the dispute. Eventually, another public nondenominational installation, not the "best" facility originally demanded, was transferred to the denominational system. Dramatic and energetic bargaining prompted the public board to comply. So did vast infusions of provincial funds to somewhat compensate that public board for its lost schoolhouse. Denominational as well as nondenominational interviewees agree the infusions were vast.

Now that we have reviewed the five modes of being for controlled implementation, selected consequences for provincial and local school administrators will be outlined. The province's politicians expect these administrators to see to it that these well-understood policies are brought off.

Language on the Department's Controlling Officials

What the average Maple resident knows as provincial policymaking, most attach to people in downtown offices of Capital City. These offices' challenges vary with elected governments. Conservative politicians, for instance, are said to work with bureaucrats *Hand-In-Hand* to develop and implement policies. Liberal politicians are said to set forth the general direction and expect bureaucrats to refine it. New Democrat politicians are said to expect bureaucrats to bargain with them over the whats and hows of new policy. These different styles of affiliation give oblique evidence of politicians' cognitive dispositions and ideals.

The nature of the bureaucrats' challenge is affected by the level of anguish within the Department of Education itself. When undergoing one of their deputies' periodic reorganizations for new missions and compatible personal ties, managers in the hierarchy resort to metaphors—such as "When *One Shoe In The Department*

Drops, we wait for other shoes to fall . . . for other *Stars To Rise";* *"After The Dust Settles,* the department just moves back to the structure it had before"; and "If you like today's restructuring, enjoy, for tomorrow's will be worse." Local officials agree that success would result more often if the middle stratum of Maple's Department of Education wouldn't have to play this *Game Of Musical Chairs* whereby the province's middle managers are reassigned to responsibilities they never anticipated. As provincial staff learn about their new jobs, locals see the department's compartmentalized and segmented headquarters as *Chaos* and *A Labyrinth* with twisting *Corridors Of Power* where visitors from the boards never see a familiar face. Whenever the department appears as *A Rudderless Ship,* blame is personalized and affixed to the government's paramount officials. A deputy might explain his new alignment as helping to develop generalists, as trying to build an organization characterized by flexibility, or as obliterating *The Corporate Memory* so that innovative things can be done. Those defenses earn catcalls from several interviewees in the lower ranks.

If the verdict of various local administrators is accepted, "I'm from the Department of Education and I'm here to help you" has to be one of the great laugh lines of education of Maple Province. Yet local administrators generally evince sympathy for the middle stratum of the department who venture out from the sometimes dispirited provincial headquarters to schools and classrooms. True, local administrators have been heard to say, "Why do we always have to hear from these guys?" Locals say that when provincial officials show up, meaning to edify with transparencies for overhead projectors, these transparencies are invariably welltyped but hard to read from the rear of conference rooms. Provincial officials bring handout documents that, the story goes, are not distributed until after those officials have read aloud to locals all the words on those transparencies. "I ask you," a local administrator says, "is that good pedagogy?"

Nonetheless, local staffs recognize that the world of the department's middle stratum typically is a sphere of circumspect middleness, a sphere where dozens of newspaper clippings about education are read over coffee rather than a world of splashy decisions about which headlines shout. Although their personality and subtlety in the use of authority does give a few department officials *An Aura,* many within that middle stratum are no longer held in awe. This is one of the firmer changes in a seemingly unchangeable Department of Education from a decade or more ago. The other is that the middle stratum is being drastically *Whittled Away,* its numbers decimated. Department officials who stay "do *Piecework* to support a politically determined perspective," in a factory metaphor that one interviewee enjoys. A local official opines, "They act in a bureaucracy that is not the product of anybody's plan or intention."

"Not so," a colleague differs, insistently:

> Members of the department look for the viable. . . . They represent [disparate] *Wavelengths* in the department. . . . They go through a *Gestation Period.* . . . Nobody has any illusions. . . . It's not *Inertia.* . . . So what if they digress from the task now and then? That's part of the process. . . . By and by, they work out something reasonable. It's hard when problems aren't neatly divided by department.

A familiar storyline is that middle-management officials of the department are people of value. They have classroom experience and master's degrees; many have passed provincial exams on the Education Act and on the supervisory officerships. Soundness usually is their long suit, while colorfulness and experience in a particular curricular area are not usually at a premium. They have self-images of trying hard, responding to notes that ask them "to read and make comments," doing their best, and being willing to subordinate their own interests for the good of the collective. They are said to respect firm standards that are fair. "We bring *Administrative Coherence* to programs," a gray-haired man explains.

An alternative symbol is that the Department of Education is a *Hive* that attracts swarms of bees trying to leverage their beliefs. Other storylines implicate a few of these department operators as *Natural Disasters*—"He went to a music festival out of province when he should've been here working" is a synecdochic example. "We're a slow-moving *Supertanker* that takes a long time to turn around," a middle manager at the department says. That speaker is playing up his organization's own myth, for he believes in gradualism and in the *Safety Valve* of deliberative processes. Another department insider self-flagellatingly indulges in perhaps the cruelest of all storylines:

> Teachers have a picture of us having nothing better to do but close one eye every morning while gazing out a window, and spending afternoons with the rested eye peering again through

the windows. In the morning, they think we don't open our curtains lest we have nothing to do in the afternoon.

A counter-story is that, once told at 10 a.m. to do something by the deputy, bureaucrats will ask, "Is noon soon enough?"

The institutional complexity and diversity of the Department of Education is recognized as a cause for some of the problems in *The Field* inhabited by local boards and neighborhood schools. Board authorities say that often the cause of some of their problems is that segments within the provincial bureaucracy are poorly linked. They tell stories about how they have had to introduce department officials to each other, even though their provincial offices are only a few floors apart in Capital City and even though their portfolios impinge on each other. They expect the Department of Education to be a totally *Rational* organization without competing bureaus. So outsiders who receive documents written by department bureaucrats on one floor express bewilderment over receiving telephone calls from a second group of department officials on another floor. This synecdoche for poor internal communication and poor boundary-spanning has the second department group asking outsiders, "Can you send us a copy of that department document, please?"

However, provincial officials resonate to the story that a productive policy can be generated and *Shepherded* through the department's midsystem, going for approval up and down that hierarchy. Those who do not exhaust their reform fervor in achieving consensus among colleagues within their own offices can have plenty to occupy them in persuading other offices. French or English counterparts, for instance, might or might not waiver under attack from perceiving altogether different consequences and principles at play. "People have a tendency," an insider summarizes, "not to fit things together beyond their language, bureau, or floor."

The paramount officials, the authorities who in more flush times would go on weekend retreats to think about strategy, occasionally are critical of the middle-echelon program officers they have inherited. The paramounts' synecdoche is that energetic educators who comprise the midstratum can be *Hyper*, too easily influenced by well-prepared briefs of interest associations. They want to *Hit The Ground Running*, even before solutions have been thought through. In this construction, the department's middle managers should have policy directions that are clear-cut. Developing this clarity takes time, not just *One-On-Ones* with lobbyists, not just empathy with local situations that department managers presumably have left behind for *The Province's Wider Purview.* Middle-level bureaucrats are, unfortunately, *Up To Their Asses In Alligators,* not always able to see the high ground, says one situated on that high ground, thinking back to when he too was alligator fodder. Top officials have a cliché that a portion of their middle-level managers come into the department intent on *Shaking It Up*—but never adjusted to the government's work flow. Another story among higher-ups is that there is a vacuum of good ideas among the middle-levels.

Away from their desks and their curtained offices, staff in the middle stratum sardonically return the compliment, occasionally shaking their heads about the two dozen officials above them. Interviewees talk most freely about those who have *Moved On* to jobs outside the Department of Education. They say how they bet each other when such-and-such new assistant deputy minister would leave, because he or she does not understand *How The System Works.* In interviews, the province's middle managers usually do not directly impugn the intelligence or ultimate morality of their peak echelon. Still, several in the middle do see a portion of their past superordinates metaphorically as *Nervous Workhorses* who transferred their insecurities down the line, as *Passive-Aggressives Or Phobics* who seldom questioned ideas of the minister or deputy, and as *Burnouts* who wasted their talents and stayed ten or more years past their primes. Sentiments of local officials, less intimately informed than those of inside the bureaucracy, seem no kinder to the *Whipping Boys And Girls* atop the department. For instance, a trustee mixes her metaphors, saying, "When you ask a hard question, *The Honchos Go Bananas.*"

Saddened but not surprised by these dour characterizations of them as almost foreigners in education land, the department's uppermost officials have their own storylines as response. Local boards overestimate options open to the Department of Education, a provincial leader says:

> There's a provinceful of auditors. They ask, "How are you making sure the money goes for the best purposes?" We have to go to the treasurer for money, and they say, "You've got to be kidding." The minister has to collaborate with members of

> caucus . . . and [with] recent policy statements from other min-
> istries. He has to abide by this or that reg, unless he wants to
> spend rare political capital. . . . From afar, I suppose it looks like
> we have scads of possibilities. Boards want to know, "How on
> earth did you ever dream that one up?" . . . They don't know the
> givens. *The Fine Line* we tread.

Unflattering aspersions come with the job, another says, thinking
back to her own ideas and past contributions to education. For
instance, well before critics "started lambasting us and demanding
site-based management, we were focusing on the principal as a
vessel for major initiatives. . . . Fourteen legal acts, regulations,
and directives are directly applicable to the principal." Another
high official says,

> We get criticized because voters are upset with all govern-
> ments. . . . Voters say we're *Being Political* when we do some-
> thing they think misses the real problems in schools. Then we
> have to turn around and criticize school people for missing *The
> Big Picture*.

Other hints arise of suspected causes for the province's top
administrators' loss of standing among followers. Thus, a provincial authority says, "Teachers like to *Shoot The Messenger*" while
another says, "Some people never learn how to deal with *Authority*." A third says:

> I feel like I'm in a western with frontier justice, where the posse
> points to me and says, "Give the man a 'fair' trial and then hang
> him." . . . The thing is, huh, if you make a policy, half the posse
> will hate you for it. Half won't. But *If You Don't Make A Policy
> At All*, rest assured, *Everybody Will Hate You*.

Once provincial politicians and top administrators authorize
the substance of controlling policies, different branches within the
Department of Education put forward their procedural options.
Notions about implementation may be floated past liaison committees, past a few well-regarded thinkers and doers in education,
and past interesting people whom authorities encounter at professional functions. Aberrant or renegade advice is scrapped. Before
final endorsement by the department's management committee,
directives are rewritten and copiously amended. Wordings that
are *Right On* are agonized over again and again and again.

If a policy idea is significant enough that the cabinet is involved, the province's middle-top administrators *Put A Good Word* into ears of friends within other ministries that might be affected. Ultimately, after submissions are cleared at the cabinet, the department sets implementations into motion if new legislation is not required. Alternatively, if the Education Act is to be revised, after the attorney general's legislative branch has approved a draft of a bill, legislators engage in raucous exchanges during committee meetings and second readings in the House. Later these legislators and their staffs might meet peaceably to devise accommodations. A wrinkle in recent years is that, without direct ties to the department, these elected politicians are seeing themselves as able on their own to vote up particular policies. Past politicians may have decided pedagogical policy for Maple's schools, while denying that they were actually doing so. These days, however, legislators are thought to be more freewheeling with their suggestions. They do not hide their handiwork as much, a somewhat gray-haired woman says.

All in all, functionaries at the Department of Education tend to see themselves more as professional educators who *Infiltrate* local networks than as *Hired Guns* appraising local performances. Yet, at the bidding of their seniors, the department's middle managers do diagnose and appraise, *Leaving Behind A Lot Of Paper* that local boards are expected to complete. A simple request for the percentage of female students in science classes can take, across an urban board, "as much as 100 hours of staff time to put together." The department's middle managers examine local schedules and operations, go over computer tapes of boards' data, and probe for depth and fidelity in implementation. Provincial officials lament that local officials see their surveillance less constructively: certain boards' administrators perplexingly regard these visitations as *Snapping At Our Heels*.

For controlled implementations, *Moments Of Truth* arrive for the provinces' managers. Once they know that deviations from posted policies are going on in boards, they are said to enact one or more of three scenes:

1. They say they *Defend The Fort*, giving the impression that the government knows full well about problems but is undertaking *Knife-To-The-Throat* actions.

2. They *"Turn a Blind Eye* . . . just this once." Stereotypi-
cally, this turning occurs because more salient issues come
onto the politicians' horizons, because *Circumstances Are
Dicey,* because politicians do not want further involve-
ments, or because politicians want to protect allies.

3. They say *They Go Back To The Drafting Board,* to adjust
the control, precision, agenda, or whatever.

Incidentally, any number of *Agendas* for systemic reform
besides the corporate and political party species exist in interviewees' lexicons. One local politician, for instance, speaks uneas-
ily of a voter with a libertarian agenda, where priority would be
given to the nonviolation of the child's freedom and protection of
that child's individual integrity.

More specifically, once Department of Education officials dis-
patch precise memoranda to board authorities, reportedly a first
impulse of those local authorities is to cooperate. Regular conflict
over control with the provincial department is not the preference
of local administrators—that would reduce their effectiveness in
other matters. *"You Can Only Carry So Much Water,"* one board
official says by way of cause and effect. Consequently, local
administrators are choosy about which controlled policies of the
province they try to defy, delay, or negotiate.

Among boards of various sizes in this study, a lack of material
resources, or the wrong combination thereof, is the justificatory
storyline of choice for inaction on controlled implementations.
That is, the cause-and-effect relationship of local top administrators is that policy success stems from the right combination of
money, personnel, and time to develop skills—and not on how
money is spent or how expertise is networked, not on how responsibilities are assigned or how confusion over roles is avoided, not
on schedules or motivations for locals to overcome obstacles or
misinformation, and not on how policies may stem from invalid
theories of cause and effect. Thus, according to more than half the
interviewees, in the face of add-ons without curtailments of other
programs, instead of taking on new duties for existing personnel,
board officials try to get "More, more, more—more staffing time,
materials, local *Input."* They want more of everything except
paperwork— "that we're already overwhelmed by." Reflecting
the way systems theory has filtered into administrative thinking,

two interviewees causally and tersely explain that schools are dependent on the external environment for their resources.

Should implementors or a constituency reject a controlled implementation, local administrators may use that provincial policy as a shield, saying, "I'd like to help, but this provincial policy won't let me," and "We'll implement, but we don't have to be *Cheerleaders.*" And on selected occasions, local officials are seen as knowingly deviating from provincial controls, finding a gap between a policy's precise and mechanical meaning and the purpose for which that policy was enacted. When these local administrators believe their action would facilitate the ultimate goal of such a policy, whether that action formally does or not, local administrators "*Micro-Manage* the policy toward the outcomes we think best.*"

CONCLUSION

Is the Talk Symbolic of Control's Style?

James Joyce, were he writing today about Maple's policy world in the manner of his *Portrait of an Artist As Young Man*, might try to reflect controlled implementations. That is, he might use words to mirror controlled implementation's qualities of high precision and close monitoring, much as he used words in successive chapters of *Portrait of an Artist* to mirror his young subject's evolving maturity of observation. With that rhetorical perspective, can we conclude that the talk by politicians and administrators about controlled implementation is itself highly precise and closely monitored? Perhaps inadvertently, are implementors Joycean?

Not at all. Storylines and synecdoches lack the prioritizations, careful formalities, rigorous and rank-ordered definitions, and tidy attentions to timetables and regulations associated with control. Interviewees do give cause-effect linkages, sometimes bespeaking a consciousness of incentives, but without the strict enumeration of variables (independent, dependent, and intervening), explaining of premises, and closeness of measurement that make for high precision. Moreover, interviewees' assertions seem to undercut as much as support the top-down authority and enforcement associated with control.

We would be remiss, however, were we to dismiss the politicians' and administrators' talk as unhelpful in understanding the nature of control. Their talk might not bring whole new perspectives into the world, but it does help communicate the speakers' intents and experiences. These people use symbols, cause-effect links, and counts of stakes to buttress their positions. That is not nothing.

Local boards are concourses where provincial policies arrive with alternative types of monitoring and precision. These alternative types bring out talk that shapes and constrains implementations. Chapter 8 explores these other concourses.

NOTES

Interviews were conducted from 1988 to mid 1993. Various students of mine have contributed to my understandings, and for editorial reactions I am obliged to several noninterviewees: Gail Anderson, Peter Baker, Bill Bridgeland, Ted Duane, Joanne Janke, Ken Leithwood, Stephen Mould, Jerry Paquette, Rouleen Wignall, Barry Wadman, and Don Werner. I am further indebted to Leo Santos for formatting the charts. Of course, to repeat an academic storyline, *I Am Solely Responsible For All Errors Herein.*

1. For insights on the linguistics of policy, I draw upon, passim, the excellent work of Deborah A. Stone (1988). The emphasis on talk extends the work on metaphors in organizations (e.g., Morgan 1993; Kushnir 1993) and education (Taylor 1984) into the field of policy. See also Hood and Jackson (1991).

2. This link is described, for the United States, by Frank Thompson (1987). A number of other sharp, well-elaborated models trace the doing of educational policies across jurisdictions (e.g., Elmore and McLaughlin 1981; Manzer 1988; Mawhinney 1993, Odden and Marsh 1989; Leithwood, Cousins, and Trider 1990; Wilson and Rees 1990; Cantlon, Rushcamp, and Freeman 1991; Bartunek 1991; Cibulka 1991; Paquette 1991), but on the basis of what interviewees talk about, I am drawn to Thompson's, itself a reworking of a matrix by Berman (1980). Thompson's figure 1 and table 1, which have not entered the educational literature, spring from a number of other commonly accepted concepts in the literature on public administration. While frameworks homegrown in Canada could contribute globally to understandings of school organization and policy, it can be argued that Thompson's general categories are worth playing with, not being limited in their usefulness to one (U.S.) milieu.

It is important to note that I did not embark on this study with Thompson's scholarship in mind. It was not until three years into this research, while wrestling unsuccessfully and unhappily with my data, in a mild moment of Eureka, that I came upon Thompson. I cheered to his inclusion of institutions that reflected implements' values. That he recognized individual politicians as having personal incentives grabbed me as well, as did his attention to the impact of interest groups. His schema did not array everything that my interviewees and I wanted to lay out, but it was a start, and the filling of the boxes in Thompson's table (table 7–1) came easily.

Unlike this account, Thompson does not look at education or a jurisdiction as an organized whole, inventory symbols associated with policies and policy processes, try to capture the language about cause-effect relationships that undergird policy and process, or consider how policy people count the political stakes of assorted options. Finally Thompson does not map the processes involving provincial and local top administrators (as they deal with symbols, causes, and stakes), but I do—and this is part of the novelty in this report.

Since Thompson's categories are not reader-friendly, I try to stay away from his jargon. Thus "conditions" (with a connection, in some minds, to successful implementation) is converted to the less evaluative and more descriptive term, *dynamics*. "Technology" hereafter becomes *method*, "overhead actors" becomes *elected politicians and their political appointees*, and "oversight" (with its intimation, in lay terms, of disregarding) becomes *monitoring*.

3. Names of potential interviewees came to light from lists that twenty-two key informants were asked to prepare of "influentials in this province's policy process for education." The informants' positions and understandings were presumed to give them ideas of who else was involved. Perhaps because of my emphasis on provincial policies and processes, lists yielded more citizens from Capital City than from other parts of the province, and that centrism is a limitation. When certain persons on those lists retired before I had a chance to interview them, I sounded out successors to whom I had entrée, when I thought those successors were street-smart.

4. The time span for policies covered here goes from the late 1960s to October 1993. Having previously worked as inspectors or consultants for the Department of Education (though sometimes selected and paid by the larger boards), many local CEOs at the start of this period tended to manage with the aims of the provincial government—CEOs' "beliefs were extensions of the department," a board chairman told me. For career growth, aspirants to local administrative positions were urged to arrange work stints within the department.

In those provincial corridors, deputy ministers watched the politicians and hence kept them within bounds. Yet by the 1990s, when nobody was watching (circumscribing and circumventing) provincial legislators and many local CEOs had achieved promotion through the ranks of school boards, naturally their loyalties tended toward the trustees who

Table 7-1
Thompson's Types of Implementation and Some Conditions Heightening Their Appeal

Type	Technology	Environmental Stability	Implementing Agency	Sociopolitical Milieu	Overhead Actors
Controlled	Certain: Not bottom-heavy	Moderately high	Absence of tempered commitment in the form of either hostility or zealotry	Substantial opposition to cost-effective implementation from groups in the task environment; in sum, a debilitating sociopolitical milieu	The capacity and incentive to formulate coherent policy is moderately high; efficacy in terms of error correction is very high
Prophylactic or Preventive	Very certain: Not bottom-heavy	Very high	A moderate level of commitment; strong	A milieu that is not strongly debilitating	The capacity and incentive to formulate coherent policy is extremely high; efficacy with respect to error correction is low
Up-for-Grabs	Uncertain: Often bottom-heavy	Low	A moderately high level of rather tempered commitment	No more than moderate opposition to cost-effective implementation from groups in the task environment	The capacity and incentive to formulate coherent policy is low, but the propensity to engage in correction is moderately high

Type	Technology	Environmental Stability	Implementing Agency	Sociopolitical Milieu	Overhead Actors
Buffered	Uncertain: Often bottom-heavy	Low	Widespread consensus within the implementing agency; very high level of tempered commitment	Limited, if any, opposition to cost-effective implementation from groups in the task environment	The capacity and incentive to formulate coherent policy and engage in error correction are low

had hired them. "The last time I looked," one attested, "the minister didn't sign my cheque." Although a few of today's younger CEOs posit that they are wired into the minister's office to get things done or "when I want something," many local executives of schools playfully see interaction with department authorities as foolish. An older top administrator is droll about this:

> Years ago, in my first week as principal, I called my superintendent and when I got off the phone, I had six new things to do. Allright? I swore then that I would never call a higher-up again unless I absolutely had to, and never did. I go ahead and make the decisions. That's how I deal with the department too.

This statement, however, is more pungent than accurate. When probed, even this local administrator admits substantial traffic with what he refers to as *Tammany Hall*. This blatantly U.S. metaphor takes me aback: the speaker is an ardent Canadian nationalist.

REFERENCES

Bartunek, F. (1991). A political response perspective on inter-governmental relations in education. Unpublished doctoral dissertation, University of British Columbia.

Berman, P. (1980). Thinking about programmed and adaptive implementation: Matching strategies to situations. In H. M. Ingram & D. E. Mann (Eds.), Why policies succeed or fail. Beverly Hills: Sage.

Cantlon, D., Rushcamp, S., & Freeman, D. (1991). The interplay between state and system guidelines for curriculum reform in elementary schools. In S. H. Fuhrman & B. Malen (Eds.), The politics of curriculum and testing. London: Falmer Press.

Cibulka, J. G. (1991). Educational accountability reforms: Performance information and political power. In S. H. Fuhrman & B. Malen (Eds.), The politics of curriculum and testing (pp. 181–201). London: Falmer.

Elmore, R., & McLaughlin, M. (1981). Strategic choice in federal policy: The compliance-assistance tradeoff. In A. Lieberman & M. McLaughlin (Eds.), Policymaking in education. Chicago: University of Chicago Press.

Hood, C., & Jackson, M. W. (1991). Administrative argument. Brookfield, Vermont: Dartmouth.

Kushnir, W. V. (1993). Frames of reference in planned consensual action: A case study of a committtee planning an innovation in a complex organization. Unpublished doctoral dissertation, OISE.

Leithwood, K., Cousins, J. B., & Trider, D. M. (1990). The process and substance of curriculum reform in Canada. In Y. L. Jack Lam (Ed.), Canadian public education system: Issues and prospects (pp. 303–37). Calgary: Detselig.

Manzer, R. (1988). The political theory and practice of Canadian school trustee representation, Canadian Public Administration, 31(1), 433–46.

Mawhinney, H. (1993). An interpretive framework for understanding the politics of policy change. Unpublished Ph.D. dissertation, University of Ottawa.

Morgan, G. (1993). Imaginization: The art of creative management. Beverly Hills, Sage.

Odden, A., & Marsh, D. (1989). State education reform implementation: A framework for analysis. In J. Hannaway & R. Crowson (Eds.), The politics of reforming school administration (pp. 41–59). New York: Falmer Press.

Paquette, J. (1991). A new policy paradigm for Ontario education?, Interchange, 22(4), 1-23.

Stone, D. (1987). Policy paradox and political reason. Glenview, Illinois: Scott Foresman.

Taylor, W. (Ed.) (1984). Metaphors of education. London: Heineman Institute for Education, University of London.

Thompson, F. J. (1987). Policy implementation and overhead control. In G. Edwards (Ed.), Public policy implementation. London: JAI Press.

Vickers, G. (1965). The art of judgment: A study of policy making. London: Chapman & Hall.

Wilson, R. J., & Rees, R. (1990). The ecology of assessment: Evaluation in educational settings. Canadian Journal of Education, 15, 215–28.

CHAPTER 8

Plucking Billiard Balls Out of Thin Air or How a Few Politicians and Managers of Education Hustle Policy: Part II

Richard G. Townsend

The Canadian media have picked up a metaphor from those in the United States who propose that educational government needs reinvention. The metaphor is that governments should *Steer, Not Row*. Steering, not rowing, is what preventive implementation is about. Involving provincial policies, it is called "preventive" because its central tendency is to prevent problems from creeping into local practice.

It is not as new as the media suggest. From the sixties on, assumptions have been working loose about the role of the province in regulating public education. A local administrator explains that, with enlarged opportunities, he has not had to *"Live or Die by provincial rule-books as much as my predecessors."* Other local administrators attribute the provincial freeing-up of selected routines to the growing competence of local administrators, such as themselves.

This chapter gives the flavor of politicians' and top administrators' language about those looser policies and routines. But first you might want to glance again at figure 7–2 and table 7–1 in chapter 7. Those graphics can serve as a general reminder of how three other types of getting-on depart from the provincial centralizations for controlled implementation discussed in chapter 7.

184   RICHARD G. TOWNSEND

GREAT PRECISION, LIMITED MONITORING

There is a "yes . . . , but . . ." tone to discussions about preventive implementation. It seems as if, *yes*, politicians are willing to delegate monitoring or enforcement to local boards, *but* these provincial officials want precise draftsmanship as a guide for warding off mistakes at local and neighborhood levels. Controlled implementation would operate if the province decreed that boards annually *shall* schedule nine professional development days, and if the exact types of professional development were specified in narrow detail. Yet "the policy memorandum isn't written that way." The document is written with leeway, so boards *may* schedule up to nine professional development days (assuming money is available). An economically pinched board can negotiate fewer days, but boards are barred from negotiating more than nine days. A provincial politician says that ten days would be a mistake—as it is, having so many nonschool days is *A Thorn* in the side of parents. Preventive implementation is shorthand for such blends of provincial precision with limited enforcement.

This kind of implementation is also known, more provocatively, with a hint of sexual implementations, as "prophylactic" (Thompson 1987). The label *prophylactic* is especially suitable when the province says that boards may allow—again not *shall* allow—the sale of condoms in schools' washrooms. (One observer sees this as an example of condom sense and then joins me in a groan at his witticism.) However named, interviewees say this approach is not as plentiful in Maple as controlled implementation is.

Three dynamics make preventive implementation attractive:

1. The approach has only to rely on moderate, not strong, commitment within implementing agencies. Local educators and communities are said to have commitment that is indifferent, for instance, to the provincial policy that students' **lunches should be supervised** in suitable quarters. The province is said to be more interested than some localities in this policy: an official from Capital City portrays the hiring of lunchroom supervisors as strongly serving student, staff, and community safety.

2. As a sociopolitical milieu tends toward support, the open

opposition of pressure groups is slight. Either the public good is served by the policy, or organized groups offset each other by giving conflicting advice. To date, about the only lay criticism of the lunchroom supervision policy has come from those who oppose the extra expense of hiring supervisors and from a few observers who think that, by not being lunchroom supervisors, teachers miss a good chance to know their students. The relative acceptance of a supervision policy enables provincial politicians to do, and continue doing, what they think best in this regard.

3. Politicians and top administrators are adroit at fostering a policy that will not collapse when implemented. A provincial policy memo can be authoritative enough, for instance, to prompt teachers' unions to press boards to set aside funds for hiring lunchtime supervisors. Of course, even if teachers' contracts free them from this *Contact Time* between themselves and students, if reliable supervisors are not available, implementation can falter, "but that's the principals' and secretaries' problem, not the province's."

Language of Preventive Implementations

The great-precision, little-monitoring policy most mentioned occurs every March through the **budget estimates** for education, introduced in the provincial parliament by the minister. A few yards away, sitting in an antechamber to the House, the deputy minister and his associates usually wait, ready to advise when necessary. The adversarial ritual of each budget debate allows opposition legislators to provoke. After they make jabs at discrediting the government's closely defined intentions, the minister typically defends the would-be disbursements. Stories are told in the House about why selected activities should thrive while others should perish.

In the shouts, catcalls, and free-for-all of parliamentary debate, exaggerations are made on both sides of the House—to grab the media's attention, an interviewee suggests. Normally no parliamentarian takes the personal attacks seriously. Theirs is expressive play, yet the occasion does provide chances to explore legislative possibilities. Since the government has the votes for the budget specifics it already has decided on, genuine political monitoring at this point usually is scant.

Preventive implementations are shaped for groups at risk, including those taunted to feel ashamed of what they were born as. Maple Province, for instance, has an **antiracism** policy to reduce any helplessness felt by victims of name-calling, slurs, insults, jokes, graffiti, threats, and physical violence. Each board is to submit a plan for antiracism that allegedly will be modestly monitored by a busy and small unit in the Department of Education. Most of *The Action,* though, is said to be at the local level, where board coordinators hold forums on equity, teachers wear buttons that say "Let's Stop Racism," and signs in schools proclaim "Welcome To Our Multicultural Community." To forestall racial and ethnic prejudice, Maple expects educators to police themselves within particular strictures of the department. Facilitators are to be trained to work in schools during and after racial incidents; discussions at the site are to be convened with offending parties; the victimized are to be encouraged to discount the incident; through plays and videos, other students are to be reminded that harassment and stereotyping are unpalatable. For all the diversity reflected in Maple, one politician emphasizes the good will of the majority: "We need to take the latent support for tolerance and make it manifest." When the minister receives a grievance about students, visitors, or staff causing "an incident," that grievance is referred back to the local board.

For the most part, as a provincial authority underlines, "we're far from *Home Free* on this one." Discipline at the site is to be meted out, even by local administrators who wonder aloud whether their actions are producing intended effects among individuals. What is the nature of this upsurge? An administrator muses:

> I don't know if the board really ought to be into antiracism. . . . Isn't it enough for us to be into the celebration of multiculturalism? We're evolving, believe me, we're evolving . . . but is racism something that can be *Weeded Out* just like that? [he snaps his fingers] . . . You see heterogeneous groupings in class, but you don't see it in the halls or cafeteria. Blacks in one corner, *Dominoes* in another, Indians in a third. What can you do about that? What can you do about views that they don't learn in school? . . . Considering the potential for violence or backlash, how smart is it for government to let Sikhs come to school with

their kirpan [knife and ethnic symbol]? How safe is the school
for other kids?

This speaker's policy prescription is to cut back on antiracism
efforts and let racism continue to dwindle on its own, without any
nudging from government. Later he reveals his storyline: *We All
Harbor Prejudices But Our Children Will Be Less Racist Than We
Are,* he hopes. Subsequently, this speaker comes close to rejecting
the province's policy that schools should use their knowledge and
power to cause individuals to learn about the dangers of prejudice.
The province's time frame for change is unrealistic, he says,
because discriminatory activities are deeply implanted and hard to
counteract. Finally, by valuing multicultural celebrations and
hinting at violence, this speaker offers a variant to the story of
school decline: through multicultural celebrations, things had
been getting better. Now a busybody government is *Legislating
Morality,* making things worse, slowing down assimilation.

A lawyer relates his story about antiracism to Canada's
decade-old Charter of Rights and Freedoms. The next decade, he
says, will have Canadians citing fairly specific court rulings on the
Charter to bolster arguments about individual and group rights.

A minor storyline of the province's antiracism education is
that out of ignorance and recklessness (cause), educators themselves may be racist (effect). Hence, they "had better look into
themselves." So on professional development days, black administrators have been known to lecture white teachers that, synecdochically, "just because you eat granola or tofu and talk tolerance doesn't exempt you from responsibility." Generally the story
of white irresponsibility has gone over badly among whites; "Not
again" is a response when meetings on the subject are called. "It's
not true that teachers are racists who need reforming," one bel-
lows at me. Serious doubt about being lectured at comes in
another cause-and-effect relationship: "Teachers learn better
about tolerance by working with their peers."

A more genial symbol seems to be the idea of *Balance,* particularly when it comes to widening ethnicity in the curriculum. An
administrator claims that math and technology departments are
bringing non-European mathematicians and inventors into their
coverage. To achieve balance, "English and history departments
have made cuts." In another interviewee's construction, antiracism's implementation is said to be working, rather like the Cana-

dian symbol of *Peace, Order, And Good Government.* A pair of activist interviewees say, however, that this policy is not eventful enough. Their cause-effect connection is that racism will be foiled only when politicians take more control and provide far better teaching, materials, and learnings for low-income communities.

The mix of control and light monitoring characteristic of preventive implementation can be an approach taken to help groups traditionally excluded from success. Women are one example. Pitifully, despite all the consciousness raising of the past decade, not one male interviewee introduces this matter of women bringing their experiences, networks, and understandings to governance. Most female interviewees initiate discussions about **gender parity in administrative positions** with a recitation of figures to suggest that the problem is big—"Canadians don't measure things unless they want to change them," explains one woman. The government has *Raised The Ante,* however—by the year 2000, half of all school administrators in Maple Province are to be female, a precise target set by provincial politicians and realizable by reaching into their gender majorities within teaching ranks. The parity target has left many males taking a hard line. A union leader, male, seems to minimize the fact that 50 percent of all positions in the hierarchy may rest with men:

> Is it fair that our generation of men has to be passed over for promotion? Do women have the experience to run our boards? Are we departing from the merit principle when boards announce, even before interviews, that of eleven new vice-principals, eight are going to be women? How successful can men be in organizational leadership once it's known that they're slated to go nowhere [up the hierarchy]? Is it really necessary for women to be a pressure group to overcome discrimination in school promotions?

The implicit storyline here is that the school system is organic. Its whole is deemed more important than the sum of its parts, and deliberate interference in promotions would be artificial and ruinous.

That, however, is hardly the story traced by female interviewees. Although one says she is angry—"Chauvinism makes *My Blood Boil*"—this interviewee calmly says, "They may not mean to, but administrators of one gender send out exclusionary message to teachers of other gender." Reacting in the margins of my draft, two male interviewees signal their general agreement. One inscription: "Since women have always been nurturers, it seems *Only Fair* that they be on the receiving end for a change."

Throughout part of the eighties, Maple was thought to be advancing the Year 2000 target by subsidizing board programs for affirmative action to prevent male domination. Now more women are seen as moving into middle-management posts—"It's *A New Ball Game* out there"—particularly as elementary principals and as secondary vice-principals.[1] Within urban neighborhoods, a growing number work as supervisory officers, and more than 50 percent of all teachers who have earned the supervisory-officer certificate are women. Yet less than 20 percent of women actually hold these positions. More women are enrolling in the department's principals' and supervisory officers' courses. In fact, more women are even running these courses. Should this equity policy succeed, a reason is thought to be the very precision of the government's target, "although boards are being *Dragged Kicking And Screaming*" and "the 50 percent figure is making boards adapt." Even so, by failing to check the numbers and by merely referring to but not enforcing possible penalties, the province's monitoring is regarded as having been too spare, the year 2000 target too elusive. Symbolically, "It's our turn to *Step Up To The Plate*." (It seems that even for women who report no direct experience of participation in it, baseball is the sport that provides the most metaphors for policy implementation.) The Department of Education may be financing research on how to revise practices that contribute to gender inequity, and its measurements of that gap may be creating subtle pressure to do something about it. Nonetheless, for some women, progress is unhappy, the policy is airy-fairy, merely an anemic piece of paper, an approach that's *A Nice Try But No Cigar*. (This cigar metaphor comes from a woman legislator who, in private, is said to smoke cigarillos.)

Other women legislators in Maple are concerned about this policy effect but observe that politicians themselves are tardy in demonstrating equal treatment. Maple's legislature is one of the province's precedent-setting organizations, and more women than ever before are being elected to its halls. Yet the inside story is that the male-dominated caucuses still "defer to ideas that come from other men."

Language about Authorities in Preventive Implementations

For more than a generation now, the department has not sent inspectors out to schools for **teacher evaluations**. Principals thus are responsible for gauging *Dead Wood* or—expressed positively—for helping judge if teachers live up to the Education Act's expectations of *Temperance, Purity, and All Other Virtues.*

To prevent inaccessibility to children's services, politicians talk about seamless days. Community, social welfare, health, education, and other government initiatives are to be treated *Holistically,* existing resources being rechanneled with the school as a hub, as a single entry point for programs. Periodically the metaphor of *Fragmentation* surfaces in this talk too, along with the storyline of *Coordination.* "We want service systems that respond in a coordinated and comprehensive fashion to the interconnected needs of the child," explains an elderly politician. "If a youth is on welfare and not attending school, welfare should cease." Toward that end, governmental statutes require—all very precisely—that **day-care facilities** be developed in new or empty schools.

In the idiom of interviewees, however, provincial monitoring at the critical moment has turned out to be little more than "a nice phrase, old ideas, a flowchart, and five or six pages in point form." Glossy, multicolored guidelines from provincial authorities have left administrators at the local level with the tasks of monitoring needs assessments, data sharing, rent collection, cost control, and the like. When parents observe that many neighbourhoods in greatest need of child-care have neither new nor empty schools that can accommodate the seamless day, board administrators find themselves being *Scapegoated.* They had thought they would be earning local credit for drawing upon other agencies' expertise. Responding, these local administrators criticize provincial officials for (1) insufficient *Debugging* of the seamless-day policy, (2) the minor contributions of staff and money that boards receive from the province's noneducation departments, and (3) the lack of coordination among the province's departments. That local "boards aren't nourished by *Crumbs From On High*" is a metaphor that a provincial politician uses in rebuttal to excuse his cabinet colleagues for not doing more.

When provincial precision is not accompanied by provincial monitoring, interviewees take critical note. In the eighties, many local boards supported an expensive policy by the province to prevent Canada from sliding into technological illiteracy. "There was all that hoopla when Maple developed its own computers. It was *An Impossible Dream,*" an opposition politician recalls. Those special computers were not widely adapted.

In addition, Maple authorites are seen as backing away from recifying problems with **partners in action,** a Department of Education policy that teachers work more closely with school librarians in developing resource-based units. Yet one higher-up reflects that the policy was doomed from its outset: "Partners was an idea that the department floated to see if it would catch on. It didn't, because this sort of action and interaction depends on the chemistry between teachers and librarians. Nobody can legislate that. Partners is another *Beached Whale.* The Department is full of beached whales." Another insider adds, "Partners just wasn't sexy enought" (sex as a metaphor for sustaining interest).

Proponents of multiculturalism say they are pleased that since 1989 Maple's government provides 80 percent of the boards' costs for teaching **heritage languages** as an in-school program (lately renamed "international education"—a politician asks, Is this part of an effort to promote cosmopolitanism?) The provision is thought to have had great political impact. Only a few interviewees are negative on these stakes: "Shouldn't we educate youth to live together harmoniously? I know it sounds simplistic, but how can we when heritage programs keep encouraging them to be distinct?" No air of finality is attached to the province's policy story, however. As one says, *"Lines Are Drawn Differently* over what counts as multicultural." Should heritage teachers be licensed? Should heritage teachers be evaluated by principals? Should heritage classes be an appendix to the program after school, or should the school day be extended by thirty minutes, as partly happens in two boards? Should these foreign languages be a part of the regular curriculum? A politician thinks these concerns may be moot: "I worry that the hysteria about The *Deficit* will mean heritage programs will go."

Inasmuch as costs figure briefly in around twenty other references to provincial policies that precisely but lightly control, that mention of cost is a fair point on which to conclude a discussion of preventive implementations. Indeed, *Costs, Costs, Costs* seem as much a theme in local boards today as *Jobs, Jobs, Jobs* in federal elections. Because Maple's Education Act is precise in allowing trustees to set the amount and timing of their own honorarium, those costs serve as symbols of waste, a trustee tells me. Costs serve, moreover, as symbols of efficiency (a small budget was "well used" to sensitize staff on handling suspected child abuse) and of quality (local funds spent on an "outstanding" program in drama). Costs serve as proxies for public compassion too. Thus, "little goes to **deaf education**" and, representing other spheres of difficulty "**AIDS education** is underfunded, like **French in the core curriculum.**

To launch preventive implementations, the Department of Education has underwritten costs for less-affluent communities. Yet only infrequently do local administrators in those communities credit politicians for expanded opportunities to serve in a new public role. Rather, the conventional scene has local administrators fretting that beyond small initial outlays from the Department of Education for supply-teacher coverage and location rental for in-servicing teachers, internal costs for new provincial projects typically are borne by local boards. "The department is *A Wicked Stepmother* who only grumpily provides for her husband's kid" is a board chairman's metaphor of parent-child relationships where the parent cannot win. "This government tells us they're going to cut between 2 and 5 percent every year. You think they're going to *Cut Off Both Your Arms,* but then [when the budget comes down] they only cut off one. You're supposed to feel grateful?" Owing to overall proportions of costs increasingly being downloaded from province to locality, local resources are *Spread Too Thinly,* as if resources were delicious homemade jams meant to fully cover pieces of toast. As a corrective to all these provincial costs, one local official clears his throat and rallies behind the hoary and populist storyline that *Those Who Are Taxed Should Control Costs.*[2]

THE TRAJECTORY OF
UP-FOR-GRABS IMPLEMENTATIONS

The up-for-grabs style provides objectives vague enough for people *To Drive Trucks Through Without Denting The Sides.* It is a bottom-up strategy where implementors of policy learn what they want in the process of experimenting. Minimizing, or *Soft-Pedaling,* their potential for coercion, politicians and top administrators at the provincial level watch proceedings closely, not quite off-stage—lest they need to step in and correct what is happening. So living with provincial disinterest, boards have shaped their own great precision for continuing (adult) education, higher-order thinking, holistic grading, language across the curriculum, media literacy, process writing, science fairs, and staff development.

Language on Limited Precision and Great Monitoring

Up-for-grabs implementation is especially inviting to authorities when the context outside the school is fluctuating, when the culture, the demography, and the economy are changing, when everything seems like that most transitional of seasons, autumn. Yesterday is summer, tomorrow is winter, and some days autumn thinks it is both. Commitment from implementing agencies need only be moderate, betwixt and between firm and soft. Top administrators at the local level can initiate as long as (1) they address broad provincial aims and (2) organized interests in the sociopolitical milieu do not try to disrupt.

Probably Maple's longest-running and most-discussed case of an up-for-grabs implementation involves allocations for constructing and expanding buildings, a matter different from the control of architectural standards mentioned in chapter 7. Should a board want new, expanded, or refurbished buildings, judgments are required, especially the judgments of provincial politicians. A signal of how control in this arena can be outside the neighborhood is that principals on some days are requested to stay out of discussions regarding the choice of their schools' new sites.

In autumn, boards tell their hard-luck stories. The very act of measuring their overcrowding, their squatty portables, and their capital needs adds some pressure for the province to come to their rescue. Middle managers and top administrators within the Department of Education analyze and align submissions in winter, applying certain formulas for space needs. These authorities' rankings of regional needs go to the cabinet not long afterward, and the question of "Who should get which facility when and how?" leads to stories of desperation and need advanced by locals on good terms with a minister, almost any minister.

Then the cabinet vigorously corrects the list of approvable projects. Chums within government are said to *Scratch Each Other's Back,* presumably along lines of "If you [as education minister] award my riding a new school, then I [as minister for

some other portfolio] will award your riding something else."
Probably this is another exaggerated cause-and-effect postulation,
but it is not as celebrated as the old political maxim about reward-
ing friends and punishing enemies. Anyway, in governmental
announcements come springtime, the cabinet's decisions are introduced as value-free, unemotional, nonsubjective, and nonpoliti-
cal. "But we all know better."

Through all this coalition building and counting of stakes,
many boards end up almost, but not quite, in *The Winners' Circle.*
Some schoolhouses may end up ranking higher than those technically more needy, according to standards of the department's
bureaucratic ranks, within the region. Occasionally, too, a capital
project succeeds that is low on the requesting board's priorities.
Stories are even told of errors where expensive schools are erected
to serve, for only a few years, in dying northern communities. Top
administrators at the local level study provincial statistics, thereafter telling stories of discrimination and inequity. Thus one
region may compute that it has received less money in the past five
years than 25 percent of the province's approved grants for capital
construction. Although they know that successful governments
skew spending patterns to favor ridings that are strategically
important for winning elections, interviewees from boards with
yardfuls of portables use, in mock innocence, the language of puz-
zlement. For example, one said to me, "What more could we have
given them" to demonstrate capital needs? For their part, provincial politicians are said to conceal their partisanship in the neutral,
technical language of space standards.

Language of Top Administrators in Up-For-Grabs
Implementations

Take **detracking** as an example of such political monitoring of
policies with limited precision. Along with ethnic parents' groups,
elementary teachers, the provincial federation of labor, selected
researchers, and a network of educational activists, two governments have supported this projected integration of students of all
ability ranges beginning in grade 9 classes. The policy, egalitarian
in intent, recognizes that disproportionate numbers of young
black, native, immigrant, poor, and second-language students
have been *On A Slow Train To Nowhere,* thanks to their stigma-
tizing placement in low tracks. Early adolescence is too early for

passing judgment on a student, and little opportunity later is available for students to maneuver themselves into the higher reaches of education, salaries, social status, and self-esteem.

Detracking is combined with redesigns of secondary curricula, the aim being to replace *Balkanized* departments and atomistic courses with mentoring programs and new teaching strategies. Allegedly, this reform can improve school climate, reduce absenteeism, better engage students, help lower dropout rates, and therefore boost socioeconomic chances. Inasmuch as minorities have tended to dominate in the lower streams, the storyline of *Vertical Social Mobility And Ethnic Harmony* simultaneously can be played out by a common curriculum, flexible mixed work teams, mental and manual integration, and diversified experiences in community service for all. That is *The Heart* of detracking's cause-and-effect chain. "This would be a *Deep, Not A Shallow, Change,*" provincewide change being one of the headiest of storylines. "If detracking were left to the schools," a small town administrator explains, "it might happen in Capital City, but nowhere else."

Two gripping portraits about that policy have competed for public support. In one, change agents see themselves as striving democratically in a just cause. Instead of developing prescriptive revisions of curriculum documents and programs, provincial politicians and their top administrators have worded the policy to permit much variety, giving large measures of control to local officials over "which bodies will go into which classrooms." Hoping that disagreements could be worked out in private, the Department of Education funded pilot projects, one for almost every board that sought a grant. These projects were intended to overcome uncertainties about learning outcomes. Nonetheless, certain secondary teachers and their department heads initially paid little heed to the first-year assessments of those demonstrations. The government did not pull back from its commitment, however. It wanted a *Big-Bang Effect To Blast Teachers Out Of Their Ruts.* In one of the more strenuous pedagogical changes of the past twenty-five years, about 20 percent of the province's high school teachers—most of the grade 9 teachers—did go with a form of detracking.

Teachers who had a chance to see detracking in operation in other schools chugged along with their own *Creative* coteaching and subject coordination, *creativity* being a term loaded with delicious affect and heard more often among Maple educators than, say, *predictability*. A storyline has denominational schools in some communities in the lead because they never negotiated subject-matter headships into their contracts. So "it's easier for them to create *Diversified Learning Environments* where students move from what they already know to what they need and would like to know." Other secondary teachers ought to do, it is said, what Maple's elementary teachers regularly do—find their own materials and develop their own units.

After *"Dillydallying* and posturing for four years while the province *Phased In* this policy," nondenominational secondary teachers needed to be stirred out of the "insulation that certain of their administrators and trustees have lulled them into. . . . They're an aging group, average age 49." Their union needed to replace recalcitrance and aggressive rhetoric with commitment to overcoming injustice in practices:

> They [teachers] campaigned to elect the government and expected it to be their *Pet*. Well, that didn't happened: "Their" politicians are independent and are standing up to the unions. The unions don't comprehend or don't care that the public, whenever it is polled, wants a more fair system.

Cabinet guidelines of what students should know by the end of grade 9 are represented as more form than substance. That very openness, however, squares with the scant provincial precision that is part of the cause-and-effect link for up-for-grabs implementation. That obscure language on the province's part is meant to empower teachers to step into the precision void and emerge as micromanagers of detracking. It is the teaching cadre who will determine how much actual mixing of students occurs; for instance, will there be three or four groups per class? "Guidelines work as long as nobody's *Nose Is Out of Joint,*" concludes an administrator, but then if this suasion fails, politicians may tighten up the policy. Not surprisingly, then, another interviewee holds that, should the province's beginning efforts at integration within grade 9 prove too hard to sustain, "directive frameworks may be necessary that have legislative power behind them."

Educators may agree with detracking's radical analysis but not its radical solution. Their storyline is that politicians are *Peddling Ideas* that are educationally unsound. For example, "Certainly, people of color are disadvantaged, grievously, but research evidence is mixed on whether detracking leads to higher academic achievement." The government's research on the policy's pilot projects is said to have scientific veneer, but to be only a mirage. Detracking is represented as a system of thought, when it is actually an absence of systematic thought. Union officials who support the change, through their regional curriculum forums and monographs they publish, are said to have no gumption (e.g., *"They Laid Down And Died"*). According to a local administrator given to alarmism, *"The Bottom Line* is that students without special needs would be deprived. Unwieldy amounts of teachers' time would be taken up attending to special-needs students." Economic causes and effects are not forgotten: "Detracking will lead to a lower quality of workforce, which in turn would jeopardize the country's economic future. . . . It's a *No-Win Situation."* Department officials are criticized for not realizing that some grade 9 youth cannot yet handle abstract thinking. The generalization is tendered in an interview, without factual support, that youngsters who are not ready will slow down bright or average learners.

The threat is subtle but present in the teachers' storyline that *"Teachers Are The Only Ones Who Can Make It Work,* and we are dubious at best." Secondary teachers of special education, technology, English, and certain other subjects also wade into the subject, asking rhetorically, *The WIIFM Question* (What's In It For Me?), alluding to themselves as harried innocents, trained as specialists but suddenly *Jerked Around* and expected to teach multiple subjects. Certain politicians—*The Enemy*—are repudiated for failing to fund the change sufficiently or to concern themselves with practicalities of formulating and making precise what materials are needed—texts, course calendars, evaluation criteria, curriculum crediting, pupil-teacher ratios, and other protocols. Findings from the second-year assessments of demonstration projects have been *Holed Up* in a slow-to-publish Department of Education, and "reports from pilot projects leave out the negatives. After all," according to a cause-and-effect link in an interview, "people in pilots are atypical, they want the pilots to succeed . . . but sooner or later the *Halo Effect* wears off." Other local administrators express fear that if detracking does not click, they and their teachers will be blamed.

A number of interviewees admit that the detracking policy is do-able, but *"Not On Top Of Everything Else* foisted on us," such as other new policies, students' unsettling behaviors, provincial cutbacks, and pension uncertainties. With suspicion, uncertainty, and divided purposes hampering their teaching, a unionist says, "When we go out in the halls, we deal with obstreperous problems that detracking advocates know nothing about." The unionist acknowledges that new routines might go far to settle the snafus he has enumerated, but he has another mini-analysis. Departing from the department's own wise and systematic model for gradual implementation, the government of the day is depicted as compressing timelines, and *Derailing The Consultation Process*. Politicians are doing this, two interviewees suggest, to be able to boast that the reform is operational when it next goes to the electorate. Detracking thus is seen by educators as politically popular, but popular democracy "isn't always the best way to make educational choices." "Nobody likes stupidity in government" is the claim by a person who says she has *Torn Up A Membership Card* for the in-power party.

The political party that first pushed for detracking now criticizes the successor government's present approach as "like *Nailing Jello-O To The Wall.*" Without the *Nuts and Bolts* of the policy and without precise images of instruction and learning outcomes, the government's capacity to implement a coherent policy for detracking is envisaged as *Piddling*. Agitation, which a unionist told me is characteristic of the labor movement, is predicted. "It'll be another illustration of the government treating us like *Tires That Have To Be Retreaded* every couple of years. We just get transformed by one bright idea, then along comes another." Giving a related explanation of the present conflict, provincial authorities have not even been effective in convincing the lay public of this and other policies' concrete benefits.

To a degree, this flare-up over detracking is reminiscent of the introduction of **special education,** an up-for-grabs implementation of which many stories are told. Again political forces, presenting themselves as citizen-democrats, were involved. A well-organized interest group of parents and educators in Maple is remembered for urging that U.S. patterns be transferred for individual treatments of children with learning disabilities. Prototypic cases were introduced, synecdochically, of handicapped children who thrived in regular classrooms; at the time, the phrase *physically or developmentally challenged* was not part of policy people's everyday vocabulary. Yet Maple's legislators did not feel confident in transferring the American experience wholesale or in precisely designing their own intricate policy. Implementing agencies signaled their unwillingness, too: surely children with behavioral or physical problems, once integrated into regular classrooms, would distract other learners. Yet, under pressure, politicians brought forward a bill that had been pulled together by a branch within the Department of Education. Lobbyists for children with disabilities thereafter sat in conferences of all-party parliamentary committees. The passage of education bills can be easy, if the opposition chooses to focus on such other sectors as health and culture, but that was not the case with special education. To opposition members of Parliament, those lobbyists handed sharply pointed questions to raise with government spokespersons. In this manner, "error correctors" were responsible for additions, clarifications, and complications later being *"Firmed-up* right on the floor of the legislature." A minority government was prepared to act on consensual advice supporting, in one of Maple's best-known educational storylines, *The Most Appropriate Student Placement In The Least Restrictive Environment.* (This is talk that comes trippingly to six tongues in my sample.)

The consequence, as recalled unsympathetically by administrators at the local level, is that "it took five years to shake the pap out of that bill and to gear up for a more inclusive style of addressing student needs." By providing time for the techniques and legally binding documents to be tried out, learned from, and better understood by staff, politicians were giving provincial and local authorities—and their staffs—what an interviewee portrays as *A Strategic Delay.* Modifications were made that bolstered the chances for achieving the policy aims, and consequently a tempered sense of commitment may be said to have grown among many implementors. Reportedly the department's middle managers became supportive colleagues, devising procedures for special-education committees, crafting guidelines for service models, upgrading qualifications for teachers of exceptional students, proposing learning outcomes, and so on.

At first, owing to the still-imprecise nature of the legislation for special education, every board was *In Compliance.* A framework had been provided for boards to start where they were, metaphorically represented by an interviewee as *Ground Zero* in some cases. As a result in this up-for-grabs implementation, educators at the local level thrashed out admissions routines, documents on reporting to parents, and variations in plans and time lines. Answers were necessary:

Where would the training take place—in wholly or partially integrated classrooms, cluster classrooms, satellite sites, neighborhood schools? For what subjects?

How would the instructional assistants, itinerant teachers, and regular teachers be trained?

How could parents avoid worry when resources were being redirected away from their children to other children deemed more needy?

Local administrators encouraged staff to augment processes and rename or add categories. Owing, for instance, to parental pressures, in some locales the province's term *Emotionally Disturbed* became a more euphemistic portrait, *Social Adjustment*.

To their credit, politicians and top administrators realized that a review on a case-by-case basis of all special-education decisions would be well beyond their competence and workload. Unwilling, however, to leave implementation totally in boards' hands, politicians established a tribunal system to independently review board decisions on the identification, placement, and review of developmentally challenged learners. Politically appointed experts on these monitoring committees closely reviewed boards' judgments. Several of my interviewees trumpet these committees as winning new educational rights for exceptional children.

Consistent, however, with loose provincial monitoring, special education is described as functioning diversely throughout Maple. Thus, "Boards do not operate with standard class sizes. They follow their own rules for what constitutes assessment." The present government has represented itself as wanting a more even implementation within the province, but a local administrator is skeptical: "We're in a recession. . . . This demand for equity comes at the wrong time." A storyline heard in rebuttal is that "this may not be *The Best Of Times,* but when is? We have to move forward." A recession-minded top administrator expresses commitment to the equity cause, but says "I wish I could afford the large special-education bureaucracies other boards have." In identifying new disabilities, these other boards have entitled more children to special services and paraprofessionals.

BUFFERED: THE LANGUAGE OF LEEWAY

A former deputy minister of education used to amuse himself and colleagues by wondering aloud why boards should continue to implement his organization's directives. His middle managers, then with a regulatory mind-set to be like *Zeus* in inspecting programs, were not amused. Nor were local administrators who had to forward information up that deputy's hierarchy. Anyhow, in the deputy's story, the province was powerful because boards allowed it to be, and ultimately the larger, self-funded boards would rise up and in effect say to the Department of Education, "This isn't the time or place for us to do what you want."

Although that deputy did not use the term, what he professed resembles buffered implementation. What Thompson (1987), the originator of the term, tells us is that—like up-for-grabs implementations—Bufferedness occurs when (1) the context is fluid, old assumptions giving way to newish assumptions, and (2) uncertainty is rife about appropriate technologies. Unlike up-for-grabs implementations, however, bufferedness has two qualities that make it more than a simple bottom-up initiative. Those qualities make bufferedness more than a situation where provincial vagueness and limited monitoring provide a window of opportunity for locals to run with local ideas. Those qualities, giving bufferedness its "cushiony" name, are twofold:

1. A softening of any bluntness in policy execution; local educators can stickhandle their own way within a provincial framework, and

2. A neutralizing of any shock that might come from opposing pressures—schools get the internal and external support they need for stability as well as change.

This is what Thompson (1987) tells us about buffered implementation; Maple's education gives us a chance to learn more. We will see signs of locals—by reducing adverse effects of the department's impact—protecting themselves from provincial policies.

Language about Provincial Authorities Coping with Buffers

For many years, local administrators placed federal funds for French programs into their boards' general revenues. Eventually

Ottawa required provinces to invent sharper accounting practices that ensured that federal grants for immersion were truly going only into immersion. The provincial implementation of **French immersion** and of **French as a second language** can be reckoned as being buffered, however. In the wake of national conversations about the future of French-English relations within Canada (always an agitated context, it seems), provincial authorities are leaving it up to local officials to settle upon the appropriate technology for sparking bilingualism:

> Is grade 1, 4, or 7 the best place to begin? Can immersion be partial? How much aural and oral is warranted? What are the implications of only a quarter of a class being academically prepared for advanced French in grade 9?

Three other signs mark immersion as a buffered zone:

1. Vigilant implementation might require that all immersion teachers had oral and written fluency. But many of these teachers do not.

2. Vigilant implementation might require that if and when texts were used, their levels of difficulty might be reasonable for immersion students. Yet science texts often are too advanced linguistically for their readers.

3. Vigilant implementation might require that immersion students benefit from classes with a fair share of a system's most experienced teachers, the sort who have learned much over time about how children learn. Immersion teachers might all have good teaching degrees, they might be keen, but often they are among the newest and the least credentialed on staff.

Context makes much of the difference in how vigilantly locals implement. In short, locals work with what they have, and I was told that some immersion programs suggest that, after some *Fits and Starts*, they can be gifted fixers. Consultations and trade-offs fill a vacuum left by a province that is not great in statutory precision or monitoring.

References to a consultative process, a hallmark of bufferedness, are hallowed in the culture of those top officials. As in other quarters, for more than twenty-five years the inclusive term *Stake-*

holders has been one of the most popular and hallowed words at the Department of Education; it is even championed by several of that organization's most authoritarian, nondivulging authorities. It is a term that has spread far: activist officials of trustee and educator organizations routinely speak about "stakeholder events," a department source keeps redefining who particular policies' "stakeholder groups" are, and one interviewee even speaks of "stakeholder theory" (where those affected by an organization influence it). Everybody, it seems, delights in being considered a stakeholder—except trustees. "We are not mere stakeholders, thank you very much. We have *Accountability* for money and standards, according to the Education Act," a trustee says, portraying his fellow board members as *A Step Up,* the province's only eyeball-to-eyeball partners.

Is the Province the Center or on the Periphery?

An important example of provincial buffering is Maple's **"play" curriculum.** In a debate of long standing, typically it is portrayed as encapsulating either all that is *Progressive,* warm, and caring about the department or all that is a dead loss. This curriculum—"unstructured enrichment," "child-centeredness," "uncompetitive"—involves manipulables that can help teach math concepts to primary students. Maple has middle-class parents who argue that the *Curriculum Pendulum* has swung too far toward a *Let-Things-Happen Permissiveness.* They favor more highly se-quenced and direct instruction, occasionally portrayed as a *Redneck* teacher working from the front of the class to children lined up in rows. Provincial politicians typically have not taken firm stands on this issue one way or the other, one acknowledging that *It's A Crap Shoot,* with pros and cons to both approaches. A perception, however, is that it is provincial administrators, not politicians, who support the play curriculum, even though the department's decades-old book on the subject purportedly has nothing more binding than the status of an advisory document.

The Department of Education's weapons for Buffering include committees, reviews, memoranda, conferences, time lines, round-tables, consultants, five-year plans, issue sheets, impersonal correspondence, rhetoric about responsibility, international connections, and local wisdom. "How effective are these interactions?" I ask an interviewee. He pitches me a lawyer's short and slippery storyline: "It depends [on the situation]." From others, the longer-winded answer seems to be that these interactions can be effective in situations when they are diagnostic, responsive, and attuned to circumstances of particular communities, educators, and students.

In essence, buffering's committees, or temporary administrative adhocracies, are organizational units created to bring together individuals at various levels to produce policy innovations. Insiders point, for instance, to such a unit, a writing team, branding a once-topical **Canada's multicultural heritage** course as not living up to its name, as being unbalanced in favor of the founding cultures, and as slighting other groups' enrichments of the national mosaic. The department's educators were *Movers And Shakers* on that committee, but history teachers later worked alongside them to develop and disseminate advice on that course's revisions. Staffs in schools would achieve curricular coherence at their own level.

Buffering for curriculum guidelines usually is not hurried, and for some that has been one of its disappointments. Once writing teams piece together highlights for courses of study, possibly in a more than year-long process of consultation, the department sends out invitations for validation from boards, lobbies, and others. To overcome "bureaupathological logjams and overload," a former government shortened validation periods and reduced the numbers of validators. In 1992, two local CEOs reflected more favorably than unfavorably on that streamlining. With the perspective that the periphery is informing the center, the first CEO says:

> There's still arrogance, but that's breaking down, and today the department is less insulated. They increasingly treat professionals in the unions and in the boards as the experts. . . . Department documents and instrument pools are compilations of what the best educators are already thinking and doing. The idea of doing practical, **hands-on [math] and family math** came from teachers who were doing that in their classrooms. . . . I have teachers who travel, who read, who think. They tried the idea out, it worked. This gives the department reason to say "More teachers in the province should know about this."

Besides ideas about change, a second local CEO had a storyline from a team-building game about the moon played in Maple's schools:

Guidelines from the department used to be isolated events, inconsistent, and done too quickly with too little support. . . . The process of implementation wasn't emphasized. Principals weren't valued as problem solvers. The *Culture Of Schools* wasn't considered. . . . The department put out a document with a flying donut on the cover and anyone who faithfully followed the ideas in four segments of the donut was supposed to "ensure" implementation. Well [chortle], it doesn't work that way. It's like that simulation [that] the kids do, "Survival on the Moon": improvement works if roles are thought through.

As part of its own thinking-through, nowadays the Department of Education seldom is portrayed as the prime sponsor of workshops to socialize staffs to guidelines. Rather, if funds are available, curricular induction is said to occur when and if classroom staff can get together to swap ideas with those consultants who developed the materials in the first place. Thus, primary teachers struggle over apt proportions of **whole-language and phonics** reading.

Now that it has *Less Of A Lock* on part of curricula with fewer *Thou Shalts*, the department's top administrators advise local officials that "if confusion exists about a course of study, then you [in the boards] should define the solution yourselves and complete the job." As a result, a teacher probably could spend a whole career in Maple without directly consulting any provincial guidelines. "Show me a teacher who's looked at a provincial document in the last two years," one interviewee teases, synecdochically, to make same point. Allegedly, many secondary teachers do not even turn to their boards' more down-to-earth outlines of study, instead relying on approaches deliberated upon at their in-school meetings. To the extent that behavioral problems and other chores do not overwhelm them, *Teachers In Every Class Make Their Own Decisions About Materials They Use.* Department as well as board officials present themselves as *In The Same Ballpark* and seldom do they go back on the storyline—it is almost a matter of faith—that discretion is central to teaching.

When the Department of Education's middle managers see boards with *Exemplary Practices* running sound programs, they disseminate. For instance, one department official told how a certain principal's hiring of more female teachers for math has led to more girl students doing well in that subject. Department managers are careful to observe, moreover, conflicts between interest groups and schools, circulating that information back to politicians and their superiors, who expect to be superbly informed. "The last thing," one politician says with almost a shudder, "that this government wants to face are demonstrations over local issues that we know nothing about."

Views from the Board Administrators

In recent years, local administrators have come to regard election campaigns as destabilizing phenomena. In one such election, a premier announced a **reduction of class size for grades 1 & 2.** Since 85 percent of the costs ultimately were borne by localities, boards had to buffer in answering questions like these:

> Is Maple's twenty-pupil figure a board, school, or classroom average? Which schools should change first? Which classes should be enlarged to compensate for teachers assigned to grades 1 & 2? Who should decide?

Often when discussing Maple's curriculum, local administrators portray themselves with watery metaphors such as "We were *Drowned* by policy" or "This policy won't *Hold Water,*" or "The principals will *Water Down* the policy in implementation." At other times, local authorities represent themselves as not out of their depth: with versatility, they project themselves as *Defenders Of The Faith* and willing to *Swim Against The Tide* to uphold a principle. While buffering provincial policies, principle is a theme locals like to return to, as they try channeling to staff resources such as release time for planning and money to visit other boards' schools. Or, in these economically spare times, local administrators, exchange published materials that support the change and send letters of commendation to teachers for any success.

Larger boards, with their administrative capacities, are said to take *Wide Berths* for their own augmentations of the province's curriculum. Despite accolades to the arts found in provincial guidelines, grade 7 and 8 **music** qualifies as an example of buffering; vocal and instrumental activities vary significantly from board to board. Educational provisions, perceived to be a natural outcome of one board's philosophy and administrative framework, are called into question in a second board, and deemed utterly unacceptable in a third. Provincial guides might call for a balance between performing, listening, and creating music, but board materials might minimize direct instruction in one or two of those dimensions. Small, northern, and tax-poor boards have buffering's flexibility in music and other arts programs, but because the provision of resources to provinces coincides with provincial control, these boards are not necessarily autonomous. To make matters worse, administrators there can find themselves with formal prescriptions that arrive *Naked In The Mail,* without warning or elaboration from the Department of Education. Back-country boards seethe if, for instance, department guides assume sufficient musical or talent are on staff, that sufficient money is available to keep instruments in good repair with monthly tune-ups, and that parents are willing to rent horns and other instruments for $200 a year. The sole allusion I heard to the province as *Big Brother* came from such a music-minded official in a sparsely settled locale.

Even in populous locales, cagey board administrators seldom admit that they circumvent nagging procedures or that general legislative grants are used off-kilter to what politicians prefer. Rather, they say something like, "We have *Systems That Are Workable.*" Thus to the disappointment of African Canadians, a department document might imply that **Black** (or African Canadian) **history** cannot be taught as a single unit of instruction. Wanting to be relevant to community needs, a curriculum administrator in one board may determine that because the Department of Education already supports modules to provide flexibility to teachers, black history can indeed be subsumed into parts of several existing modules. Other boards' administrators may learn of this handy resolution through consciousness-raising of the *Grapevine.* (That grapevine, interviewees keep saying, is almost a quintessential image of the essence of policy implementation.) Of course, stock solutions might start out being transferred from one board to another, but contexts and specifics in situations vary enough that a number of interviewees hasten to point out that *There Is No One Right Answer.*

With the open-endedness of buffering, local authorities value their staff's networking for the adoption of provincial policy. One goes as far as to even cite the actual research (Hannaway 1993; Meier 1992) that decentralized development of curriculum is most effective at making teachers enthusiastic and responsible for what occurs in their classrooms. Aware that staff usually will welcome only a modicum of direction from the top, supervisory officers say they know how hard to push their *Strategic Plans* that incorporate provincial, local, and neighborhoods' hopes. It is an ancient storyline that top administrators advise principals to begin reforms with a few classes and then let change grow, gradually, in the process accustoming people to the new technology. Parents may be surveyed and authority may be vested with in-school officials, on the understanding that they too are *Accountable*, "whatever" "accountable means this year," a cynical youngish superintendent says.

Consensus on Student Evaluation Is Elusive, Even with Buffering

These days provincial politicians and their top administrators seem less into policing and more into *Throne Speeches* about elementary science as a new focus, or about the importance of teachers' sharpening their work in cognitive disciplines such as math. Much also revolves around endpoints for describing and improving what students learn in grades 3, 6, and 9. While academics and Department of Education officials propose broad skills for student achievement, a story is that local educators and subject-matter associations would be the local stars of endpoints to make their boards more measurement-minded. Were that to happen, the provincial endpoints policy would have the provincial imprecision and local monitoring requisite to buffering.

In one board, teachers are doing the *Grunt Work* of developing endpoints' new sequencing, pedagogies, and boardwide indicators. In a neighbor board, deliberations on endpoints "are not being asked of teachers." After the department widely circulated a newspaper heralding the general elements of the new endpoints curriculum and its attendant evaluation, teachers questioned the amount of voice they would have, *In The Real World*, were they to take issue with any of those elements. Consistent with buffered implementation's relative openness, provincial documents are silent about particular matters, like great literature. "Can we still assign Shakespeare?" teachers ask.

According to a half-dozen interviewees, teachers see themselves as soon losing that sort of discretion and having to enact the most senseless and hoary of storylines: They will have to *Teach to the Provincial Tests*, training youth who can spout information but not think. An administrator speaks for others who have a grievance over such a direction:

Parents demand all, that their children pass tests *With Flying Colors*, and we will have to give all. We will have to prep [for the band of test questions]. Developmental activities will *Go By The Board*. . . . We're not even being prepared for this. It's here. It's *Production-Line* time. It's time to *Spoon-Feed Widgets of Information*. . . . School will be for those who like to *Obediently Follow Instructions*. . . .

Such would hardly be a buffered stance.

In addition to those in the media who think schools are awash with *Fads And Not Content* (such as environmental studies), groups in the sociopolitical milieu who are singled out as most restive for the endpoints evaluation are the business and industrial elite. The chamber of commerce "crowd" allegedly wants to push further, so that the media can publish annual learning assessments of all schools. Boards are being expected to revise their forms of reporting to parents, hitherto a local board prerogative rather than a provincial one—and the new forms are said to have the markings of *An Outcomes Orientation*. A trustee dismisses that movement:

> You'd think that *Captains of Industry* would want education to continue working on many fronts with many types of clients, like their own dynamic companies. Their "captains" want schools for everyone to be like the schools they went to. These men forget that they were the top 20 percent of a smaller [population] base. . . . If these businessmen win out, it won't be *A Picnic* for the other 80 percent.

It would be premature, however, to write off the buffering potential of the province's endpoints evaluation policy. Despite all the push by external forces for stricter evaluations of student learnings, people internal to schools still do have some say-so in the matter. A small sign of this discretion is the range of terms used by boards—*culminating* outcomes, *exit* outcomes, *performance* outcomes. Qualifying the policy as more, rather than less, buffered, provincial interviewees add that more-substantive variations may exist from board to board. For instance, open to wide interpretation by boards is the provincial expectation that students, by the end of grade 9, be able to "visualize and evaluate possible futures for themselves and their world." Variations on this "self and society" dimension can exist from classroom to classroom, too.

In a sense, all policies generated at one level are lost at another. In a field like education, where teachers need control of their jobs, those who rev up policy engines in provincial circles can not fully possess local policy. With limited precision and monitoring, buffered policies are the ones wherein the province relinquishes most. The basic provincial impulse to control will exist as long as policies remain vital, but each locality will also need to reinterpret certain policies in light of its particular setting. To point out that buffered implementations have great local variability and that certain provincial policies sometimes are not quickly completed in particular boards is merely to phrase a situation in negative terms. It is just as objective to recognize, through buffering, the continuing need of locals to adapt provincial messages.

CONCLUSION

The Language of Intergovernmental Relations

When 120 old and middle-aged politicians and administrators in Maple Province speak at length with me about what it is like to govern, in effect they say, '"If our accounts can profit you anything, take them. This is part of what we bring back from our policy travails. "

What have these 120 interviewees brought back for us? It is clear that policy people do more than problem-focus on technical criteria (e.g., "What will solve this problem?") and politics-focus on public receptivities (e.g., "What does the public want now?"). Beyond those foci, policy people interplay between their own situations and already-developed symbols of storytelling others. In this interplay, policy people do not particularly use a special arcane language of policy. They do not, for instance, speak of coupling problem, policy, and political streams (Kingdon 1984). Nor do they speak of other classic notions such as muddling through (Lindbloom 1959), assumptions analysis (Dunn 1981), backward mapping (Elmore and McLaughlin 1985), policy gambling (Dror 1986), or policy instruments and design (McDonnell and Elmore 1987).

Instead, what they evoke are more commonplace symbols such as the Department of Education as a *Spiderweb* that can entangle the naive. Or interviewees somewhat link cause and effect with easy explanations of doings, such as "When we recruit for immersion teachers, we get either adventurers who don't last long or those who can't get a job in Quebec." Expenditures and effects are calculated, but in more everyday than technocratic terms, as in "Professional development days are wrongly handled—what other public organization would risk the bad public relations of shutting down completely for most of its staff to learn?" Talk such as this not only reflects their ways of seeing but provides frameworks for their actions (Morgan 1993). An elaboration of those summary points follows.

Language of Symbols Revisited: Packaging for Acceptability

Educational authorities relate outlines of stories that are in good currency, metaphors, and synecdoches. They concern themselves with strategy and with substance, transformation, and flux. Through these symbols, they share their pleasure and sadness in their jobs, they demonstrate their misunderstandings, they make sense of stability and reform. Their portraits of conflict and collaboration are meant to elicit, in themselves and others, déjà vu and vertigo—the fictions can be as familiar as that doleful caution not to throw the *Baby Out With The Bathwater,* a metaphor droningly repeated by as many as eight of my interviewees.

A central point is that policy people do imagine themselves as fighting the good fight, which means that they slip into language that could heighten tension between themselves and those in other roles at other levels. They remember themselves and their colleagues as dueling nobly for causes. Local top administrators of education, portraying themselves as valiant and their protagonists as only mediocre duelists, tell how provincial politicians "blow in, through elections, with what they think are trendy proposals." To adapt Sartre's storyline about the despair caused by "other people," *Hell Is Other Levels Of Educational Government.* No one directly uses the metaphor of "turf," "territory," or "white picket fences" to describe their policy situations—but their descriptions suggest a terrain marked by division.

In light of that competitiveness, it is not surprising that sport imagery is used, and unsinisterly. Sinisterly, the athlete's concept of "fair play" might have been introduced, for instance, into a discussion between the government and an underfinanced parents' group. Then the speaker might have insinuated that a loss by the parents was the acceptable result of a fair process. Similarly the term *professional* might be used, not in the sense of holding oneself and one's colleagues accountable, but to insinuate that only the preferences of the speaker count. Fair play and professionalism are mentioned by interviewees, but none overindulge in this cloaking and unidimensional distortion of language.

Tone is a tricky quality to estimate, and it certainly has not been scientifically measured here on a five-or ten-point scale. Government initiatives may be laced with defeat, as in "By the time important provincial policies reach the classroom, they're so diluted that they make little difference." Nonetheless, peeking through the chagrin over policies that are *Hard To Swallow* is a guarded hopefulness. After marathon negotiations, agents for provincial and local levels see themselves as striking honorable compromises, and for them *Compromise Is Not A Dirty Word*. A pervasive storyline is of mutual sacrifice, of resistance and accommodation, of warriors sacrificing to integrators and vice versa, of politicians' sacrificing to top administrators and again vice versa, of provincial authorities' sacrificing to locals and again vice versa.

No one is so simpleminded as to say, "There are no problems, only opportunities." Yet as they discuss issues, leading policy formulators and implementors fall back on fairly chipper, if glib, storylines, metaphors, and synecdoches such as these (implicit on earlier pages): "One has to care for tomorrow." "Happiness in governance is not extinct." "The province has a golden past in superb education." "Moral identities have continually to be discovered." "Experience is a costly but worthwhile commodity." A spunkiness exists within the implementation class against unexplained policies. Unique joy is found in bemoaning the department of education, since such-and-such provincial policy is typically retrograde. Laboring for board or department success is not monomania ("even Retreads care"). "One can't simply wash one's hands of obligations and practice virtue by oneself." "There is no reason to assume that what is true of an implementation today will remain so indefinitely." "The paths to great success or great failure in a particular policy are close." "The school is an enterprise where everyone is an investor, stockholder, or the like."

References to well-established stories in the culture at large can be explicit and highbrow. For instance, while arguing that the province's funding levels impose crippling constraints, one politician sound-bites without mentioning Iseult by name: "Policy perfection is about as remote as *The Unattainable Lady In German Opera.*" Usually, though, storylines are much more down-to-earth, as when an interviewee depicts himself as *Johnny On The Spot;* he says he *Takes Care Of Problems.* With him, "taking care" appears to mean personally deciding how to handle emergencies.

Such projections of political or educational activity and the provincial-local seesaw somewhat falsify reality, omit key facts, and even miss the most telling plots, the most atmospheric settings, the most integrative characters. Any one portrait may be incomplete and therefore partially untrue. For instance, as in the Kurosawa movie *Rashomon,* where four people tell their own different versions of a rape and murder, conflicting accounts can be told about the same episode. That is the case, for example, in this report's account of two storylines about detracking, each capable of being believed, each invoking separate criteria, each revealing a separate experience.

When taken together, these policy portraits resemble an extended and not very original family. Symbols are related by the common characteristic of evoking their tellers' experiences. They interact familiarly in representations of policy formulation, reformulation, and implementation. One by one, these storylines, metaphors, and synecdoches strike us as clichés. Heard only once or twice, most seem monotonous. Heard many times, however, politicians' and administrators' symbols seem like old, comforting friends, lending continuity to policy life. When a hundred or more of these bromides burst forth, as they have above, it is almost like a family get-together.[3] We see that policy hustling has characteristics in common with other understandings we have. We see that the policy process acknowledges many symbols that have come before. We see that policy people use a clichéd style to look at complicated material and that the complicated material turns out to have elements of cliché.

Why do policy people rely on established storylines, synecdoches, and metaphors to punch across their visions and processes? One explanation: to make fresh demands seem less intimidating, interviewees dress those demands in old clothes. Perhaps they have no more aptitude for original conversation than they have for original ideas. A more charitable explanation is that while their language is hackneyed, a part of each of us is hackneyed: extreme originality, like extreme anything, tends toward singular-ity and isolation. By role, if not by personality, though, policy people are so interactional that too much of such isolation could be debilitating. An official in a northern town gives a third explanation for this commonness: "We're all *Busy, Busy.*" Authorities are so preoccupied, she implies, that they do not have the time to be imaginative in conjuring new symbols. Synecdochically, where the whole of a thing is represented as a part or a part is represented for a whole, they may lack the literary art of Alice Munro or Mordecai Richler. Still, at least their toolkit of words rates as familiar and down-home—even in a world bulking with newness.

Language on Causes & Effects Revisited: Notions of Human Nature

A second major portrait is of human causes and effects for an entire arena and province. Cameos are shown of Maple's top administrators and politicians being competitive and bonded, closed and open, digging in and kicking over the traces, talking to and past each other, and challenging and affirming others' cause-and-effect scenarios. Greeting provincial policies with varying degrees of receptivity, board administrators say they are leery of being trapped or immobilized; the province has offended by not consulting them at the conceptual stage of policymaking, only at the final stage of ratification. For their part, survivors at the provincial level also present themselves as human—approaching and withdrawing, asserting and responding, engaging and disentangling, stimulating and dampening agitation, asserting the self and worrying about education's direction, operations, and costs.

Portraits of cause and effect array themselves to some degree by roles in the system. Talking about implementation, several provincial interviewees bespeak authoritarian, controlling ways of an earlier time that have not disappeared simply because an evolving democratic process and great public scepticism say they should. Gutted with precepts from above, certain local politicians and top administrators say they "have *Had It Up To Here*—we want to *Pull The Plug* on all the advice we hear." Simultaneously a key understanding among many top administrators is that politicians generally overrespond to pressure groups and special interests. These educators say politicians won't be able to change classrooms fundamentally, for "unless there's a revolution, *Change Isn't Normal.*" Thus provincial legislators are said to have "their

Heads Screwed On Sideways if they think educational realities are the same as political realities."

On occasion, provincial politicians claim they control or try to force certain implementations more than others. The department's managers and local CEOs claim they are more multifaceted than mere *Tools* of the province's politicians. By asserting that these and other causes and effects are important, local and provincial authorities help to make these relationships important. Somehow, out of the murk, implementations begin to take form, expressing to some degree what politicians, top administrators and others have seen and what they want. My first interviewee accepts that "it's like plucking billiard balls out of thin air."[4]

Any out-and-out tension in this slice-of-life here may unsettle those who assume that (1) central politicians and their bureaucracies simply make policy and do not implement it, and (2) local top administrators simply put managerial processes and procedures into effect for the province. According to interviewees, nothing in education is that black and white, that simple in cause or effect.

Revisiting the Language on Stakes: Who Benefits? Who Pays?

Retrieving implementation experiences from the past twenty or more years of Maple's education, this report sought to peg out a plot on the common borders of politics and education at provincial and local levels, an arena that is not a frequently researched. Such a view thereby has a wider, more macro, perspective than research on superintendent-community relations and improvements in schools, both elementary (Crandall and Associates 1982) and secondary (Louis and Miles 1990). In remembering particulars, interviewees provided data for a more person-centered, micro vantage than overviews of provincial or state realignments (such as the one by Firestone, Fuhrman, and Kirst 1991).

Linkages were etched between (1) policy precision/clarity and (2) policy monitoring/control for 57 provincial policy soups, like Heinz's 57 or more varieties of soup. The "57" metaphor is referred to by an interviewee who claims that the department's policy implementations are not monolithic.

Interviewees would appear to deviate from scholars who suggest that only one or two or three different approaches to reform, or to understanding reform, are working (e.g., Darling-Hammond 1992). Drawn upon words from interviewees, five dynamics are

Table 8–1

Propositions on Managers' Interactions, by Implementation Types

Type	Ministry Managers' Interactions	Local Managers' Interactions
Controlled	Plan expertly; draft precise procedures; don't fully trust the discretion of local managers; evaluate implementations for system errors; use the hierarchy and be more assessment-oriented than process-oriented; usually value uniformity and convergence with definitions of the public interest by provincial politicians; usually recognize but don't emphasize negotiation as characteristic of the intergovernmental process.	Rail against provincial prescriptions; if disagreements with ministry have little impact, begin a "rear guard" effort to have previously uninvolved parties infiltrate assorted networks to persuade provincial politicians to make changes for "the kids' sake"; if still no change occurs, put pressure on staff to go by the book; perhaps gather data on local results/reactions to argue for redesign or less surveillance of provincial policy; see self as an administrative agent for central authorities.
Preventive/ Prophylactic	Value vague policy systems; trust local systems and try to infiltrate their networks; infrequently evaluate for major errors at local level; tolerate diverse approaches; emphasize that deliberative judgement is required at both ministry and local levels.	Emphasize local system as functional partner of ministry; work out local approaches that enhance local professionalism and needs; manage, streamline, and tinker with the details of principles enunciated by central actors; see self as functional partner with ministry.

Type	Ministry Managers' Interactions	Local Managers' Interactions
Up-for-Grabs	Draft imprecise procedures; attach accountability strings; frequently monitor for local errors and hints of what works; value the partial success; emphasize functional partnership and need for deliberative judgment by all levels.	Firm up the imprecise policy, compensating for statutory looseness in provincial policy by designing a more elaborate local policy; circulate data to the province about "fixes" that work.
Buffered	Fine-tune imprecise policy that delegates control; lightly and infrequently monitor for local errors; value diversity; recognize others as politically interdependent.	Encourage staff initiative and accountability in adopting and augmenting policy; see self as bargaining for advantage with ministry officials.

shown as operating somewhat divergently for four types of implementation (ranging from the technocratic controlled implementation to the populist buffered implementation). Those dynamics are policy technique, environmental stability, sociopolitical milieu, commitment of implementors, and capacity of politicians and their top appointees. It is impossible to imagine which of these variables is the least important or dispensable. Each dynamic seems to help and constrain the others. Awareness of these distinctions has the potential to help and constraint policymakers and their advisers to think more carefully about diverse mixes of precision and monitoring for their implementations.

This inquiry's stronger conceptual rationale is its convergent-forces perspective (Thompson 1987), the stuff of figure 7–1 of chapter 7. We have glimpsed the utility of controlled implementations' precision and monitoring, even where teachers (say) lack commitment and groups in the milieu churn with opposition. In the company of political and administrative authorities, we have glanced back at preventive implementations; they seem to work because the strong clarity and precision makes implementation sequential, just as they seem to excite resistance when boards are expected to absorb internal costs. In up-for-grabs implementation, we have noticed how local boards are in good positions to "read" the climates of their localities and to adjust procedures to meet local demands. Buffered implementations encourage a sense of professional autonomy among local education, but can circumvent difficult goals.

Thompson's ideas about implementation thus are not only applied and confirmed but materially expanded. From observing what is said about policy content, processes, and outcomes, the following rendering of recent transactions in Maple's education is discernible.

That is, in the interests of explanation and prediction, table 8–1 brings together the dynamics outlined in table 7–1 of chapter 7 with activities of top administrators at several levels. Often these people have distinct, loose interpretations of policy purposes and means. They play with different information. What we have here are several linkages of an *if-then* nature: they suggest how forces converge in this intergovernmental case of politicians and top administrators implementing educational policies. For instance, if politicians have decided on a new controlled implementation, then the department's top administrators may use the hierarchy and be more assessment-oriented than process-oriented. Then too, top administrators at the local level might begin their own rain dance by railing against provincial prescriptions. This set of interactions helps these policy people move beyond their divergent talk about the meanings of policies to more or less consensual implementations.

Because people are infinitely more spontaneous than these patterns suggest, almost the last thing I want to do is claim that intergovernmental relations in education everywhere can be managed by these beginning precepts. But in the course of arriving at implementations of provincial policies, interviewees in Maple say they see themselves and others as exhibiting these yings and yangs of action and reaction.

Much as policy people have perspective on their roles, this report needs to be put into perspective. Education leaders may talk symbolically, cause-effectually, and stake-countingly, as if they are committed to a cause like efficiency or excellence. But then they may fail to allocate sufficient resources, or to enhance their systems' capacities to realize particulars, or to revise certain taken-for-granted practices that frustrate those commitments. Still, leaders' talk might not be wasted. Preferences that are talked up can linger, and remind.

NOTES

For an explanation of my use of italicized capitalized terms and of boldfaced terms, see chapter 7.

1. The vice-principalship appears easiest to achieve, for in 1988, women represented a mere 10 percent of Maple's superintendents, 11 percent of secondary principals, and 17 percent of elementary principals. Another common storyline is that affirmative action has extensive ramifications for boards in terms of dollars. Recent provincial legislation requires that staffs represent the diversities of their communities' visible minorities, handicapped, and Natives, but allegedly not many qualified individuals from those groups are on the job market. Consequently, boards are having to look at internal means for training members of those groups for work in their academic and nonacademic sectors.

2. Besides having to trim financial costs, local CEOs today have another constraint: more local interests are needing to be persuaded that all local costs are necessary. Hence, trustees are spending time in board central offices, largely to better acquaint themselves with options for

financing provincial initiatives. Particularly in urban areas that are growing, new groupings of ratepayers and a number of "reform" trustees are
making program review and cost-containment their causes, wanting to
know the hidden stories in budget and enrollment numbers; occasionally
(it is said) they negatively affect program and teacher-student ratios
(*Loading The Classrooms,* in one educator's metaphor). Accustomed to
being the ones who choose what to cut, to phase out, to phase in, or to
expand, local administrators now are having to learn how to satisfy their
internal and external groups' thirsts for information on costs and other
matters. Counting the stakes, several local CEOs deplore the Department
of Education's allowing trustees to have enough power to distract educators from *Getting On With The Job.* These CEOs prefer working internally, tailoring learning programs to schools' different needs and to their
increasingly diverse clienteles.

    3. For another treatment of this phenomenon of archetypes, see Eco
1988.

    4. Reacting to this paragraph at our second meeting, my first inter-
viewee leaned forward to ask, "Last time [when I first interviewed him,
years before], did I really say that about billiard balls?" My field notes
from that interview are not irrefutable (I was just getting into this study,
I had forgotten what a slow notetaker I was, I was not yet using a tape
recorder, and all I have about that remark of his is: ~*to plu. b. balls out
of t. air*). I replied to the practitioner that I believed others would agree
with what I wrote down as his sentiment: at bottom, it may be no easier
to formulate and implement policies than to pluck billiard balls out of
the thin air.

REFERENCES

Crandall, D., & Associates (1982). *People, policies and practices: Examining the chain of school improvement.* Vols. I–X. Andover, Massa-
chusetts: The Network.

Darling-Hammond, L. (1992). Reframing the school reform agenda:
New paradigms must restore discourse with local educators, *The
School Administrator,* 10(49), 22–27.

Dror, Y. (1986). *Policymaking under adversity.* New York: Transaction
Books.

Dunn, W. (1981). *Public policy analysis.* Englewood Cliffs: Scott Foresman.

Eco, U. (1988). Cult movies and intertextual collage. In D. Lodge (Ed.),
Modern criticism and theory (pp. 446–55). London: Longman.

Elmore, R., & McLaughlin, M. (1985). Forward and backward mapping: Reversible logic." In K. Hanf & T. Toonen (Eds.), *Policy imple-*

mentation in federal and unitary systems (pp. 33–70). Boston: Martinus Nijhoff.

Firestone, W., Fuhrman, S., & Kirst, M. (1991). State educational reform since 1983: Appraisal and the future, *Educational Policy, 5,* 223–50.

Hannaway, J. (1993). Decentralization, social control and technical demands: Two cases in education. In J. Hannaway & M. Carnoy (Eds.), *Decentralization and education* (pp. 135–62). San Francisco: Jossey-Bass.

Kingdon, J. W. (1984). *Agendas, alternatives, and public policies.* Boston: Little Brown.

Louis, K. S., & Miles, M. B. (1990). *Improving the urban high school: What works and why.* New York: Teachers College Press.

McDonnell, L. M., & Elmore, R. F. (1987). Getting the Job Done: Alternative Policy Instruments, *Educational Evaluation and Policy Analysis, 9*(2),133–52.

McLeod, G. T. (1984). The work of school board chief executive officers, *Canadian Journal of Education, 9*(2), 171-190.

Meier, D. H. (1992). Reinventing teaching. *Teachers College Record, 93,* 594–609.

Morgan, G. (1993). *Imaginization: The art of creative management.* Beverly Hills, Sage.

Thompson, F. J. (1987). Policy implementation and overhead control. In G. Edwards (Ed.), *Public policy implementation.* London: JAI Press.

CHAPTER 9

How CEOs Influence
School System Culture

Donald Musella

Most concerns about schooling have stimulated school-level improvement efforts. So we read about changing the role of the school principal so as to provide instructional leadership, improving teacher and administrator preparation, increasing teacher and parental participation in school site governance, organizational decentralization in the form of site-level management, and a host of instruction-related changes intended to increase levels of learning.

Less attention has been paid to changes in the central office. Those who focus their attention on the school as the unit of change agree with this de-emphasis. Others say it is a mistake. For example, Barr and Dreeben (1983) remind us that "education would be a strange organization indeed, if the parts were hermetically sealed off from each other, if superintendents had no impact upon principals"(p.3). Yet, they claim, it is precisely the failure to come up with satisfactory answers to questions about the impact of senior administrators that is the source of so much of our inability to understand school effects. Concerning this lack of research about senior levels of administration, Pfeffer (1984) notes that leadership effects may vary with level in an organizational heirarchy, but for the most part leadership research has been overconcentrated upon first-line supervisors. He argues for more research on the impact of central office administration on the organization. "If leadership has any impact, it should be more evident at higher organizational levels or where there is more dis-

223

cretion in decisions and activities" (p. 9). Murphy (1989) argues for research and reform at all levels in the organization: "It would be a serious flaw of reform to believe that one must chose between centralization and decentralization. Rather, the likelihood is that local schooling will move increasingly toward a more balanced system of both centralized and decentralized control, with changed images of top-executive leadership along side new visions of school-site autonomy and teacher professionalism" (p. 808).

Previous attempts to better understand administrative roles and relationships seemed to offer new insights but eventually proved disappointing. For example, Crowson (1990) reminds us of the once-widespread acceptance of the efficiency movement (Callahan 1962), increased bureaucratization (Cronin 1973; Rogers 1969), "loose coupling" (Weick 1976), and "organized anarchy" (March and Olsen 1976) as "solutions" to top-down and bottom-up relationships that would improve administrators' effectiveness in "reforming" schools (Corwin and Borman 1988; Firestone and Herriott 1982).

Of course, there have been other studies focused on the role of the chief education officer. Although sometimes not explicit, the purpose of these studies often has been to identify what constitutes "effectiveness" and how one might become an effective leader. For example, Murphy and Hallinger's (1986) study of 12 superintendents in "carefully defined instructionally effective districts" concluded that these superintendents were successful instructional leaders because they controlled the development of goals at both district and school levels, were influential in the selection of staff, supervised and evaluated principals, and established and monitored a district-wide instruction and curriculum focus. In a national study of 194 superintendents, Salley (1980) concluded that the priority of importance given to each job function by superintendents is influenced by personal, district, ethnic, and/or socioeconomic characteristics. These conclusions indicate understandable human preferences, but they contribute little of substantive value. Ellen Wolf (1987), in an attempt to discover what superintendents do to meet the demands and expectations of their role, found major disagreements as to "what is considered important" in their work lives. Superintendents indicated that a working relationship with the school board is their highest priority [see also chapters 2 and 3—Editor] and ranked improvement in educational opportunities last; school principals in this study reversed this ranking. Coleman and LaRocque (1990) found that, through "reaching out," superintendents in successful districts were able to foster a "positive district ethos," an ethos that supported district improvement and school effectiveness. In a comparison of superintendents of high-performing and low-performing school districts, the former "seemed full of confidence about their ability to make a difference to students, teachers, and schools. On the other hand, superintendents of low-performing districts seemed passive; they felt that important work and decisions were in other hands" (p. 84).

Compared to Coleman and LaRocque, Musella and Leithwood (1990) found much less top-to-bottom "reach" into classrooms on the part of a cross section of CEOs in one Canadian province. Although CEOs appeared to have minimal direct effects upon schools, their work created many of the organizational conditions giving rise to quality education, particularly through its contribution to the improvement of school-level administrator effectiveness.

As this review of a small sample of previous research points out, little evidence has been generated about the impact of the chief education officer on school district effectiveness. Few attempts have been made to examine the perceived or real impact of CEOs' activities on school systems and their outcomes. Nor has much attention been given to situational variables that affect system quality. The study reported in this chapter addressed these neglects by inquiring about the impact of two newly-appointed CEOs on school district effectiveness, especially district culture, and CEO practices associated with such impact. Four questions were asked: What was the culture of the organization prior to the new CEOs' taking office? What was the culture of the organization one year later? What impact did the new CEOs have on districts' cultures as perceived by those who worked there? and What did the CEOs do, if anything, that was considered effective in improving the district and its culture?

FRAMEWORK

Collection of data to use in answering these questions was guided by a framework that included concepts and propositions about the relationship between culture and organizational effectiveness;

226   DONALD MUSELLA

how culture is changed; and forms of leadership that generate such change.

Culture and Organizational Effectiveness

The importance attached to culture by modern organizations is based, in part, on the belief in a strong relationship between organizational culture and organizational performance. But there is little empirical evidence to support this connection, at least evidence in the form of such measurable outcomes as economic performance (Wilkins and Ouchi 1983; Schein 1990; Denison 1990). However, there is support for the belief that understanding culture can assist in greater understanding of organizational behavior; this, in turn, can assist in shaping the beliefs and actions of those who work in or are affected by the organization (Musella and Davis 1991; Buono and Bowditch 1989; Patten 1988; Morgan 1986; Huse and Cummings 1985; Deal and Kennedy 1982).

Although cultures manifest themselves in many forms, cultural norms were the focus of this study. People from a broad range of backgrounds and educational levels can readily understand the meaning of norms and how they are applied in their organization. As Allen (1986) claims: "Since norms are the elements of culture least dependent upon abstraction, most readily recognizable in all aspects of daily lives, and most general in their applications, they provide an excellent vehicle for helping people understand and manage the cultural aspects of organizational life" (p. 334). The definition of norms used in the study is a simple one: Norms encompass all behavior that is expected, accepted, or supported by the group, whether the behavior is stated or unstated. "The norm is the sanctioned behavior, and people are rewarded and encouraged when they follow the norms, and chastised, confronted, and ostracized when they violate them" (Allen, 1986, p. 334).

How Culture Is Created and Changed

According to Schein (1990), culture is created through two means: critical organizational incidents and identification with leaders; through leaders' modeling, group members identify with leaders and internalize their values and assumptions, thus effecting cultural change. Two approaches to cultural change also are identified by Schein, one focusing on *primary embedding mechanisms,* and the other on *secondary articulation and reinforcement mechanisms.* Primary embedding mechanisms include (a) what leaders pay attention to, measure, and control; (b) how leaders react to critical incidents and organizational crises; (c) deliberate role modeling and coaching; (d) operational criteria for the allocation of rewards and status; and (e) operational criteria for recruitment, selection, promotion, retirement, and "excommunication." Secondary mechanisms for cultural change include (a) the organization's design and structure; (b) organizational systems and procedures; (c) the design of physical space, facades, and buildings; (d) stories, legends, myths, and symbols; and (e) formal statements or organizational philosophy, creeds, and charters (p. 115). Another key factor in the reproduction of culture is the socialization of new members. They can be selected on the basis of having the "right" set of assumptions, beliefs, and values. In addition, however, they must also be trained and "acculturated" (Feldmann 1988; Ritti and Funkhouser 1987).

Cultural Change and Transformational Leaders

Organizational culture in general, and shared norms in particular, are crucial determinants of organizational change. Further, as the highest-ranking official in the organization, it seems evident that the CEO will have a significant influence on these determinants of change. There is growing support for the position that the chief education officer in school systems ought to provide the type of leadership necessary to change the culture in ways that lead to greater organizational effectiveness.

Just what type of leadership is this? Increasingly, "transformational leadership" is being proposed as the answer to this question (e.g., Tichy and Ulrich 1984). Practices associated with such leadership include a systematic focus on the leaders' entry process, cultural assessment, creation of a vision, mobilization of commitment and the institutionalization of technical, political, and cultural change. Coleman and LaRocque (1990) explain in the following terms changes in organizational culture resulting from transformational leadership behavior exhibited by superintendents:

> The current research leads us to expect district leadership in high performing districts to involve creating and sustaining a positive

district ethos which indirectly affects principals and through them teachers, students, and parents. This is achieved through "reaching out", which includes both "vision" (norms which shape and guide the activities towards a desired future state) and "range" (the scope and variety of activities and issues to which the superintendent devotes his time and energy). (p. 67)

However, Leithwood, Jantzi, and Fernandez (1994) argue there is still much work to do. "The development of a well-tested theory of transformational leadership in education seems overdue" (p. 27). This study provides additional data intended to help develop such a theory useful to leaders in their efforts to improve the effectiveness of their school systems. It is based on the premise that organizational effectiveness depends on the culture of the organization and changes in such culture will usually depend on action by the leader. To change the culture, one must first assess it, as well as the perceived effectiveness of the school system. This will reveal aspects of the culture and other aspects of the organization in need of change.

METHOD

Two case studies were completed in an effort to determine the nature of the relationship between school system culture and school system effectiveness; and to identify administrative practices useful in changing school system culture and improving its effectiveness. These were case studies of two Ontario CEOs (directors), both of whom were beginning their second year in the position and who were appointed from senior central administration positions in other school systems. In part, this was a study of their effectiveness in bringing about changes in the culture and the perceived effectiveness of their respective school systems.

Each case study involved the collection of responses to a partly closed-ended survey and to an open-ended interview. The population for the survey was all professional and support staff in the school systems. A random sample of 25 percent of this population was asked to complete the survey. Interview data were obtained from 21 and 28 members of staff, respectively, in the two school systems. These interviewees were selected to reflect all categories of staff in each school system. In addition, each CEO was interviewed four times over the course of one year. These interviews, largely open-ended, were designed to uncover the CEOs' views of their plans and activities.

The survey for staff consisted of 48 items asking about perceptions of current norms in the school system and changes in those norms over the previous two years. Eleven open-ended questions were included in the interview, which required about 45 minutes. Descriptive statistics were calculated for survey responses across each case, as a whole. Individual, school, and group scores were not reported separately. A content analysis was performed on interview responses by staff also aggregated to the school system level.

RESULTS

The Survey Responses: Norms

Table 9–1 indicates the achieved sample and response rate in both cases. Based on these responses, this section describes the comparative perceptions of the two school system staffs concerning the norms of their systems.

Norms Changed during the Last Year. There was a significant change in the norms operating in both school systems (case 1 and case 2) as perceived by the respondents to the survey. In almost all

Table 9–1
Summary of Achieved Sample and Response Rate for Survey

Position	Achieved Sample (#)		Response Rate (%)	
	Case 1	Case 2	Case 1	Case 2
Trustee	5	4	28	27
Supervisory officer	5	3	63	75
Principal	23	17	62	81
Vice-principal	14	7	67	70
Consultant	22	5	88	45
Teacher (elementary)	92	31	82	48
Teacher (secondary)	41	22	68	48
Support staff	45	32	61	64

cases there was an *increase* in the number and percentage of responses *agreeing* with the same norm statements over those of one year ago. In both cases 90 percent or more of the respondents agreed that three norms reflected their present situation: In each case the number and percentage of respondents *agreeing* was *greater* than the number and percentage describing the situation one year earlier. The three norms were (a) to continue to seek better ways of doing things, (b) for people to feel that the school board offers good job security, and (c) for people to take pride in their own work. In case 2, the same percentage of respondents also said that it was the norm for people to feel responsible for doing their own jobs right and for people to like the kind of work they are doing. These same respondents also indicated that it was the norm for people to avoid placing blame and concentrate on looking for constructive solutions; for people to have an effective means of communication with peers and supervisors; for people to work together effectively; and for people who work together to meet regularly on important issues.

In both cases, 75 to 90 percent of respondents agreed that eight norms reflected the present situation. In each case, the number and percentage of respondents *agreeing increased* over those reflecting the situation one year earlier. Respondents reported that it was a norm in their board for people to

- Regularly plan their work goals and review progress
- Feel satisfied with their pay
- Feel that their work is important
- Have good feelings of accomplishment from their work
- Help each other with on-the-job or personal problems
- Follow through on activities that they begin
- Care about and strive for excellent performance

It was also considered a norm for leaders to demonstrate their own commitment to what the organization is trying to accomplish. Respondents in each school system also reported high levels of agreement about norms unique to each of their systems. Those norms are listed in table 9–2.

Sixty to 75 percent of respondents in both cases agreed that thirteen norms reflected the present situation. In each case, the

Table 9–2
Norms Unique to Each School Board: High Agreement

Case 1	*Case 2*
To confront negative behavior constructively	For people to feel that the school board offers good job security
To feel satisfied with the programs offered by the school board	For people to feel satisfied with the programs offered by the school board
To have some input on decisions that affect their work	For people to have some input on decisions that affect their work
For leaders to be equally concerned for people as well as results	For leaders to be equally concerned for people as well as results
To review policies and procedures regularly and change them as needed	To review policies and procedures regularly and change them as needed
	For people to have good feelings of accomplishment from their work
	For people to take pride in their own work
	For leaders to make a strong effort to involve and motivate people
	For authority to be delegated appropriately

number and percentage of respondents *agreeing increased* over those reflecting the situation one year earlier. These norms were as follows:

- For new people to be properly oriented and prepared for the job
- For leaders to take time to follow up on the jobs they have assigned to people
- For school board policies and procedures to be helpful,

well understood, and up-to-date

- For people to get feedback on how they are doing so they can develop as individuals
- For people to feel "turned on" and enthusiastic about what they are doing
- For selection and promotion practices to be fair
- To understand the school board's programs
- For a spirit of cooperation and teamwork to be felt throughout the organization
- To point out errors constructively
- To use time and resources effectively
- To give and receive feedback in helpful ways
- For people to share responsibility for what happens in the organization
- For groups to define goals clearly before a task is begun.

Table 9–3 lists norms unique to each school system for which there was above-average agreement.

Fifty to 60 percent in both school districts agreed that three norms were reflective of the present situation. Again, in almost all instances, the number and percentage of respondents *agreeing* *increased* over those reflecting the situation one year earlier. In case 1, these norms were (a) for workloads to be fairly and equitably distributed, (b) to feel really involved in the work of the organization, and (c) for people to feel that the organization keeps them informed on matters that directly affect them. In case 2, the three norms were (a) for people to share responsibility for things that go wrong, (b) for workloads to be fairly and equitably distributed, and (c) to have a clear way of measuring results.

Although there was an increase in agreement about most norms, there was considerable (60–70 percent) disagreement, in case 1, about training needs being adequately met, about having a clear way of measuring results, and about people getting whatever training is needed to help them succeed in their work.

In case 2, four norms were reported to be unchanged in terms of consensus or agreement. These included people confronting negative behavior constructively and people following through on activities that they begin. Also unchanged were the norms of peo-

Table 9–3
Norms Unique to Each School System: Above Average Agreement

Case 1	*Case 2*
For people to confront negative behavior constructively	For people to avoid placing blame and concentrate on looking for constructive solutions
For people to feel satisfied with the programs offered by the school board	For training needs to be adequately met
For people to have some input on decisions that affect their work	For people to have an effective means of communication with peers and supervisors
For leaders to be equally concerned for people as well as results	For people to work together effectively
To review policies and procedures regularly and change them as needed	To feel really involved in the work of the organization
For people to share responsibility for things that go wrong	For people who work together to meet regularly on important issues
For leaders to help their team members succeed	For people to get whatever training is needed to help them succeed in their work
For improvement efforts to be based on facts	For people to feel that the organization keeps them informed on matters that directly affect them
For leaders to make a strong effort to involve and motivate people	
For authority to be delegated appropriately	

ple sharing responsibility for things that go wrong and caring about and striving for excellent performance.

The Survey Responses: Improvements to the System

Three open-ended questions were asked of those responding to the survey: What changes leading to improvement were made during the last year? What factors impeded improvement during the last year? and What changes would you recommend to improve the effectiveness of this school board?

Respondents in case 1 identified the appointment of a new CEO with excellent leadership skills, a clear plan of action, and strong people skills, who has made many positive changes, provides initiatives and support, and has a fresh outlook on education. They also cited an improved leadership selection process and the introduction of a "supervision for growth" form of staff development and supervision. Improved and increased inservice for teachers, more resource persons for schools, and clearly defined areas of authority and levels of communication were also identified.

Case 2 respondents cited changes including a reorganization of administration and more involvement in decision making by trustees and staff. They also pointed to decentralization of authority and school-based management, more fair hiring procedures, the new CEO, and a five-year plan for the board. Also mentioned were greater commitment from all levels of staff and the addition of resource persons. Greater clarification of responsibilities and improved communication were also noted.

In case 1, responses to the question about factors impeding improvement were similar to the recommendations for change offered to the final question asked on the survey. In sum, most frequently they included inadequate resources and the continued fast pace of growth. Funds were needed for buildings and related facilities, for staffing and professional development for some new and existing programs, for necessary new initiatives, to reduce overcrowding, and to reduce pressure caused by trying to meet student, parent, and teacher needs with limited human resources. With respect to the pace of change, cited were changes in personnel, communication delays, some peoples' attitudes of resistance to change, increased demands in face of limited time and resources, perceived loss of community, large classes, continual need for inservice, portables, increased stress, lack of adequate time for planning and implementation, insufficient personnel, and sheer volume of issues and needs that require efforts leading toward resolution.

Respondents in case 1 recommended that there be improved teamwork and an examination of goals, directions, and philosophy for the coming years. The board, it was believed, should be more proactive in dealing with change; the time is right for putting it together. Case 1 respondents also felt the need for more supportive behavior that acknowledged the value of an individual's work. More funds for school programs, new classrooms, and more support staff would be helpful, as would a better sense of community, increased trust, and better relationships. These people also wished for increased involvement in decisions and improved communication between board/central office and schools and between departments.

In case 2, impediments to change were perceived to be individuals' resistance and too many changes introduced too quickly. Lack of funds, inadequate facilities and lack of communication were also cited. These respondents recommended that change continue, but at a slower pace. More and better inservice programs and improved communication would also help.

Interview Responses: Both Cases

Although the instruction to the interviewees was to respond to the situation in their school system as it presently exists, it became clear that a much different response would have been given if one were considering a period of time prior to the term of the present CEOs. Although high satisfaction with the previous CEOs was often expressed (particularly in one of the cases), the present situation was described as much improved and more positive in all respects. Many respondents reasoned that present conditions in their school system warranted a different type of leadership. The basic message was a positive one and the recommendations can be interpreted as a call for even more change.

Responses to interview questions suggest very positive attitudes toward the school systems. In both cases the words used by respondents conveyed the sense that they felt their efforts were appreciated and supported and that the systems provided changing and challenging environments in which to work. Respondents identified competence and commitment, rather than politics and connections, as the keys to getting ahead in their systems. Respondents identified a focus on student service as among the major successes. Case 1 respondents noted, as well, good working conditions and interpersonal relations; case 2 respondents pointed at reductions in student dropout as well as successes with school-based management and special education initiatives. Respondents in case 2 could not think of any system "failures"; case 1 respondents clearly felt a bit overwhelmed by the speed and challenges of change.

Facilities, maintenance, and construction were common perceived priorities across the two cases. The two new directors were considered the source of a major proportion of the changes introduced into the system in both cases. These changes, in sum, pushed the two systems toward more participatory forms of decision making, more facilitative and inclusive styles of leadership, as well as better management practices. The consequences of these changes were perceived to include better staff morale, improved educational services, and a better working environment for staffs in both cases. These changes, however, were considered by some respondents to be too much too fast, increasing workloads beyond what could be coped with. Nevertheless, the bulk of respondents clearly believed that the change was worthwhile and that its momentum should continue.

CEOs' Descriptions of Their Own Plans and Activities

The CEOs in the study had developed and implemented similar entry plans upon their appointment. The plans included interviews, held prior to the beginning of their appointment, with a sample of persons at various levels in the organization. For positions—such as school board members, supervisory officers (e.g., assistant superintendents), principals, supervisors, and federation and union leaders, all persons were interviewed. For other positions (teachers, consultants, support staff of various categories, parents, students) a sample was selected. Two major questions were asked of all interviewees: What would you like to change in the system to improve it, and What would you not want to see changed? Follow-up questions were individualized according to responses.

One CEO summarized the basic needs of the system identified by various groups as follows:

- Communication patterns that are open
- Participative decision making
- Greater involvement of principals/vice-principals associations in decision making
- Greater involvement of teachers' federation in decision making

- A process for capital projects construction
- Policy development in the human resources area
- A higher profile for the fine arts
- Policy development in areas of principal selection

This was followed by the development of objectives for implementing these changes. In the first year, these objectives included the creation of a climate of change and excitement, the establishment of structures to assist change, and the articulation of a vision. Objectives for the second year included translating the vision into practice, emphasizing staff development, and creating ownership of the intended changes. In his third year, this CEO intended to evaluate individual schools and the system as a whole.

This set of three-year objectives was followed with the implementation of specific sets of activities that the CEO believed would help in their achievement. One set of activities derived from this CEO's having identified the improvement of leadership as a priority. In response to this, he began to institute a better system of selection and promotion for positions of responsibility and increased liaison with the principals' association. He also expanded his executive council, provided information on the growing need for better education of the 5 to10-year-olds in the system, instituted affirmative action policy and plans, and initiated plans for dealing with the fact that a large number of staff were near retirement. Another of this CEO's priorities was creating expectation for change. To do this, he began to approach principals/vice-principals associations to encourage applications for transfer. Appropriate transfers of principals and vice-principals were made; all such transfers were discussed with trustees prior to announcement. This CEO also initiated the establishment of a three-year staffing projection. Communication was a third priority, pursued through the following initiatives:

- Institute a director's meeting for all principals and vice-principals (focus on leadership, learner, servant leaders, trust)
- Liaison with principal's association (focus on development, finance, inspirational speakers, live-in retreat)
- Meet with teachers' federation

- Focus on leadership and trust, solicit input regarding the new selection and promotion process, explain the selections
- Seek advice (focus on policy matters, hiring panels, bus policies, budget process)
- Visit the cluster meetings of teachers and principals (a vehicle for open forum and small-group discussions)
- Meet with trustees, individually and as a group
- Ensure that all reports have staff recommendations
- Meet with consultants/coordinators
- Focus on the importance of the role and vision of the learner

The CEO in case 2 , using a similar process, summarized as follows his actions to change the system:

- Interviews held with key stakeholders (staff, principals, federation representatives, parents, students)
- Discussion held with community leaders concerning educational needs and processes
- Board discussions held (as a group and individually) on a variety of issues
- All matters formulated into a long-range plan were discussed thoroughly with the superintendents through the administrative council
- A major directional paper was presented to the full board in December of year 1, and a discussion of recommendations took place at a retreat of trustees and administrators in February of year 1. Trustees had two months to think about the plan and discuss it informally before the retreat
- Final board-approved recommendations were distributed to appropriate committees for action in March of year 1
- Priorities were established mutually with school administrators in May of year 1. School plans were designed in conjunction with these systemwide priorities for operation in September of year 2
- Action on most recommendations was begun during the fall of year 2

- A second retreat was held in November of year 2 for trustees and senior administrators to review the procedures and actions to date.

"In addition," said this CEO, "there have been a multitude of meetings with principals, staffs, individuals at every level of the system. Proper communication is necessary to the implementation of change; most impediments we experienced were caused by lack of understanding of intent and results."

Underlying the actions of both CEOs was a similar, explicit model for how they would contribute to the improvement of their school systems. The model can be conceptualized as consisting of six phases:

1. *Development of a preentry plan.* This plan called for learning about the history, culture, and expectations of the school system from those in positions to know. The two CEOs carried out this phase in a similar manner.

2. *Entry.* During the early stages of being on the job, each CEO continued to build his understanding of the new situation and to set priorities. Expectations were developed with key persons, and the basis for effective working relationships was established. During entry, each CEO faced the dilemma of judging how quickly to act on problems. Acting too quickly, they acknowledged, increased the risks of making a poor decision because of lack of adequate knowledge or of taking actions that constrain subsequent decisions that cannot be anticipated. They also acknowledged that acting too slowly risked losing advantage of the "honeymoon" period, losing credibility because of apparent indecisiveness, and losing valuable time.

3. *Immersion.* Following the early entry stages, each CEO worked to develop a deeper understanding of his situation and the people in his system. This involved assessing consequences of actions that they anticipated taking and reassessing initial priorities. Questions and problems concerning key persons were resolved, and their initial understanding of their organizations were refined.

4. *Reshaping.* At this stage, both CEOs implemented refinements to the design of their systems. They also tried to

address underlying causes of residual problems but remained open to unanticipated problems that emerged as a result of a second-wave change.

5. *Consolidation.* At this stage, the CEOs concentrated on follow-through to firmly embed changes they had made in the design of their systems.

6. *Refinement.* The CEOs anticipated they would need to make continuous refinements in their school systems following their initial changes. Some of these were likely to be, in their view, responses to new "opportunities" likely to arise.

CONCLUSION

Evidence from the two cases suggests a strong relationship between staff perceptions of changes in organizational culture and perceptions of increased effectiveness. Furthermore, the means used by the two CEOs bear strong resemblance to proposals offered by others, several of which are examined by way of conclusion.

Both CEOs went about their mission paying close attention to the sets of questions identified by Allen (1986) as crucial for culture change:

1. *Rewards.* What behaviors are supported? Rewarded? What behaviors lead to confrontation and formal or informal penalties?

2. *Modeling Behavior.* Which people have the greatest influence, and what type of behavior do they model for the organization? Are others expected to model this behavior, or is the philosophy projected, "Do as we say, not as we do"?

3. *Information and Communication Systems.* What information is being communicated? Do mixed messages sometimes cause confusion? Is it the norm for people at all levels to seek out the ideas and opinions of others?

4. *Interactions and Relationships.* In what ways do present interactions and relationships influence the culture? What opportunities exist for improving these interactions and

relationships? Do organizational units and teams work effectively together?

5. *Management and Supervisory Skills.* Do managers and supervisors have the skills necessary for effective leadership? How can they be helped to develop these skills if they do not have them?

6. *Organizational Structures, Policies, and Procedures.* Is the organization structured in a way that helps it achieve its objectives? Are there ways that the organizational structures, policies, and procedures can be modified to help them contribute more to the achievement of the cultural goals?

7. *Training.* Are training opportunities sufficient to support the desired culture? Are skills developed in the training process, supported in the day-to-day life of the organization?

8. *Orientation.* Are the right things being communicated during the orientation process? Do the people responsible for the orientation process exhibit positive behavioral norms, attitudes, and work habits?

9. *Allocation of Resources.* On what are money, time, and resources spent? Are expenditures in line with the cultural goal? (pp. 341, 343)

The practices of these CEOs also appeared consistent with the method of cultural change identified by Schein (1990). Among other things, the CEOs encouraged their organizations to believe that change was possible and desirable. They also articulated new directions and new sets of assumptions, thus providing a clear and new role model. Key positions were filled with new incumbents who held these new assumptions; and people were systematically rewarded for the adoption of new directions. Organizational members were persuaded to adopt new behaviors that were more consistent with the new assumptions. The two CEOs *shaped* the organizational culture in much the same way as Firestone and Wilson (1984) and Smircich and Morgan 1982) propose, that is, by first identifying what cultural content is preferred, by assessing the existing culture with respect to content, symbols, and communication patterns prior to moving to change the culture, and by exercising the leadership appropriate for the *context in action*. The findings of this study are also congruent with claims by Tichy and Ulrich (1984) that "the successful leaders . . . articulate new values or goals to meet changed environments" (p. 78), and by Bennis and Nanus (1985) that "leaders set the moral tone by choosing carefully the people with whom they surround themselves, by communicating a sense of purpose for the organization, by reinforcing appropriate behavior and by articulating these moral positions to external and internal constituencies" (p. 186). Evidence from this study, however, calls into question Hoyle's (1989) variety of well-known skills—human, technical, and conceptual—for the twenty-first-century superintendent. In an extensive description of these skills, he neglected to identify the skills associated with the processes undertaken by these two CEOs to change their organizations' cultures and improve their organizations' effectiveness. He also failed to identify transformational leadership practices as powerful for these tasks.

As Bolman and Deal (1991) assert, in *reframing* the organization, leadership is the art of good judgment, the art of choosing the right *frame* to fit a particular organizational situation. Such reframing is integral to the process of changing organizational culture. Using Bolman and Deal's terms, the CEOs included in this study sought to keep the organization headed in the right direction (structure), kept people involved and communication open (people), provided opportunities for individuals and groups to make their interest known (politics), and developed symbols and shared values (symbolic). These CEOs were transformational leaders: They deliberately set out to change the culture as a means for improving organizational effectiveness and were perceived to be successful in doing so.

REFERENCES

Allen, R. F. (1986). Four phases for bringing about cultural change. In R. H. Kilmann, M. J. Saxton, & R. Serpa & Associates (Eds.), *Gaining control of the corporate culture* (pp. 332–50). San Francisco: Jossey-Bass.

Barr, R., & Dreeben, R. (1983). *How schools work*. Chicago: University of Chicago Press.

Bennis, W., & Nanus, B. (1985). *Leaders: The strategies for taking charge.* New York: Harper & Row.

Bolman, L. G., & Deal, T. E. (1991). *Reframing organizations.* San Francisco: Jossey-Bass.

Buono, A. F., & Bowditch, J. L. (1989). *The human side of mergers and acquisitions.* San Francisco: Jossey-Bass.

Callahan, R. E. (1962). *Education and the cult of efficiency.* Chicago: University of Chicago Press.

Coleman, P., & LaRocque, L. (1990). Reaching out: Instructional leadership in school districts. *Peabody Journal of Education, 65(4),* 60–89.

Corwin, R. G., & Borman, K. M. (1988). School as workplace: Structural constraints on administration. In N. J. Boyan (Ed.), *Handbook of research on educational administration* (pp. 209–37). New York: Longman.

Cronin, J. M. (1973). *The control of urban schools.* New York: Free Press.

Crowson, R. (1990) The local school district superintendency, under reform. *Peabody Journal of Education, 65*(4), 1–8.

Deal, T. E., & Kennedy, A. A. (1982). *Corporate cultures.* Reading, MA: Addison-Wesley.

Denison, D. R. (1990). *Corporate culture and organizational effectiveness.* Toronto: Wiley.

Feldman, D. C. (1988). *Managing careers in organizations.* Glenview, IL: Scott, Foresman.

Firestone, W. A., & Herriott, R. E. (1982). Two images of schools as organizations: An explication and illustrative empirical test. *Educational Administration Quarterly, 18*(2), 39–59.

Firestone, W. A., & Wilson, B. L. (1984). What can principals do? Culture of a school is a key to more effective instruction. *NASSP Bulletin, 68(476),* 7–11.

Hoyle, J. (1989). Preparing the 21st-century superintendent. *Phi Delta Kappan,* (January), 376–79.

Huse, E. F., & Cummings, T. G. (1985). *Organizational development and change* (3d ed.). St. Paul: West.

Leithwood, K., Jantzi, D., & Fernandez, A. (1994). Teachers' commitment to change: The contributions of transformational leadership. In J. Murphy & K. Louis (Eds.), *Reshaping the principalship: Insights from transformational reform efforts.* Newbury Park, CA: Corwin.

March, J. G., & Olsen, J. P. (1976). *Ambiguity and choice in organizations.* Bergen, Norway: Universitetsforlaget.

Morgan, G. (1986). *Images of organizations.* Beverly Hills: Sage.

Murphy, J. T. (1989). The paradox of decentralizing schools: Lessons from business, government, and the Catholic Church. *Phi Delta Kappan, 70*(10), 808–12.

Murphy, J. T., & Hallinger, P. (1986). The superintendent as instructional leader: Findings from effective school districts. *Journal of Educational Administration, 24*(2), 213–36.

Musella, D., & Davis, J. (1991). Assessing organizational culture: Implications for leaders or organizational change. In K. Leithwood and D. Musella (Eds.), *Understanding school system administration* (pp. 287–305). London: Falmer Press.

Musella, D., & Leithwood, K. (1990). The influence of chief education officers on school effectiveness. *Peabody Journal of Education, 65*(4), 90–112.

Patten, T. H., Jr. (1988). Organizational development: The evolution to "excellence" and corporate culture. In J. Pfeiffer (Ed.), *The 1988 annual: Developing human resources* (pp. 189–200). San Diego, CA: University Associates Ltd.

Pfeffer, J. (1984). The ambiguity of leadership. In W. E. Rosenbach & R. L. Taylor (Eds.), *Contemporary issues in leadership* (pp. 4–17). Boulder: Westview Press.

Ritti, R. R., & Funkhouser, G. R. (1987). *The ropes to skip and the ropes to know* (3d ed.). New York: Wiley.

Rogers, D. (1969). *110 Livingston Street.* New York: Vintage.

Salley, C. (1980). Superintendents' job priorities. *Administrator's Notebook, 28*(1), 1–4.

Schein, E. H. (1990). Organizational culture. *American Psychologist, 45*(2), 109–19.

Smircich, L., & Morgan, G. (1982). Leadership: The management of meaning. *Journal of Applied Behavioral Science, 18*(3), 257–73.

Tichy, N. M., & Ulrich, D. (1984). SMR Forum: The leadership challenge—a call for the transformational leader. *Sloan Management Review,* (Fall), 59–67.

Weick, K. E. (1976, March). Educational organizations as loosely-coupled systems. *Administrative Science Quarterly, 21*, 1–16.

Wilkins, A. L., & Ouchi, W. G. (1983). Efficient cultures: Exploring the relationship between culture and organizational performance. *Administrative Science Quarterly, 28*, 468–81.

Wolf, E. L. (1987). *A comparison of superintendents' perceptions of their role with an exemplary model of the superintendency.* Unpublished doctoral dissertation, University of Washington, Seattle.

CHAPTER 10

Educated Dissent: Implications of Policy Disagreement for Educational Leadership

Mark Holmes

CONTEXT AND PURPOSE

Education in the Western world is in crisis. If critics can agree on little else, that at least is common ground. Unfortunately, such agreement does not take us very far, for what is lacking is agreement on the particularities, the causes and the cures of the malady.

Two earlier phases of the research described here found that Ontario's chief education officers (CEOs) had opinions about educational policy matters that were distinctly different from those of their similarly educated peers not employed in education (Holmes 1991b, 1991c). The differences were either based on or reflected in differing educational philosophies, the most obvious difference being the CEOs' enthusiasm for progressivism, with which the comparison group was distinctly disenchanted. This fundamental difference was made further evident in views on testing and on secondary education policy. Likely, the CEOs' denial that there was a problem with the discipline of secondary students (in terms of unwillingness to work and unacceptable behavior) was not unrelated. Alternatively, one could hypothesize that the CEOs, defenders of the status quo, are among those who do not agree that education is in crisis. Probably both explanations have some validity. CEOs do believe their critics are misguided and they do believe that their progressive policies are beneficial.

One important point on which there was considerable agreement within both samples was unhelpful. Most agreed there
should be only one school system with one program, but they
sharply disagreed about what that program should be. Beneath
the superficial agreement, there seemed to be willingness to except
their own favorite causes, such as Roman Catholic education or
French immersion. Support for Roman Catholic education by no
means always (or usually) extended to support for Jewish or Protestant education, just as support for French immersion does not
imply support for education to support a minority culture.

I concluded that the current classic model of educational delivery, adopted by Ontario, no longer suits the pluralist and dissenting nature of the province. The problem is symbolized by the status of the CEO. CEOs are expected to have a strong educational
philosophy (and many do); they are expected to act with integrity;
they are expected to be sensitive to the interests of minorities; and
they are expected to deliver equal opportunities to all, so that all
may have an equivalent chance to gain the better things of life,
whether these be more education or a good job or something less
material. Clearly, when the larger society is riven by dissent and
pluralism, there are some incompatibilities among those high-
sounding sentiments.

Suppose one CEO believes Seventh Day Adventists should be
permitted their own religious education (which is not permitted in
Ontario), while another believes Roman Catholics should not be
(its offering is mandated in Ontario); yet another believes girls and
boys should be given identical education; another believes all young
people should have a common program in elementary school; one
believes that children should choose their own programs; and so
on. As dissent grows, the number of people who can take on the
role of CEO declines; either the CEO has elastic ideals, or the ideals
are those that fit the politically correct model of the time.

The conclusion was that the large school board, which typically contains as much dissent within its boundaries as there is
between its clientele and another board's, can no longer function
as a buffer between central prescriptions and local needs, because
that traditional role (in North America) for the school board
implies consensual agreement at the local (community) level.
Rather than tempering a high-level consensus, the large school
board is increasingly forced to provide a lowest common denom-
inator of schooling in an attempt to minimize offense.

Here I examine the policy opinions of other demographic groups among the educated and consider the implications for educational leadership and provision. Both the CEOs and the comparison group were of a kind (deliberately so). They were middle aged and middle class—and mostly male. The CEOs, it turned out, were even more conspicuous in their normalities and their abnormalities. Public CEOs were preeminently affiliated with the United Church, the middle of the Canadian middle religious ground—and Canadians are not renowned for their radicalism. They also strongly opposed capital punishment, unlike most of the rest of the population. As already pointed out, educationally they were progressive (in the philosophical, Deweyan sense of the word). Even some of those who were most evidently not progressive, it was discovered, were by their own account overseeing the imposition of progressive dogma in their schools (Holmes 1991b).

To what extent do CEOs simply reflect the teaching force? Does the comparison group reflect educated Canadians generally? An initial hypothesis was that CEOs would be close to the center of public (or educator) opinion, because it would be intolerable for a school system to have a person, particularly one of high integrity, who strongly dissented from the central norms. Imagine an Orthodox Jew or a Jehovah's Witness or a fundamentalist Muslim overseeing a contemporary, secular program teaching the advantages of the condom and the relative convenience of abortion. (There was no one remotely like those examples among the ranks of the sampled CEOs, although a Jew, presumably not Orthodox, has been appointed since the research was completed). Do principals reflect a halfway position between teachers and CEOs, with slightly more tolerance of diversity being permitted? Do teachers lie between CEOs and the public in terms of educational philosophy and public policy, or are CEOs forced to compromise more with the public? Does the comparison group reflect the major professions (and the intelligentsia), or are there differences among the professions with respect to educational matters? These are the questions addressed in this piece of research.

Beneath these questions lie some fundamental issues. Members of a dissenting, pluralist society do not necessarily like their societal reflection. While they might take pride in their society's tolerance and its multicultural aspect, they might, at the same time, not necessarily consistently, yearn for some greater central meaning, demanding commitment and loyalty. On the one hand, they may want the schools to welcome all children, irrespective of their social status and their cultural background. On the other hand, they want their society to be supportive of cultural difference. They want all children to have the same chances, but they do not want to impose a single regimen, curriculum, and structure. They want all children to succeed, but they want to measure success by access to limited opportunities for professional and corporate careers (and they want to be free to help their own children in a special way). They want to be respectful of religious differences, but they do not want them to be reinforced in such a way that some children, and their future, may be differentiated from others. If such competing, sometimes incompatible goals do reflect current reality in pluralist democracies, it is small wonder that schools are wracked with dissent—and retreat to a bare minimum of tolerance, consideration of the other person, and nonviolence, a doctrine that is thin emotivist gruel rather than the clarion call for action desired by so many. My purpose here is to explore these complex issues further by inquiring into the educational opinions of samples of educators, engineers, and nurses in order to put dissent within a broader perspective. Until the breadth and depth of dissent is understood, it is impossible to plan sensibly for the kind of choice and the kind of senior administrative leadership we shall need to serve a multicultural, multiethnic and multifaith society. Although this research is limited by the specificity (in legal, historical, and ethnic terms) of Ontario, I believe that the fundamental issues faced in Ontario are reflective of the democratic English-speaking world.

METHODOLOGY

The two previous samples (of CEOs and a comparison group) were taken in the early summer of 1988. The comparison group consisted of graduates of the University of Toronto of about the same age as the CEOs. Two questionnaires were developed for this third phase, based principally on those used in the first phase of the research. Nurses and engineers were selected because they were considered to be most similar in professional status to teachers and because, like elementary and secondary teachers, they have been traditionally segmented by sex. Samples, all graduates of the University of Toronto, were selected to produce a comparable cross section by age among the three samples. Four hundred and fifty questionnaires were mailed to each group (nurses and engineers), with return rates of 48 percent and 42 percent, respectively. Eight hundred and eighty-nine questionnaires were mailed to the education sample (including both bachelor and master's degree recipients), with a 39 percent return rate. The larger sample was used for educators so that scores for subgroup samples could be reported.

The usual cautions with respect to mailed questionnaires apply. Although the return rate was quite good (a 30 percent return is probably a useful minimum to work with), one cannot generalize to different universities and different faculties. Making comparisons among different samples must be treated with great care. In particular, it is arguable that the views of CEOs and the comparison group may have changed in the intervening thirty months. This is undoubtedly the case with voting intentions, which are notoriously fickle. (They are not reported here, as the complications in their interpretation outweigh any value for the research). It is assumed that most other opinions, about educational policy and philosophy, are more stable.

No tests of statistical significance have been applied to the data. With *Ns* above 70, a difference in means of about 15 percent would be statistically significant at the 0.05 level. Furthermore, differences in the 15 to 20 percent range do appear to be substantively important. Only differences greater than 15 percent are noted. Particular care should be used in interpreting the small samples—public CEOs, separate CEOs, separate teachers and principals, and principals, only the last of which, with an *N* of 60, is important to the study's conclusions. The CEOs are not a statistical sample in any sense of the word; they are simply all members of the population who responded. Statistical tests could be defended for the remaining samples, but in general the magnitude of difference is considered to be a better guide than statistical significance in the policy area. Some of the more interesting differences run well over 25 percent.

THE OPINIONS OF EDUCATORS

Tables 10–1 through 10–5 summarize the responses of different subgroups of educators to the questions found to be of greatest importance in the first phase of the study, together with responses to some new questions designed to complete gaps identified in the analysis of the earlier questionnaires. The complete questionnaires with overall response rates are obtainable from the Department of Educational Administration at OISE.[1]

Five important conclusions may be drawn from table 10–1. In the public system, a lower proportion of teachers (including principals) (56.7 percent) belongs to mainstream Protestant denominations than is the case with CEOs (80.9 percent). This finding is consistent with the hypothesis that teachers are more reflective of the general population than are CEOs. In the previously published research, it appeared that CEOs were centrist in their opinions—not so much that they reflected the center of public opinion (they did not), but that there was much less variance among them.

Male educators (80.3 percent) are more likely to be married to their first spouse than are female educators (53.8 percent). The sample of educators is based on all returned questionnaires and therefore includes all qualified educators, irrespective of their current employment status. A possible explanation is that, although many educators marry other educators, active professional women are more likely than active professional men to postpone or not entertain marriage. Consistently, male educators (34.7 percent) are more likely than female educators (13 percent) to have more than two children. CEOs (69.7 percent) are even more likely to have three or more children. The latter finding may be partly a function of age, but CEOs are also more fecund than the comparison group (46.3 percent). Once again, there would appear to be less variance among CEOs.

In table 10–2, there is further support for the hypothesis that CEOs are more progressive—that is, more Deweyan and child centered (but not more left-wing)—than are their similarly educated peers and also that they are more defensive of the educational status quo associated with their organizations. Thus the earlier research showed that CEOs are not at all left-wing; they had no sympathy for an egalitarian philosophy of education and gave virtually no support to the NDP (socialist) federal and provincial parties. They were, however, far more supportive of progressive policies in education than was the comparison group. Educators (53.0 percent) and principals (55.2 percent) favor capital punishment more than do CEOs (31.9 percent). Over many years, consistent majorities of the Canadian public have favored capital punishment in public opinion polls. Thus, CEOs are distin-

Table 10-1
Educator Samples: Personal Characteristics

	N	Sex Male	RC	Prot	None	Other	First	Children (>2)
CEOs	73	98.6	43.8	52.1	4.1	0.0	78.1	69.7
CEOs Pub	47	97.9	12.8	80.9	6.4	0.0	74.5	70.2
CEOs Sep	26	100.0	100.0	0.0	0.0	0.0	84.6	69.2
Princ	60	93.3	18.6	66.2	5.1	10.9	89.8	37.0
Teach+P	231	60.2	29.5	46.3	10.1	14.1	74.2	24.5
Teach Pub	184	66.9	13.3	56.7	12.8	17.2	73.8	21.8
Teach Sep	47	34.0	91.5	2.1	0.0	6.4	76.1	34.9
Teach El	76	30.3	37.8	35.1	6.8	20.3	69.3	12.5
Teach Sec	95	63.2	29.8	40.5	16.0	10.7	68.4	48.5
Educs	345	61.7	25.4	48.0	9.6	17.0	70.1	53.4
Educs M	213	100.0	21.0	53.3	9.0	16.7	80.3	34.7
Educs F	132	0.0	32.6	39.5	10.6	17.3	53.8	13.0

Samples:
CEOs: Chief Education Officers (directors)
CEOs Pub: CEOs in public boards of education
CEOs Sep: CEOs in Roman Catholic separate boards of education
Princ: Principals
Teach+P: Teachers and principals (excluding senior administrators)
Teach Pub: Teachers and principals in public schools
Teach El: Teachers in elementary schools
Teach Sec: Teachers in secondary schools
Educs: Educators (the entire sample, based on educational qualifications)
Educs M: Male educators
Educs F: Female educators

Columns:
N: Number in sample (the precise N varies slightly from question to question)
Sex Male: Percentage of sample male
RC: Percentage of sample stating religion to be Roman Catholic
Prot: Percentage of sample stating religion to be United, Anglican, or Presbyterian (interpreted as mainstream Protestant)
None: Percentage of sample describing themselves as atheist, agnostic, or skeptic
Other: All others (with Baptists, fundamentalist Christians and Jews forming the largest constituents)
Married First: Percentage married to first spouse
Children>2: Percentage with more than two children

Table 10–2
Educator Samples: Public Policy Issues
(in percentages)

| | CapPun | Abort | Spending Priorities | | | |
			El/sec.	Health	Def.	Less Tax
CEOs	31.9	—	48.6	21.4	8.6	5.7
CEOs Pub	42.9	—	43.2	22.7	13.6	4.5
CEOs Sep	16.0	—	57.7	19.2	0.0	7.7
Princ	55.2	71.9	23.3	30.0	23.3	6.7
Teach+P	52.7	63.8	22.5	34.6	15.4	6.6
Teach Pub	54.4	73.3	22.5	33.4	15.4	6.6
Teach Sep	45.7	25.0	41.3	41.3	13.0	8.7
Teach El	45.3	60.0	25.3	32.0	10.7	9.3
Teach Sec	57.0	62.0	18.3	39.8	5.4	12.9
Educs	53.0	67.3	21.2	30.8	17.4	7.6
Educs M	56.1	68.3	22.5	29.6	19.2	7.0
Educs F	48.1	65.7	19.1	32.8	14.5	8.4

Samples: See table 10–1
Columns:
Cap Pun: Favor capital punishment
Abort: Favor liberal policies on abortion
Spending priorities: First priority for additional provincial spending—
　elementary secondary education; health; reduction of deficit; tax reduction

guished in this respect from their educational counterparts as well as from the general public.

Educators (21.2 percent) and principals (23.3 percent) give spending on elementary/secondary education a lower priority than do CEOs (48.6 percent). One explanation is that the time interval between the administration of the two questionnaires has allowed for greater public awareness of the importance of budgetary deficits. However, that is not supported by the responses of engineers in table10–6, which are similar to those of the (largely male) comparison group two years earlier. It seems at least possible that CEOs are exceptional in their attachment to the need for additional funding for Ontario's school systems. It is not unusual, for example, for teachers to be critical of the level of spending by school boards outside the school, a level that increased greatly during the 1980s.

The different response between separate school teachers and principals (41.3 percent giving priority to elementary/secondary spending) and public teachers and principals (22.5 percent) is possibly explained by the difference in levels of funding of the two systems at the time of the questionnaire.

The major focus of the research has been on educational philosophies. The same six philosophical statements were used as in the earlier research, and respondents were asked to rank-order the philosophies down as far as the last one with which they felt some sympathy. Typically, three, four, or five were ranked. Important differences about means of attaining ends can sometimes be successfully compromised. But if differences about means overlie substantial differences concerning the purposes of education, then the divisions are less likely to be readily bridged.

The six philosophies and their accompanying descriptive statements are these (the labels in square brackets were not included in the questionnaires):

1. *The child at the center.* The prime purpose of education is to allow children to grow healthily, to express themselves as individuals, to be tolerant of others, and to feel at one with themselves. The school should be seen as providing the field of opportunity rather than imposing a prescribed set of outcomes. [This is referred to as "the progressive philosophy."]

2. *Success in future life.* The prime purpose of education is to prepare children for their future lives as citizens and workers. The school's responsibility is to provide them all with the basic skills, habits, and attitudes required for future success and good citizenship in Canada. [This is referred to as "the technocratic philosophy."]

3. *Intellectual and cultural development.* The prime purpose of education is to cultivate the intellect, together with the aesthetic and social senses. The school's responsibility is to develop children's ability to think clearly, to express themselves and to appreciate our culture and environment.

[This philosophy is referred to as "the cultural philosophy."]

4. *Development of good character and personal responsibility.* The prime purpose of education is to help children grow into good adults who will help the development of our society and culture through their work and through their family and community activities. The purpose of the school is to provide instruction in the skills, disciplines, and other attributes of our culture, within a clear moral framework. [This philosophy is referred to as "the traditional philosophy."]

5. *The development of individual freedom.* The prime purpose of education is to educate every individual child to the limits of his or her abilities and interests, within a framework of parental wishes. The purpose of the school is to challenge every child with the possibility of excellence and to encourage reasonable competition, particularly in the academic and vocational fields. [This philosophy is referred to as "the individualist philosophy."]

6. *The search for social equality.* The prime purpose of education is the development of a better society characterized by much-reduced social and economic division. The purpose of the school is to promote the harmonious development of children, without regard for social background, ability, gender, and race, so they may learn to participate in an equal and cooperative manner. [This philosophy is referred to as "the egalitarian philosophy."]

The earlier research found that the CEOs ranked the progressive philosophy first. The comparison group ranked this philosophy fifth out of six but, like the CEOs, this group ranked the egalitarian philosophy sixth. The combined first-and second-ranked choices of philosophy are shown in table 10–3.

Secondary teachers rank the progressive philosophy (37.6 percent rank it first or second) lower than do elementary teachers (58.0 percent) and CEOs (57.2 percent). This sharp differentiation in philosophy suggests that the gap between educational leaders and the public is also reflected internally within the profession. The current Ontario attempt to introduce an ideologically loaded form of "destreaming" into grade 9 and the strong encouragement

Table 10–3
Educator Samples: Educational Philosophies (ranked first or second) and
Testing (in percentages)

	Prog	Tech	Cult	Trad	Ind	Egal	Ach T
CEOs	57.2	26.6	39.2	29.2	33.6	4.2	11.4
CEOs Pub	47.8	28.2	52.2	26.1	43.5	2.2	15.9
CEOs Sep	74.0	23.5	15.8	62.8	15.8	8.0	3.8
Princ	46.0	44.6	46.1	37.6	18.9	6.8	15.3
Teach+P	45.4	39.5	50.0	39.2	18.8	8.0	24.6
Teach Pub	45.2	38.4	43.5	39.0	18.9	7.9	24.9
Teach Sep	50.0	43.5	50.0	45.7	6.5	15.2	23.4
Teach El	58.0	31.6	39.5	40.8	12.4	11.2	17.1
Teach Sec	37.6	42.0	52.0	40.9	17.7	10.0	36.6
Educs	42.7	42.4	47.8	38.2	16.1	10.5	25.3
Educs M	33.5	41.8	51.0	42.2	18.0	11.2	23.7
Educs F	57.4	43.4	42.6	31.8	13.2	9.3	27.8

Samples: See table 10–1
Columns:
Prog: Progressive
Tech: Technocratic
Cult: Cultural
Trad: Traditional
Ind: Individualist
Egal: Egalitarian
Ach T: Favor annual external testing of basic skills

of collaborative learning methodologies in all the high school grades can be seen as an attempt by educational leaders to extend their progressive influence from the elementary to the secondary grades. ("Destreaming" in Ontario is being interpreted as a mechanism to change teachers' instructional methodologies from their traditionally teacher- and subject-centered approaches).

Educators (42.4 percent) and principals (44.6 percent) are more technocratic than are CEOs (26.6 percent). The progressive and the technocratic philosophies appear to be the main battleground for ascendancy in Ontario. There is also strong support for the cultural and traditional philosophies. It can be argued that the current economic difficulties favor technocratic ideas and that the CEOs see the larger picture, less local and time oriented. Against that, it should be noted that CEOs and elementary teachers are the only groups (among educators and noneducators) to rank the progressive philosophy notably ahead of all the others (see tables 10–3 and 10–7).

Two possibly important details are that public CEOs favor the individualist philosophy (43.5 percent) notably more than do separate teachers and principals (6.5 percent) and separate CEOs (15.8 percent). The small sample sizes call for careful interpretation, but it is interesting to speculate that secular educators are attracted more to the individualism inherent in progressivism (to Rousseau's ideal of the natural child pursuing her or his own interests in the pursuit of self-realization) while Roman Catholic educators are more attracted to the friendly, caring, detailed structure inherent in Rousseau's ideal. Both are strongly progressive, the Catholic even more so than the public CEOs. The Catholics combine their progressivism (74%) (inconsistently?) with traditionalism (62.8%) ranking one of them first or second. The public CEOs combine their progressivism (more consistently?) with individualism (91.3 percent rank one of them first or second).

Educators and the two professional samples of noneducators were given five choices with respect to school choice within the publicly funded system. Table10–4 shows that, overall, a single common school serving the neighborhood was most favored, accompanied by the opinion that separate (Roman Catholic) schools should not have received public funding. (In Ontario, Roman Catholic elementary schools have been funded since Confederation in 1867. In 1985, a decision supported by all three political parties extended full public funding to the end of high school).

The second-favored choice was the status quo, with two systems and limited choice within each—including French immersion, gifted, and vocational programs. These responses imply that a majority of Ontario educators in Ontario might like no choice at all, simply a local common school for all.

Principals (74.1 percent) agree more strongly than do elementary teachers (43.4 percent) that there should be just one common school, suggesting that part of the opposition to choice is organizational—choice is a threat to the organizational entity. This interpretation is consistent with the finding that separate teachers and principals (34.0 percent) support the status quo more than do public teachers and principals (14.9 percent). Nonetheless, it is interesting to see how low the support of the status quo is even among the supposed beneficiaries. Consistently, separate teachers and principals (19.1 percent) support parental choice of school more strongly than do public teachers and principals (3.3 percent).

Table 10–4 also shows how little support there is among educators for partial or full funding of independent schools. Once again, this is particularly so in the case of the public schools. Public teachers and principals (85.6 percent) agree that independent schools should not receive funding more than do separate teachers and principals (56.7 percent).

Christian (i.e., Protestant) education was long a mandatory part of Ontario public education. It is now illegal. Table 10–5 shows the strong level of support among educators for that change (with only 13.1 percent of educators favoring the funding of Christian schools on the same basis as Roman Catholic schools). Educators are strong supporters of the demand for the secularization of schools.

Currently in Ontario, secondary schools are structured on the basis of three levels, or "streams," with students choosing from among an advanced, a general, and a basic level of instruction in most major subjects. In practice, not all schools provide all choices, and in some urban areas different schools offer different levels—with the result that there are essentially "advanced" and "basic" schools. The recent Radwanski report (Radwanski 1987) advocated the establishment of a single common program to the end of high school, somewhat along the lines of Mortimer Adler's ideal. The third option provided was what can be described as "the Danish system," whereby there is a common program until the end of grade 10, followed by discrete program (as distinct from subject) options leading to different vocational and academic futures.

There is not consistently strong majority support for the current structure of secondary education, with only public CEOs (63.8 percent) and secondary teachers (59.1 percent) giving the status quo majority support. Elementary teachers are much less supportive (27.0 percent). There is very little support among educators for the Radwanski plan. The Danish option is generally a close second to the status quo.

Table 10–4
Educator Samples: Choice and Independent Schools
(in percentages)

| | Publicly Funded Schools | | | | | Independent Schools | | | |
	ComS	CoRC	As is	MorC	Rel	None	As is	$$$	More $
CEOs	—	—	—	—	—	—	—	—	—
CEOs Pub	—	—	—	—	—	—	—	—	—
CEOs Sep	—	—	—	—	—	—	—	—	—
Princ	74.1	6.9	10.3	5.2	3.4	1.7	86.4	3.4	8.5
Teach+P	57.9	9.2	18.9	7.5	6.6	3.1	76.7	12.3	7.9
Teach Pub	69.6	4.4	14.9	7.7	3.3	3.3	82.3	9.4	5.0
Teach Sep	12.8	27.7	34.0	6.4	19.1	2.2	54.3	23.9	19.6
Teach El	43.4	14.5	26.3	6.6	9.2	2.6	71.1	15.8	10.5
Teach Sec	59.6	6.4	18.1	9.6	6.4	4.3	75.0	15.2	5.4
Educs	57.0	10.5	16.6	7.3	8.7	2.0	74.3	13.5	10.2
Educs M	62.1	10.0	11.4	7.1	9.5	2.4	78.5	7.7	11.5
Educs F	48.9	11.3	24.8	7.5	7.5	1.5	67.7	22.6	8.3

Samples: See table 10–1

Columns:

Choice of Publicly Funded Schools

ComS: Favor just one common school for all

CoRC: Favor common school plus Roman Catholic schools

As is: Favor status quo, with public and separate systems and further limited choices, such as French immersion

MorC: Favor more choice (e.g., academically intensive and child-centered schools) but not other religious schools

Rel: Allow parental choice (including religious and ethnic schools) under strict conditions

Treatment of Independent Schools

None: Do not permit them

As is: Allow them, but no funding—status quo

$$$: Provide partial funding

More$: Full or almost full funding, if they meet certain criteria

Table 10–5
Educator Samples: Minority Schools and Secondary Structure
(in percentages)

| | Extended Funding | | Secondary Structure | | |
	Christian	No other	Danish	Radwanski	As is
CEOs	8.1	75.7	30.1	2.7	54.8
CEOs Pub	2.1	89.6	19.1	0.0	63.8
CEOs Sep	19.2	50.0	50.0	7.7	38.5
Princ	7.0	76.7	46.6	5.2	41.4
Teach+P	11.6	75.5	38.2	5.8	44.0
Teach Pub	10.0	78.3	38.5	5.0	46.4
Teach Sep	18.2	63.6	37.0	8.7	34.8
Teach El	14.5	69.7	55.4	9.5	27.0
Teach Sec	11.6	73.7	19.4	3.2	59.1
Educs	13.1	74.7	41.9	6.2	40.4
Educs M	13.7	76.6	41.1	4.8	41.6
Educs F	12.2	71.8	43.1	8.5	38.5

Samples: See table 10–1
Columns:
  Extended Funding
  Christian: Christian school should be funded as well as public and
    Roman Catholic
  No other: No additional schools should be funded

  Secondary Structure
  Danish: No streams before grade 11 (common core)—then program choice
    depending on future plans
  Radwanski: One common program through to the end of high school
  As is: Status quo—make current three-level program work better

THE OPINIONS OF NURSES AND ENGINEERS

Tables 10–6 through 10–11 summarize the important policy differences between educators and noneducators. They also serve to
test the idea that differences between educators and noneducators
are just a subset of the dissent found throughout society. It is pos-

sible that the differences between nurses and engineers, chosen partly because of the marked gender difference between the two groups, are explained as much by gender as by occupation. Unfortunately, just as there were not enough male secondary teachers in the sample to make gender differentiation feasible, so is gender differentiation impractical among nurses and engineers. The purpose of the study, however, was not primarily to determine the cause of differences in opinion, a task generally beyond an opinion survey of this kind (although it is interesting to speculate about possible causes). The major purpose was to provide a finer-grained analysis of dissent than has been shown heretofore. The issue of gender and its influence on the findings is briefly discussed later.

Some demographic differences emerge from table 10-6. Educators (53.4 percent) are more likely to have at least three children than are nurses (28.1 percent) and engineers (22.6 percent), but the difference is explicable in terms of the greater fertility of male educators, particularly those not involved directly in teaching. Does this mean that organizationally successful male educators love children more than do engineers, but that female educators have no greater love for them than nurses? Or does it mean that females necessarily make a greater sacrifice of family for career than do males?

Public CEOs (80.9 percent) and principals (66.2 percent) are much more likely to belong to mainstream Protestant denominations than are engineers (33.4 percent). Engineers (27.3 percent), nurses (21.0 percent), and educators (16.8 percent) are more likely to belong to other religions than are CEOs (0.0 percent). This finding is consistent with the hypothesis that CEOs are selected on the basis of their middle religious ground, or choose to stay in that middle ground after having been selected. I noted in the earlier research the problem, in a multicultural society, of there being large segments of the population who, despite being potentially qualified in terms of educational knowledge and commitment, are necessarily excluded from senior (or even junior) positions in the educational system because of the incompatibility of their worldviews with what is believed to be or actually is required for responsibility in a public, secular school system. Such exclusion raises questions as to the possibility of true representation.

I have suggested previously (Holmes 1991a) that the progressive philosophy in education is an extension of contemporary lib-

Table 10–6
Educators and Professionals: Background Characteristics
(in percentages)

	N	%M	M#1	>2c	RC	Prot	None	Other
CEOs	73	98.6	78.1	43.8	52.1	52.1	4.1	0.0
Princ	60	93.3	89.8	37.0	18.6	66.2	5.1	10.9
Educs	345	61.7	70.1	53.4	25.7	47.9	9.6	16.8
Comp	83	86.4	84.1	46.3	17.1	59.8	11.0	12.1
Nurses	214	1.9	65.6	28.1	23.0	51.2	4.8	21.0
Engineers	187	91.9	75.3	22.6	22.6	33.4	16.7	27.3

Samples:
 CEOs: Chief Education Officers (directors)
 Princ: Principals
 Educs: Educators, including all those in the qualified sample
 Comp: CEOs' comparison group—similar age, similar education, employed
  full-time not in education
 Nurses: All qualified in sample
 Engineers: All qualified in sample

Columns:
 N: Number in sample (number varies slightly from question to question)
 %M: Percentage male
 M#1: Married to first spouse
 >2c: Has more than two children
 RC: Roman Catholic by religion
 Prot: United, Anglican, or Presbyterian by religion—mainstream Protestant
 None: Atheist, agnostic or skeptic
 Other: All others

eralism of a form best described as "therapeutics." The nine-teenth-century liberalism of John Stuart Mill has been replaced by a managed form of individualism, by which kindly therapists help those in need—such as children, criminals, and others (including aberrant teachers) whose ideas and behavior do not fit well with contemporary ideology, but professedly in a nonjudgmental way. In table 10–7, the strong opposition to capital punishment among CEOs (31.9 percent support it), compared with support for the idea among the comparison group (65.9 percent) and engineers (65.6 percent), is consistent with this claim; that is, CEOs might be more therapeutic in outlook than is the average layperson. If the gender factor is considered, the differences become even more marked. Support for capital punishment is likely stronger among males than among females, yet CEOs (31.9 percent approve) are more opposed than are nurses (with 52.8 percent approval).

CEOs are also the only sample to place elementary/secondary education (48.6 percent) as a first financial priority for the provincial government, compared with engineers (13.0 percent), nurses (8.0 percent), and educators (23.3 percent). Consistently, they are least likely to place tax or deficit reduction as a first priority, with 14.3 percent selecting one or the other, compared with 32.4 percent of nurses and 30.0 percent of educators. One explanation is that the later questioning of the lay groups (i.e., in 1990) permitted more time for greater sensitivity to these two issues to develop. Another explanation is that CEOs are the most committed to their organization and its continuing growth. The latter explanation is probably the more parsimonious. It is also worth nothing that the decade of the 1980s showed a marked increase in the proportions

Table 10–7
Educators and Professionals: Political Issues

| | Cap Pun | Abort | Funding Priorities | | | |
			El/Sec	Health	Deficit	Tax Red
CEOs	31.9	—	48.6	21.4	8.6	5.7
Princ	55.2	71.9	23.3	30.0	23.3	6.7
Educs	52.8	67.1	21.2	30.7	17.4	7.5
Comp	65.9	—	11.0	17.1	35.4	14.6
Nurses	52.2	74.8	8.0	30.5	8.9	23.5
Engineers	65.6	62.8	13.0	14.1	34.2	12.0

Samples: See table 10–6
Columns:
Cap Pun: Percentage approving capital punishment
Abort: Percent approving a liberal position on abortion

Funding Priorities
El/sec: First priority elementary/secondary education
Health: First priority health
Deficit: First priority deficit reduction
Tax Red: First priority tax reduction

of qualified teachers working outside the classroom (as consultants and administrators) in Ontario—an indicator of the triumph
of therapeutics and organizational bureaucracy, two ideas that
support each other. It may be objected that CEOs are concerned
about finance simply because they know the real needs and they
see the consequences of cutbacks. Yet it is difficult to understand
by what standard Ontario's educational system can be seen to be
objectively needy. Certainly, Ontario is one of the biggest spenders
in Canada and internationally, and growth of per pupil spending
over the last two decades has far outpaced inflation.

Table 10–8 shows that CEOs (57.2 percent rank progressivism first or second) are more progressive in philosophy than any
of the lay groups (22.8 percent, 41.1 percent, and 21.0 percent for
the comparison group, nurses, and engineers, respectively) and
that educators and principals are also more progressive than the
lay groups, except in the case of nurses. Although nurses are more
progressive than both the predominantly male comparison group
and the engineers, they are less progressive than elementary teachers (58.0 percent) and female educators (57.4 percent). Thus gender appears to be only, at most, a partial explanation for difference in philosophy, and we must bear in mind that the most
progressive of all, the CEOs, are essentially a male sample.

CEOs (only 26.6 percent give it first or second priority) are
less technocratic than the comparison group (49.3 percent) and
the engineers (51.8 percent), but also less so than principals (44.6
percent) and educators and (43.1 percent). There are some sugges-
tive differences within the traditionalist and individualist philosophies, but none is of sufficient substantive importance to warrant
a conclusion.

In table 10–9, the widespread agreement that it would be better if it were possible to dismiss mediocre teachers more easily is
interesting; even principals, who normally are responsible for such
dismissals, showed 65.5 percent agreement.

By subtracting the strongly-disagree percentage from the
strongly-agree percentage one gets a sense of the strength or fervor
behind a particular opinion. A high difference, positive or negative, shows considerable agreement on a policy direction; a low
difference means either there is little strong opinion or that the
strong agreement is largely canceled by the strong disagreement
(or vice versa). Principals (19.0 percent more agree strongly than

Table 10–8

Educators and Professionals: First- and Second-Ranked Educational Philosophies
(in percentages)

| | Prog | | Tech | | Cult | | Trad | | Ind | | Egal | |
	1	1+2	1	1+2	1	1+2	1	1+2	1	1+2	1	1+2
CEOs	37.5	57.2	13.9	26.6	16.7	39.2	15.3	29.2	16.7	33.6	0.0	4.2
Princ	30.5	46.0	15.3	44.6	25.4	46.1	16.9	37.6	6.8	18.9	5.1	6.8
Educs	26.2	43.0	19.6	43.1	22.6	48.2	19.0	38.8	8.9	18.2	3.6	10.6
Comp	11.1	22.8	27.2	49.3	27.2	52.0	18.5	38.0	16.0	34.2	0.0	3.9
Nurses	26.7	41.1	16.2	39.4	28.6	53.3	13.3	34.9	11.4	21.7	3.8	9.5
Engineers	9.8	21.0	34.4	51.8	24.6	49.3	15.8	39.4	14.8	33.3	0.5	5.0

Samples: See table 10–6

Columns:

Prog: Progressive
Tech: Technocratic
Cult: Cultural
Trad: Traditional
Ind: Individualist
Egal: Egalitarian

disagree strongly) are less enthusiastic than are nurses (37.9 percent) and engineers (44.6 percent).

CEOs (20.5 percent) are less in agreement and much less enthusiastic than all other groups (-5.5 percent; i.e., more CEOs strongly disagree than strongly agree) concerning the proposition that it has become too difficult to suspend and expel from high schools students who are unwilling to work and who create many problems for others. Discipline is believed by the public to be one of the major priorities for the public school, particularly at the secondary level. That concern does not appear to be shared by those responsible for administering the system. As in the case of finance, it may be argued that CEOs know the reality—that it is not difficult to suspend or expel students. But if that is the case, the problem remains. Secondary educators and the public evidently believe that severe misbehavior goes comparatively unpunished. The possibility that students' behavior outside school is as bad or worse does not erase the importance of the belief that schools are not maintaining reasonable standards of discipline.

There is general agreement (except among engineers, of whom only 47.2 percent agree) that teachers should have final authority in most situations in determining how to teach their programs. What is surprising about these responses is the comparatively low level of fervor given by teachers to the endorsement of their right to teach. For example, 61.7 percent of principals endorse this opinion, and 63.0 percent of nurses. A similar item asked who should have the greatest say about pedagogy (teaching methodology). The difference between principals (35.0 percent naming the teacher) and educators (61.2 percent) is mirrored by that between engineers (37.9 percent) and nurses (60.5 percent). Perhaps engineers see teaching as a science more than as an art. If that is the explanation, the findings are ironic. Engineers, if this interpretation is correct, believe that teachers should be expected to teach the scientifically proven best way (this would be consistent with their ranking technocratic philosophy first). Yet principals, who agree with engineers that teachers should not have the greatest say about pedagogy, are philosophically as likely to be progressive as technocratic. So what they impose may, at least half the time, be inconsistent with what the engineers would like.

The issue of testing is often a crucial dividing point between educational leaders and the public, with majorities among the public usually favoring regular external testing of achievement in

Table 10–9

Educators and Professionals: Opinions on Accountability

(in percentages)

	Fire T		Expel S		T Prof		T Ped	Ach Test	
	A	SA-SD	A	SA-SD	A	SA-SD		Ann	Occ
CEOs	78.0	31.5	20.5	-5.5	64.9	3.9	—	11.4	65.7
Princ	65.5	19.0	46.7	10.0	61.7	0.0	35.0	15.3	52.5
Educs	68.9	23.4	62.5	25.4	68.2	10.7	61.2	25.2	44.9
Comp	—	—	62.6	21.9	54.2	-1.2	—	58.5	31.7
Nurses	82.6	37.9	44.9	14.5	63.0	5.6	60.5	21.2	50.9
Engineers	82.3	44.6	52.2	22.7	47.2	-5.9	37.9	50.3	32.1

Samples: See table 10–6

Columns:

Fire T: A—Agree it is too difficult to dismiss mediocre teachers

Expel S: A—Agree it is too difficult to suspend and expel students

T Prof: A—Agree teachers should have authority over teaching their programs

SA-SD: Difference between number strongly agreeing and strongly disagreeing on same items

T Ped: Classroom teacher should have greatest say about pedagogy

Ach Test: Occ—one or twice and as needed (as distinct from on only special occasions)

Table 10–10
Educators and Professionals: School Policies
(in percentages)

	Small Classes		More Voc		Secondary Organization		
	A	SA-AD	A	SA-AD	Danish	Radwanski	As is
CEOs	41.7	0.0	35.6	0.0	30.1	2.7	54.8
Princ	67.8	13.6	53.4	5.0	46.6	5.2	41.4
Educs	58.4	19.1	58.8	13.0	41.8	6.2	40.6
Comp	62.4	21.2	50.6	8.5	47.5	13.8	27.5
Nurses	60.2	17.0	37.4	-3.7	51.9	6.1	35.8
Engineers	60.2	10.4	59.9	10.7	47.0	9.8	38.3

Samples: See table 10–6

Columns:
Small Classes: Agree that there should be fewer special programs and smaller homeroom classes
More Voc: Agree more students should be taking vocational programs
Secondary Organizations: Danish—common program for ten grades followed by distinct programs in the last two grades; Radwanski—a common program for all until the end of grade 12
As Is—current situation with three levels in high school

schools. The CEOs (11.4 percent), principals (15.3 percent), and educators (25.2 percent) consistently do not favor annual testing in the elementary grades, whereas such testing is supported by the comparison group (58.5 percent) and by engineers (50.3 percent), but not by nurses (21.2 percent).

Table 10–10 shows that CEOs are further removed from lay opinion about educational policy than are other educators. Principals (67.8 percent), the three lay groups (62.4 percent, 60.2 percent, and 60.2 percent), and educators (58.4 percent) support the opinion that elementary schools would be better off with fewer special programs and smaller homeroom classes, while CEOs do not (41.7 percent). CEOs (35.6 percent) and nurses (37.4 percent) are the only samples not to agree that more students should be taking vocational courses (related to possible employment opportunities) in secondary schools (the other samples vary from 50.6 percent

Table 10–11
Educators and Professionals: Religion and Choice
(in percentages)

	Fund Schools		Fund Independent Schools		
	Christian	None	No Support	Partial	Full
CEOs	8.1	75.7	—	—	—
Princ	7.0	76.7	88.1	3.4	8.5
Educs	12.6	72.2	76.3	13.4	10.2
Comp	—	—	—	—	—
Nurses	15.9	12.2	61.5	23.5	15.0
Engineers	13.9	9.1	71.4	17.3	11.4

Samples: See table 10–6

Columns:
Fund Schools
Christian: Should fund Christian as well as public and Roman Catholic schools
None: No additional schools should be funded

Fund Independent Schools
No Support: No funding for independent schools
Partial: Partial funding if they meet certain conditions
Full: Full or almost full funding if they meet certain conditions

agreement to 59.9 percent agreement). This division is generally consistent with the philosophical preferences of the samples.

Asked to choose among three policy options for the structure of secondary education, there was general disagreement with the common program to the end of high school, but there was difference in reaction to the Danish model. The Danish model was selected by a plurality of all three lay samples, notably so by the comparison group and by nurses, and was strongly opposed only by CEOs (54.8 percent of whom selected the status quo).

In table 10–11, there is strong consensus among lay and educator groups that Christian (i.e., Protestant) schools should not be funded, while there is strong disagreement about the funding of schools other than those currently funded. Approximately three-quarters of educators agree that there should be no funding of any other schools (dissent comes mainly from separate school educators), but only about one-tenth of nurses and engineers share that opinion. On the other hand, there is less support among lay groups for the status quo. Principals are more certain that there should be no funding for independent schools than are nurses and engineers, with educators being similar to the engineers rather than nurses (who are most supportive).

IMPLICATIONS OF EDUCATIONAL DISSENT

CEOs

A major question addressed by this phase of the research is whether CEOs' educational philosophies and opinions reflect those of educators generally, and whether the comparison group (of similarly aged and educated noneducators) reflects those of educated noneducators. A generalized answer to that question must be a qualified negative. It is an oversimplification to state that educators and noneducators differ systematically on educational questions. Nurses and engineers themselves differ on some educational issues, and CEOs are very different from other educators on numerous issues. In some cases, nurses are more like educators than like engineers; on some issues secondary educators are not far removed from engineers; and on several important issues CEOs are closely aligned with elementary, but not secondary, teachers and principals. Perhaps the clearest finding emerging from this study is the existence of distinct subgroups with distinctive opinions on some, but by no means all, educational issues. One can expect that other subgroups, not identifiably involved in this study, such as mothers of primary-aged children, guidance counselors, lawyers, Muslims, and those without permanent employment, might also have collective opinions that distinguish them from others on some policy issues.

There is no automatic implication that such diversity demands schools of choice. One could make the contrary argument, that the diversity is so widespread and particularistic that no imaginable set of schools of choice could possibly capture its complexity, that what is needed is a consensual, socializing experience. Choice, it could be argued, forces parents to make an educational decison on the basis of differentiating criteria that are not even particularly salient from their worldview. Some of the grand lines of dissent will be described before implications for the delivery of publicly funded education are explored.

The earlier finding that CEOs are at once centrist and distinctive is supported by this study. They are more centrist than any of the other samples in the sense that they are more likely to belong to mainstream religions (Catholic or major Protestant) than is any other sample except the principals. CEOs are not notably more progressive in philosophy than some other educators (in particular females and elementary teachers and principals), but they are the only predominantly male educator sample to be notably more progressive than all the lay samples (including nurses). CEOs are particularly defensive of the organizational status quo, including, for example, the current secondary school structure. CEOs are centrist, but in a very specific way. They are not more representative of the public than are educators in general, as might have been expected. Their worldviews (with the important exception of their being opposed to capital punishment) are middle of the road, but their educational opinions exaggerate the difference between layperson and educator—that is, they are more extreme in their progressivism than are educators as a whole. One explanation for this is that they are recruited heavily from elementary education backgrounds, as elementary educators are also strongly progressive. Another explanation is that bureaucratic monopolies create a funneling effect. Once an idea gains ascendance, adherence to it quickly becomes mandatory as groups of superiors choose whom to promote from down below. There is minimal competition, so public support for technocratic, cultural, or traditional schools is unable to break the monopolistic grip of those with central authority.

CEOs are also readily distinguishable from the other samples, for some of the same reasons that they are centrist. They are sharply opposed to capital punishment, unlike the majority of the population (including educators and all three lay groups). CEOs are the only sample apparently unconcerned about school discipline; there is more strong disagreement than strong agreement with the idea that it has become too difficult to suspend and expel those students from high schools who are unwilling to work and who create many problems for others. Their overall level of agreement (20.5 percent) contrasts with that of secondary teachers (85.3 percent) as well as with that of the lay samples.

Overall, the earlier conclusions are consistent with the new findings. The characteristics of Ontario's CEOs pose two problems for the future of senior educational leadership. CEOs currently represent a comparatively narrow ideology that is not shared by significant numbers, perhaps a majority, of the population at large. Their educational ideology is not close to the center of that of the population as a whole and is farther removed from the center than is that of educators as a whole. They can be seen as mandarins in the educational empire, remote from those they control.

Principals

It was hypothesized that principals would fall between teachers and CEOs in their educational outlook. One could argue that principals will become even more conformist than their superordinates, partly because they have been chosen by them and partly because they may have hopes of promotion. On the other hand, principals live in a daily world of teachers, and fellow-principals, and have comparatively little social involvement with CEOs, particularly in large systems typical of Ontario. The rather small sample size ($N = 60$) indicates caution in interpreting these data, particularly if differences are close to the 15 percent cutoff used in the study.

On questions of public policy (table 10–2), principals are generally not distinguishable from other educators, whereas they are distinguishable from CEOs on two key indicators. Like teachers and unlike CEOs, they favor capital punishment and give a higher priority to deficit and tax reduction (as compared with funding of elementary and secondary education).

A similar pattern emerges in educational philosophies (table 10–3). Like educators in general (except for elementary teachers) and unlike CEOs, principals rank the technocratic and the progressive philosophies equally. They also rank the individualist philosophy relatively low (a poor fifth out of six), as do educators generally, while CEOs rank it third, ahead of the technocratic and traditional philosophies. The same pattern holds over policy for secondary education, with principals sharing educators' relative support (with the exception of secondary teachers) for the Danish model over the Ontario status quo (table 10–5).

One explanation of these findings is that the greater one's responsibility for the status quo, the higher one's level of satisfaction with it. If CEOs effectively exert considerable control over educational policy, then it is understandable that they would be generally approving of the status quo. One might infer that such approval might not follow if government were to impose policies that go strongly against their own philosophical worldview.

The findings are not generally consistent with the hypothesis that principals lie between CEOs and educators, although there are occasions when that is the case. Overall, principals appear to be much more representative of educators as a whole than are CEOs.

Teachers

An initial hypothesis was that CEOs would be most distinctive, principals slightly less so, and teachers least of all. It was thought that while it would be difficult for a Seventh Day Adventist or a Conservative Jew to deliver a secular program as a CEO, it might be possible, in some distinctive social settings, for them to act as a principal—and similarly, that it might be difficult for a fundamentalist Christian or Muslim to act as a secular principal, but it might be possible, in a congenial setting, for them to work as a teacher—of music or computer programming, for example.

In the important area of religion (table 10–1), the findings are generally consistent with that idea, in that both elementary and secondary teachers are more likely than CEOs to belong to nonmainstream faiths. Where there are other differences between teachers and CEOs, the differences are either mainly between secondary teachers and CEOs (with elementary teachers being more like CEOs than are secondary teachers) or they appear to result from different hierarchical responsibilities as much as from a fundamental difference in worldview.

Simply, the difference between secondary and elementary teachers, although slight on most issues of general application, is as important as that between teachers and principals. Elementary teachers are as likely to be as progressive in philosophy as are CEOs, notably more so than their secondary colleagues, and they are correspondingly less likely to be technocratic. Elementary teachers (as well as secondary teachers) differ from CEOs in their ranking of the individualist philosophy, which is not favored by educators other than the CEOs.

Nurses and Engineers

The first phase of the study used a comparison group with which to assess the educational world views of CEOs. A purpose of this phase has been to validate that sample and to determine the degree to which that sample could be said to represent educated opinion in Ontario.

A conclusion of the earlier phases was that CEOs are distinctive in their worldviews. The opinions of the comparison groups of nurses and engineers in tables 10–6 through 10–11 are consistent with that finding. Nurses and engineers (compared with CEOs) are less likely to belong to mainstream religions, are less likely to be progressive in philosophy, are more supportive of capital punishment, put a lower priority on spending for elementary and secondary education, are less favorable to the proliferation of special programs in the elementary school, are more concerned about discipline, and are more interested in changing the structure of secondary education.

Another important finding is that there are important differences between nurses and engineers as well as between the lay samples and samples of educators. On the other hand, there are few systematic differences between educators as a whole and both nurses and engineers. Generally, nurses' opinions are closer to educators' than are engineers' and on many items the nurses' are closer to educators' than they are to engineers'. The implication of this finding is that it is very possible that the use of different samples from a variety of occupational and interest groups would elicit even more dissent and variation. Overall, the use of the lay samples emphasizes both the distinctiveness of the CEOs as well as the general level of dissent on many important educational issues.

Gender

The study was not designed to generate and explain gender differences. Its focus was instead on the opinions and worldviews of samples of educators and other similarly educated people. Although there is obvious interest in the reasons for and origins of such differences, the purpose was to consider the existence of dissent and its implications.

The reader is cautioned against assuming that gender is the most important factor at work, on the basis of the remarkable differences between female nurses and male engineers and between predominantly female elementary and mainly male secondary educators. It is just as possible that the different opinions result from the nature and context of the job as from the sex of its occupants.

One thing is certain. Gender, important as it may be, is not an overriding variable. The CEOs, the most predominantly male sample, are as progressive as female educators and are notably more so than female nurses. Female educators are as technocratic as male educators.

CONCLUSIONS

The Leadership of the CEO

An earlier phase of the study speculated as to whether CEOs were selected on the basis of their distinctive worldview or whether they became more distinctive as a consequence of their role and social context. The recent phase does not contribute directly to that question. It is arguable that experience and responsibility do bring about some changes. If selection processes rather than experience and socialization processes are the major cause, then one would expect principals to be more like the CEOs than they appear to be. Having to defend the system and its policies against external attack may help to consolidate CEOs' belief in the status quo. The new data suggest an elaboration of the social contextual explanation. The similarity between the worldviews of CEOs and of elementary teachers might be partially explained by a predominance of elementary backgrounds among CEOs. That explanation appears particularly plausible in the case of separate CEOs (in such boards, full secondary programs are relatively recent). That hypothesis is also also consistent with the finding that principals have opinions similar to those of teachers, except in those situations where they have or believe they have more direct hierarchical responsibility (e.g., the imposition of teaching methodology and the handling of discipline).

This argument (of the significance of social context to administrators' worldviews) leads to the hypothesis that Ontario administrators' worldviews are quite malleable, sensitive to their social context. The assumption is that leading educators—consultants, professors of education, other supervisory officers, officials of teachers unions and ministry officials—are, like CEOs, predominantly progressive. Principals share the perspective of teachers except in those situations where their interests are affected by hierarchical differentiation, when their opinions are situated between those of their superordinates and their subordinates.

This hypothesis is consistent with recent findings of Raun and Leithwood (in press), although my interpretation of the import of their findings differs significantly from theirs. Raun and Leithwood (using a sample based on a similar but more recent base of Ontario CEOs) find that CEOs rank integrity and honesty (two values inconsistent with malleability) seventh and fourth, respectively, in terms of their own behavior, while they rank them first and third, respectively, in the case of their expectations of students, and first and second, respectively, in their expectations of staff. For themselves, CEOs place respect for others, loyalty, solidarity, and fairness ahead of integrity and helping others, and general CEO responsibilities and consequences for clients ahead of honesty.

The worldview that emerges is, unsurprisingly, a progressive one, one I have described elsewhere (Holmes 1991a) as being "therapeutic," as favoring the authority of expert helpers (whose mission is to improve and help without conceptualizing the good) over the authority of strong, fundamental values. Raun and Leithwood take issue with Hodgkinson's view that Type One values (i.e., "trans-rational" fundamental principles) should have precedence over Type Two rational values (based largely on an assessment of consequences) and Type Three emotivist preferences.

Raun and Leithwood argue that CEOs find a defensible balance between being true to their own values and serving the values of the organization by giving precedence to a set of values that honors the values of others, examples of which are respect for others, participation, and consensus.

Alternatively, what Raun and Leithwood see as admirable flexibility can be seen as a stellar example of what MacIntyre (1981) sees as the fusing of values arising from performance of a role with those of the person unrelated to a professional role. Thus, once fundamental principles are suppressed, it becomes possible for administrators to change values according to the administrative context and to impose policies supportive of that context, provided they can be shown, by some combination of rational argument (based on alleged consequences) and emotivist preferences, to be likely to lead to some vaguely defined improvement. If integrity and honesty are secondary values, flexibility is certainly assured, but at what cost?

An earlier phase of this study (Holmes 1991b) illustrated some CEOs administering the mandatory imposition of progressive ideas in elementary education when they did not share that philosophy themselves, even in the absence of any clear direction from the Ministry of Education that progressive ideas and practices were official policy. Consideration for others is of course an admirable value, but when its value context is "general responsibilities" and "solidarity" rather than truth it can easily be transmuted into fealty to those "others" with either clout or the ability to hurt the organization or its leaders. CEOs, unlike the comparison group and the majority of Ontario citizens (as expressed in frequent opinion polls over the last decade), do not favor annual use of external tests for elementary children. Clearly, their "consideration for others" does not extend to those others, even clear majorities, if they lack the authority to enforce their ideas. Similarly, their consideration does not extend to those with educational philosophies differing from those normative among their colleagues.

If the common school is to become the new norm (a most unlikely eventuality, despite the professed desire for it by significant proportions of most of these educated people), then the CEOs of the future will have to be much closer to the norm of the population at large—much less progressive, and more technocratic.

A more likely future is very different. If I am right in supposing that schools are becoming more differentiated rather than less (with the growth of French immersion, gifted programs, and academic academies, all within the public system), then one must ask how practice, apparently in response to public demand, can be so different from what the public says it wants. The most likely explanation is very simple: Most people want there to be a single common program, but with two conditions. The two conditions nullify the wish. The first is that the common education reflect the individual's own educational philosophy. The second is that if the individual's child has a special need, that child be exempted from the common program and be given special help. As individuals' philosophies vary enormously, and as parents frequently believe their children have special needs, the future of a common school is not bright. It is not surprising, then, that current trends are to increased, rather than less differentiation—the destreaming of grade 9 notwithstanding.

If this assessment is correct, then the leadership required of the CEO changes drastically. Far from having to represent and model a central consensus, the CEO of the future will be required to represent a great many perspectives, most of which she or he will not personally share. From being a chameleon required to modify coloration in terms of collegial pressures, the CEO becomes the center of a variety of competing choices, some but not all of which will be successful in gaining representation. In this future, the requirement for someone in the middle of the road becomes much less important. What is important is that the CEO have the imagination and breadth of mind to recognize a variety of different ways to truth, only some of which will represent his or her personal philosophy. There will no longer be a single set of criteria for all principals and teachers; instead there will be a variety of criteria depending on the particular requirements of the school in question. This will require a major change in the CEO—from paternalistic and therapeutic authoritarianism to an authentic acceptance of pluralism, within the limits of a liberal democracy.

Teacher Professionalism

This study has been carried out in a province that has been imposing, by means of administrative authority (within school districts) and the influence of educational experts, a child-centered (progressive) educational regime in the public and separate elementary schools. The vigor with which this imposition has taken place, including the evaluation of teachers on the basis of whether they are using the prescribed methods, raises the question of teacher professionalism. Table 10–9 illustrates the difference in views between teachers and principals about who should have greatest say on pedagogy in the classroom.

If, as I believe to be the case, professionalism lies in the discretion one has over the processes used to achieve agreed-upon goals, then it will become increasingly important for teachers to gain more control over their central function. This increased control should also be placed in the context of increased parental influence over, and choice of, schooling for their children. CEOs will run into severe problems if they continue to enforce monolithic control over the program and teaching methodology, without allowing flexibility for parents to choose the kind of education they want for their children and discretion for teachers to have control over their teaching. Strong administrative skills will be required to facilitate parental choices compatible with teachers' styles, without having open warfare over teaching techniques in decentralized schools. Differentiated schools and programs, with clear choices for parents, are clearly indicated.

The Administrator of the Future

The traditional administrative pattern in Ontario has been bureaucratic and centralized. The working assumption has been that the local school board will modify a central offering from the province and deliver it uniformly to the local geographical community comprising the school district. That model has already broken down in most urban and suburban areas of the province as a result of open enrollment, French immersion, growth of the Roman Catholic alternative, special programs, and increasingly differentiated demographic characteristics from subcommunity to subcommunity. Demographic differences within school districts often equal or exceed those among school districts.

The skills required of future administrators will be very different from those required to find and deliver a uniform model. Instead, care will have to be taken to develop policies to determine acceptable and unacceptable models of education and to provide help and leadership to those who are moving in directions not particularly approved by CEOs themselves. The desire to appoint people like oneself (to build a happy ship) should change to a recognition of the need for people of very different outlooks and philosophies, so that nearly all parents may see their own worldview represented in the school board. This research illustrates most dramatically how far we have to go, from a system of governance where CEOs are isolated from their clients to one where they defer to clients and cooperatively build a variety of programs to meet the needs of a pluralistic, multicultural, and multifaith society. A policy of divide and rule should be replaced by one of developing a series of consensual visions of education, all of which remain consistent with society's overarching educational purposes.

NOTE

1. Requests for a complete set of five questionnaires with annotated responses is available from the Administrative Officer, Department of Educational Administration, Ontario Institute for Studies in Education (OISE), 252 Bloor Street West, Toronto, Ontario M5S 1V6, Canada. Please enclose a check or money order, payable to OISE, for $20.00 CAN.

REFERENCES

Holmes, M. (1991a). Bringing about change in teachers: Rationalistic technology and therapeutic human relations in the subversion of education. *Curriculum Inquiry, 21*(1), 65–90
Holmes, M. (1991b). A delicate balance: Leadership or stewardship?" In K. A. Leithwood & D. Musella (Eds.), *Understanding school system administration: Studies of the contemporary chief education officer* (pp. 241–72). London: Falmer Press.
Holmes, M. (1991c). The values and beliefs of Ontario's chief education officers. In K. A. Leithwood & D. Musella (Eds.), *Understanding school system administration: Studies of the contemporary chief education officer* (pp.155–74). London: Falmer Press.
MacIntyre, A. (1981). *After virtue*. Notre Dame; IN: University of Notre Dame Press.
Radwanski, G. (1987). *Ontario study of the relevance of education and the issue of dropouts*. Toronto: Ministry of Education.
Raun, T., & Keithwood, K. A. (in press). Pragmatism, participation and duty: Value themes in CEOs' problem solving. In P. Hallinger, K. A. Leithwood, & J. Murphy, (Eds.), *Cognitive perspectives and school leadership*. New York: Teachers College Press.

CHAPTER 11

Toward Improving the Structures for School System Leadership

Stephen B. Lawton, Joyce Scane, and Shihui Wang

Administrative hierarchies play a central role in the operation of virtually all contemporary organizations, transmitting the orders from the top to those on the bottom, and relaying information from the front line to the central commanders. Or at least this is the way textbooks describe the proper functioning of bureaucracies based on the Weberian model derived from the highly efficient Prussian Army.

This picture is not altogether inaccurate if one is describing key aspects of the operation of school systems in Canada. In Ontario, marching orders are regularly sent down from "Queen's Park" or the "Mowat Block," shorthand for the government (the Ontario parliament buildings are located at Queen's Park Circle) and the Ontario Ministry of Education and Training (the ministry is quartered in a towering office building named after a former Ontario premier, Sir Oliver Mowat). In the past decade, central authorities have mandated special education, extended public finance to Roman Catholic high schools, and reduced class sizes in grades 1 and 2, and have been "destreaming" grade 9. Their orders have been, and are being, followed, albeit not without complaints and a level of resistance that a Prussian general might not have thought acceptable in his lieutenants and enlisted men. [For example, see chapters 7 and 8, by Townsend—Editor.]

Canadian and American school systems are not, of course, centralized in provincial and state capitals; with the exception of

Hawaii, all have followed the practice of delegating the authority to operate schools to local school boards composed of elected or appointed school trustees. The trustees oversee their own administrative hierarchy, which stretches from their chief administrator's office to the classroom teacher. School districts, although corporate entities in their own right, are heavily regulated by provincial or state laws, regulations, and memoranda, which usually number in the hundreds of pages. Nevertheless, school boards enact their own sets of rules to direct their staff and have developed a reputation much like those of provincial and state authorities. The "central office," "downtown," 110 Livingstone Street (New York City), or 155 College (Toronto), like Olympus, are populated, in the minds of teachers and school-site administrators, with perfidious gods who, in their feuding but well-intentioned way, intercede in the affairs of mortals who conduct the daily business of educating children. Principals are rotated, schools demolished, and children reassigned other schools, all at the unseen whim of the gods. To be sure, rules are followed and one can divine a rational order to these mandates, but decisions are often experienced as arbitrary and inappropriate by those who, from their own experience, know better.

The inadequacy of bureaucratic hierarchies in confronting contemporary problems, whether in business or in the public sector, has become a central thrust of the management literature over the past two decades. Weick (1976) spoke of the need for "loosely-coupled" organizations, Peters and Waterman (1982) of the advantages of "tight-loose control" and the need for both intrepreneurs and entrepreneurs; Deming (1986) promoted the interests of the customer, quality management, and teamwork; and Osborne and Gaebler (1992) combined these elements to "reinvent government" for the 1990s. While it is unlikely that administrative hierarchies will disappear entirely to be replaced by self-managing networks or some other social form of organization, the evidence is clear that layers of middle management are disappearing as organizations "delayer" and "right-size" themselves (1990s Newspeak for firing white-collar workers and shrinking the organization) in order to become more cost-effective.

Restructuring has already occurred in a number of jurisdictions (Lawton 1992). New Zealand disbanded its elementary school boards, replacing their political function with elected governing boards for each school, and their administrative function with privatized school service agencies. In the future, services provided New Zealand schools must be "contestible"; that is, schools must be able to obtain competitive bids from more than one source. Debureaucratization could hardly go further! The United Kingdom, in a reform with similar consequences, is allowing schools to "opt out" of their local education authority (LEA); even those choosing not to do so have elected governing boards that are served by, rather than being directed by, their LEAs. In the United States, greater administrative and governing authority has been delegated to elected school councils in a number of jurisdictions, most notably Chicago, although none of these changes are as extreme as those in New Zealand and Britain. Even in Sweden, the ministry of education has been reduced drastically in size and redirected toward policy (i.e., as "steering") rather than direct service (i.e., "rowing"), a reform paralleled in the New Zealand reforms.

All of the aforementioned reforms were initiated by central governments (by the state of Illinois, in the case of Chicago, and by national governments in the other cases), but some school districts have tried to reform themselves. The school-based management program introduced in Edmonton, Alberta, by its superintendent, Mike Strembitsky, is among the most notable. Strembitsky's reforms are controversial within Canada, where some unions have condemned his reforms as "franchising education," but have been referenced in policy documents from Britain to Tasmania. Collaborative efforts between school boards and teachers unions are notable, and controversial, in Dade County, Florida, and Rochester, New York; those advocating choice in education see majoritarian control of schools by teachers as equivalent to letting the fox guard the chickens.

The failure of educational bureaucracies to achieve social and educational objectives has been widely voiced, although it is not clear that society has not been guilty of moving the bar, so to speak, by raising its expectations of schooling. Be that as it may, the impetus is still present, from a number of sources, for members of educational systems to reassess their administrative apparatus in order to learn where the problems lie and what types of reforms might be used successfully. It is too late for some systems to do this; had educational administrators in New Zealand, Chicago, and Britain, been alert to the severity of developing problems, and been willing and able to act, they might have found solutions for themselves rather than had "solutions" imposed upon them.

The purpose of this paper is to report such an assessment. In general terms, this study describes an appraisal of the administrative apparatus used by school boards (i.e., local school districts or systems) in Ontario, Canada. This appraisal consists of (1) describing central administrative structures according to an existing classification system, (2) assessing the adequacy of the central structure in serving school system needs, (3) describing the nature of relationships between various pairs of actors in the administrative system, (4) diagnosing the problems underlying the least-effective sets of relationships, (5) describing the actual decision-making authority of various actors in the system, and (6) describing the preferred levels of decision-making authority of these same actors. Taken together, this appraisal of structures, relationships, and authority patterns by key actors within the system indicates both how existing administrative hierarchies function and the direction that changes in these structures may take.

RESEARCH DESIGN

Survey data for the study of Ontario's administrative structure for education were collected between May and September 1991 (Wang 1991). A random sample of 40 school boards stratified by size was selected; 10 principals, 5 elementary and 5 secondary, were selected from within each board, except where there were fewer than 5 in the board. In all, the final sample included 353 school principals, 200 elementary and 153 secondary. The return rate for directors (i.e., superintendents, CEOs) of boards of education was 85 percent while that for principals was a 52 percent. For most analyses presented here, the complete sample of 217 respondents was used; in one case, responses were broken down by role. Although board-level analyses had been intended, with data aggregated by board, the spotty returns within a given board did not make this feasible.

CENTRAL ADMINISTRATIVE STRUCTURES

Ontario's approximately 170 school districts, referred to conventionally as "school boards," use a variety of administrative structures, although almost all except the very smallest have an appointed director of education assisted by one or more superintendents (second-level senior administrators). The number of superintendents, and other administrators, varies considerably from board to board, as do the roles the incumbents play in carrying out the work of the organization. In some, a strict administrative hierarchy applies, with a clear chain of command, descending downward from the director through the superintendents to the school principal. In others, more of an administrative matrix is used: Individuals play a variety of roles in which they have supportive rather than hierarchical relationships with principals and others. Hickcox and Ducharme (1972) developed a useful scheme for categorizing what they termed the "administrative staffing patterns" found in Ontario (figure 11–1). They suggested that staffing patterns could be classed into one of four types: pure area, tiered structure, combination, and functional.

Pure area school systems have a director of education, a business superintendent, and a number of area superintendents responsible for a geographic area, including all elementary and secondary schools, or there might be one area superintendent responsible for all the secondary schools and one responsible for all the elementary schools. "Principals report to the area superintendent directly, depending on the geographical area in which their schools are located. In this situation the area superintendent is a generalist, responsible for program, personnel and facilities within the area" (p. 102). In very small systems, directors themselves might supervise all schools.

Tiered-structure school systems "are characterised by a director at the top with a second echelon of functional superintendents including a business superintendent . . . [who have] titles such as superintendent of instruction, superintendent of operations, superintendent of personnel and the like. Below this level . . . are area superintendents who generally report to one of the functional superintendents. . . . [T]here are often dotted lines in the organization charts indicating that the area men [sic] can go directly to the various functional officials as the need arises. Principals in a tiered system report to their particular area superintendent and tend not to have direct access to the functional superintendent" (p. 102).

Combination types of administrative structures have superintendents with functional and area responsibilities. "Principals in such a structure report to a particular superintendent in his role as

Figure 11–1
Varied Types of Administrative Staffing Patterns

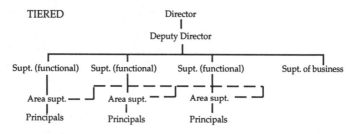

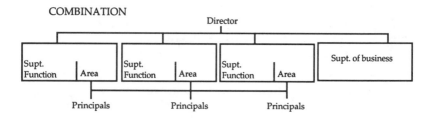

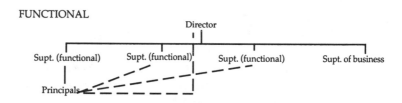

area supervisor. If assistance is required in functional areas other than the one for which the particular area man *[sic]* is responsible, the principal has only indirect access through his own supervisor. For example, if information about budget is required by a principal, he would probably ask his area supervisor to obtain it for him rather than going directly to the business office himself" p. (104).

Functional structures are found in systems where the position of area superintendent is omitted. "In this case, principals report directly to the functional superintendents for particular services. . . . [S]mall systems then to look like functional types because they are not large enough to support a substantial central office staff" (p. 104).

Hickcox and Ducharme found that the type of administrative organization was related to the size of the school system, with larger boards favoring a tiered structure and smaller boards a functional structure; of the sixty-three school boards in their survey, 77 percent had one of these two structures. Combination type administrative structures were next most common (10 percent) and pure area types the least common (7 percent); the structure of 8 percent was not determined (see table 11–1).

The present study, conducted almost twenty years after the Hickcox and Ducharme study, indicates that there has been a significant shift in the relative popularity of the various types of administrative structures (table 11–1), although differences in the size and distribution of school boards in the present sample from that of Hickcox and Ducharme may account for some of the differences. Whereas their sample was uniformly distributed across the five size categories used, ours was somewhat concentrated in the midsize group. In any case, we found that the combination type of administrative structure was the most common, reported by 33 percent of the 34 boards in our sample; tiered structure was reported by 30 percent, functional by 18 percent, pure area by 9 percent, and other by 12 percent. It appears, then, that there has been a shift away from tiered structures, in which the upper tier is solely concerned with functional responsibilities, and the middle tier with supervisory matters, toward the combination model in which the same individuals play both types of roles; this change is particularly notable among midsize boards enrolling between 5,000 and 20,000 students. Smaller boards retain a preference for a functional structure, and large boards for a tiered structure.

An additional structure, beyond the original four, was identified in the current study; this new type is a mixture of functional and combination types (see figure 11–2) with some functional superintendents with no area responsibilities, and other superintendents with both functional and area concerns. Three of the four that fell in the "other" category were of this mixed type.

Usually school boards have a management committee or council at the central level that is used to air current issues, advise the director on policy options, and assist in formulating plans to implement decisions taken by the school trustees and administration. In the Hickcox and Ducharme (1972) study, 20 of 63 boards provided information about their executive councils. "In all cases, these councils include the director, second echelon academic

Table 11-1
Types of Organizational Structures in School Boards of Different Sizes

Pupil Pop.	Pure Area (%)		Tiered (%)		Combination (%)		Functional (%)		Not Known (%)		Total (%)	
	PS	CS	PS	CS	PS	CS	PS	CS	PS	CS	PS	CS
40,000 and over	2	0	18	12	2	0	0	0	0	0	22	12
20,000 to 39,999	2	3	13	6	2	3	3	0	0	6	20	18
13,000 to 19,999	0	3	13	9	3	15	3	3	0	6	19	35
5,000 to 12,999	3	0	3	3	3	15	8	3	2	0	19	21
less than 5,000	0	3	0	0	0	0	16	12	6	0	22	15
TOTAL	7	9	47	30	10	33	30	18	8	12	102	102

Average board enrollment : 19,464 (current study)
% is greater than 100 because of rounding error
Previous study N = 63; Current study N = 34
(PS = Previous study (Hickcox and Ducharme 1972, p. 104); CS = Current study (Lawton 1993)

Figure 11–2
The Mixed Type of Administrative Staffing Pattern

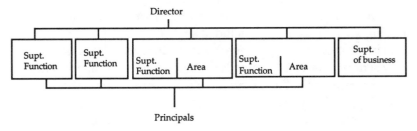

superintendents and the superintendents and the superintendent of business or business administrator. In only one case were area superintendents included" (p. 109). This situation raised some interesting questions for the authors: "In particular, what effect does restricting the membership of the executive council have on decision-making? Would there be more commitment to decisions if some representatives of the lower echelons were included on this council? Would it be useful to have in-school administrators and teachers represented on the executive council?" (p. 109).

Our study indicates some modest change in the direction indicated by the questions that Hickcox and Ducharme raised. In all, 11 of 31 boards (or 35 percent) responding to this questions indicated that their central administrative decision-making body included principals or others. Only one of eight tiered boards indicated staff other than the director or superintendent on their executive council. The phenomenon was more common for other types: two of three pure-area-type boards; two of ten combination-type boards; three of six functional boards; and three of the four mixed-type boards.

In administrative theory, the inclusion of lower levels of administration—and especially those from the front line—on central decision-making bodies has been advocated as a means of improving bottom-up communication. Traditional hierarchies seem much better at sending information and decisions down than receiving information and advice up from the grassroots. In turbulent environments, those in direct contact with the client are seen to possess the special knowledge that is critical to informed decision making. From this perspective, the inclusion of principals and others on central councils makes sense; the fact that the most inclusive councils were associated with the innovative, mixed-type administrative structures suggests that there may be a trend toward flatter, more integrative management structures.

Administrative councils also exist in areas, in families of schools, and in the schools themselves. Most boards had reported having area councils that included superintendents and principals; and in most boards, there were councils for secondary and elementary school education, councils that included both superintendents and the principals. Such structures were absent, however, in functional type administrative structures, no doubt in large part because this structure is found most frequently in small school systems.

ADEQUACY OF THE
CENTRAL ADMINISTRATIVE STRUCTURES

Hardly a day goes by without a report on the restructuring of a major corporation; for example, in the three months prior to completion of this chapter corporations such as IBM, General Motors, and Westinghouse announced major plans to decentralize and streamline their businesses. Old management practices and structures are not working; almost in desperation, attempts are being made to instill greater dynamism into subordinate units so that they can adapt to turbulent environments and pull their corporate hierarchies out of their current crises. Given the fiscal problems besetting school boards and other government-funded agencies, one can only wonder if they too sense a need for change—a readiness to look for new management strategies.

To assess how well current administrative structures work, directors and principals were asked, "In your view, how well is the current administrative structure serving your school system?" They responded on a six-point scale, ranging from very poorly to extremely well. Their responses revealed a substantial difference of opinion between those at the top and those at the bottom. The directors' mean rating was 4.6, or "very well"; the elementary principals' mean response was 4.1, or "fairly well"; the secondary principals were least satisfied, with a mean of 3.8.

Respondents who had marked 1 to 4 on the six-point scale were asked to indicate how the current administrative structure was not serving the school system very well, and to suggest changes that would improve the system; of the 87 comments made, 11 were from directors. Seven themes were identified: communication, administrative barriers, elementary/secondary knowledge, personal competence, workload, experience, politics, and school-level authority.

Communication Problems

A number of factors tend to impede the flow of information in school boards; one administrator suggested the problem was "linked to the size of the system, the time of year, and the number of issues." Another commented that in his/her board, the "director does not work effectively with the superintendents; as a result, system communication is poor." Another perceived this problem in reverse: "Most complaints or problems must still reach the upper tier, but by being involved, the area superintendent slows up and interferes with this communication."

Administrative Barriers

Sometimes, communication and action virtually cease: "Superintendents are mostly 'blockers' not facilitators; there is very little support for schools in terms of financial support, resources or morale." Another found that "some functional responsibilities are not completed because approval and/or support are needed by area superintendents. As a result, programs don't get implemented and plant repairs are not expedited." Bureaucracy, it appears, too often won out over action: "A memorandum to a functional superintendent with a copy to the area superintendent sometimes gets lost in the shuffle without the problem being addressed. If a problem is stated in writing, the initiator should get a reply in writing within a reasonable time!" One analysis of this generic problem concluded that "the indirect access to other functional areas through the area superintendent wastes time; for example, educating an area superintendent about a problem he cannot solve, correcting misinformation because of middleman superintendents creates an unnecessary level of decision-making. The superintendent becomes the rate-determining step in the reaction—a superintendent who is largely superfluous to a decision thus becomes a 'clog in the wheel of progress.'" On the other hand in another board, it was suggested that "principals indicate some frustration in having to go to different superintendents for different purposes. They express a preference for one supervisor."

Elementary/Secondary Knowledge

Secondary school principals reported a lack of either interest, expertise, or appreciation for their schools' needs on the part of superintendents, most of whom had elementary school backgrounds. This problem seemed particularly noticeable in situations where an area superintendent exerted authority over secondary schools. One respondent noted that "secondary school principals once had much more influence with functional superintendents. Of late, a move to re-empower the area superintendents has had the effect of shrinking the secondary school principal's sphere of influence." Several others simply commented, as did one, that the "area superintendent whose only experience is elementary is in charge of secondary schools." Specifically, in one board, "an imbalance of elementary to secondary superintendents was a problem: there were 16 superintendents with equal voice of whom only 5 had a secondary background; there is no distinct secondary component." Nevertheless, it was recognized elsewhere that "the elementary secondary split does not serve the system well as restructuring issues, such as the transition years [integration of grades 7 to 10], emerge."

Personal Competence

Rather than administrative structure and processes, on occasion the real problem was skill of the person filling a role. Some superintendents, one principal said, "are more conscientious than others"; and in one board, "most S.O.s [supervisory officers] are new to their positions and there seem to be some growing pains." But as one noted, "the current S.O. is outstanding; problems might develop if a weaker S.O. is appointed."

Workload

There seemed to be a widespread perception that a significant portion of administrative problems—inadequate communication, delays in approvals, and the like—reflected excessive demands upon senior administrators or, conversely, a failure to appoint sufficient numbers of supervisory officers. One principal commented, "The superintendent in charge of staffing has enough to do with that function alone, yet he also has area schools to supervise. The staffing responsibility alone is enough." Another, also in a board where the combination type of structure was used, suggested that the superintendents "either burn out or the area schools suffer neglect." In a small board, "one superintendent has a lot of ground to cover, even in a one-high-school board; however, we're really not large enough to warrant another superintendent." Some principals offered sincere concern: "I believe that they are extremely overworked and understaffed. With numerous personal problems at this level during the past two or three years, their jobs have been unbearable." Others place the blame elsewhere, either with the provincial government, which seems to be creating "an excess of bureaucratic requirements that impinge on the primary responsibility of the S.O.s," or the trustees who "want to be involved in daily operations of the school."

While superintendents may carry a very heavy workload, data do suggest that there are more of them to do it. The number of supervisory officers per 10,000 students, averaged across school boards of all sizes, has increased from 4.54 in 1972 to 5.26 in 1991, a 16 percent increase; this trend has occurred in school boards of all sizes.

Politics

More superintendents might assist the principals; but then again, some saw larger supervisory staffs as fertile ground for organizational politics: "The greater the number of superintendents, the greater the political activity and intrigue. Camps exist where loyalties supercede competence and good judgment. Much time is wasted in conferencing, communicating with trustees, and plotting." Others saw power struggles between superintendents that were counterproductive.

School-Level Authority

A combination of heavy superintendent workloads, division of authority between area and functional superintendents, and office politics resulted in what some principals felt was neglect of the interests of individual schools. Superintendents were often "unaware of school happenings and have little contact with the staff and pupils." "The words and philosophy of how we [are to] behave in our system do not match the actual behaviour; senior administration say they believe in a school-based curriculum model, but tell us what is good for kids and how we should perform our responsibilities." Sometimes distance is the problem: "The board office is over 80 kilometers from here; we're low on its list of priorities."

Overall satisfaction with a board's administrative structure was not a function of the type of structure or the size of the school board. The six classes of problems noted tended to be endemic to educational systems throughout Ontario. Some problems were related to the type of structure, but reforming the structure along conventional lines seems to replace one set of problems with another. Tiered boards, for example, appear more likely to experience administrative delays due to the number of levels, with delays (or barriers) being caused by intervening area superintendents. Combination boards and mixed boards, however, seemed to report "role overload" more often than the tiered boards did, with functional superintendents finding too little time to attend to the schools in their assigned geographic areas. Other possibilities for reform of administrative structures will be dealt with in the conclusion.

THE NATURE OF RELATIONSHIPS

Many of the comments concerning the problems with administrative structure bespoke problems in relationships—inadequate communication, neglect, disinterest, inadequate responsibility, and the like. As anyone knows who works in a large organization, the character of relationships, including trust, respect, and other often unstated traits, are fundamental to making organizations work. We constantly depend on others, whether for minor matters such as ensuring that letters get mailed or a chalkboard gets cleaned, or major ones such as ensuring an organization's future or protecting our safety. Curiously, the literature on organization behavior is relatively silent on the nature of relationships other than those within immediate workgroups. Terms such as *superordinate* and *subordinate* are used, as if that is all that needs to be said.

Our focus was upon authority relationships; that is, relationships in which there exists the "power to influence or command thought, opinion, or behavior" (*Merriam-Webster's Collegiate Dictionary*, 1993). Although our primary interest was in the relationships between supervisory officers and principals, since this is the key link in the administrative hierarchy, we explored other pairs of positions in order to map the exercise of authority within the entire school system. Even this, of course, is not entirely possible given the complexity of school systems, so we focused on the following pairs of relationships: (a) principals' to superintendents, (b) superintendents' to principals, (c) directors' to superintendents, (d) directors' to trustees, (e) principals' to teachers, (f) communities' to principals, and (g) administrations' to the regional offices of the Ministry of Education.

We asked about the perceived nature of the relationships in general rather than the individual's personal relationship, for several reasons. First, we were not surveying all the parties about whom we were asking, so these relationships could be assessed only in terms of the general perception of the respondents about the nature of the relationships. Second, when policies are changed, the motivating force is more often the general perception about where problems lie rather than with an individual's personal experience. This distinction may seem a fine one, but survey researchers have repeatedly demonstrated that people often hold different assessments of their own experience (as with the quality of their child's school) than they do of the general situation (as the quality of education overall).

In one case, we asked about both directions of the relationship; namely, principals to superintendents and vice versa. Relationships, particularly authority relationships, are rarely balanced or symmetric. A principal who cowers before a superintendent is unlikely to have a superintendent who cowers in his or her presence. All of the relationships might have been explored in both directions; we did not do so due to interests of economy, both fiscal and temporal.

How does one characterize authority relationships in a way that is more complex than that between sergeant and private? We chose eight adjectives that seemed to add subtlety to the nature of what is often treated as a simple matter of giving and taking orders. With our definition, they were as follows:

Subordinate: submissive to, or controlled by, a person in authority

Demanding: exacting, onerous

Resistant: opposing, in word or deed, directives or suggestions

Distant: reserved or aloof

Directive: guides, prescribes, or instructs in a clear and firm manner

Accepting: receives guidance or instructions with little or no opposition

Supportive: gives assistance, help, backing, and encouragement

Constructive: promotes improvement and development

These eight adjectives describe the follower's status as well as that of the leader, but they also allow for more of a mentoring, counseling, or advisory relationship between two parties. They even allow a reversal of roles, as in a customer-centered operation, wherein the client places demands upon the agent, rather than vice versa. In this way, we hoped to be able to discern whether what appears to be an administrative hierarchy on paper might in fact be something quite different in practice.

Of the eight characteristics of authority relationships that directors and principals rated, three (accepting, supportive, and constructive) might be said to have positive connotations, and five (subordinate, demanding, resistant, distant, and directive) somewhat negative connotations, at least as far as contemporary interpersonal relationships are concerned. This difference in "social desirability" of the characteristics is reflected in the responses reported for the seven sets of relationships assessed (table 11-2). For the most part, those with positive connotations were assessed more highly (4 = "much"; 5 = "very much"), whereas those with negative connotations were seen as less characteristic (1 = "not at all"; 2 = "little"; 3 = "somewhat"). All relationships therefore tend to be revealed as "soft" rather than "hard." Incumbents in none of the roles appear like the mythical Victorian father—distant, directive, and demanding; instead, all appear to have close, neighborly relations—they are accepting, supportive and constructive. Given that this underlying pattern applies across almost all of the relationships, it is necessary to attend to modest and perhaps rather subtle differences in patterns to understand the nature of the relationships.

Principals and superintendents, whose relationships often appeared frustrating in the diagnosis of system problems, turned out to differ from one another substantially on only two characteristics: principals were more subordinate to superintendents than superintendents were to principals (means of 2.9, or somewhat subordinate, vs. 1.4, or not at all), and principals were a bit less directive of their superintendents than the latter were of the principals (means of 2.6 and 3.0, respectively). Otherwise, they seemed to relate to one another in a symmetric manner—somewhat demanding of one another, a little resistant and distant, and quite accepting, supportive, and constructive.

Both directions of the other relationships were not assessed. Overall, the director's relationship to superintendents seems to be perceived as being more rigorous than the superintendents' relationship with the principals. Directors are seen as somewhat demanding, a bit distant, somewhat directive, and a bit less accepting than was the case for superintendents. Since our sample included principals and directors, but not superintendents, it may be that this firmer portrait for directors reflects the perspective of individuals not in regular contact with directors; perhaps superintendents would have had a different view.

Directors were perceived as being somewhat subordinate, demanding, directive, and accepting of their school trustees, a bit resistant and distant, and quite supportive and constructive. This profile suggests a relationship that is tense. The subordination evident in the principals' relationship to superintendents, and of superintendents' to directors, is not present in this relationship. It would appear—and this is an inference that may be overdrawn—that there is more bargaining and give-and-take among equals: directors with their professional expertise and the trustees with their political legitimacy.

Principals' authority relationships with teachers appear very much like those between superintendents and principals, except more intimate. Principals are slightly subordinate, resistant, and distant, somewhat demanding and directive, and quite accepting, supportive (a mean of 4.3 on the 5-point scale) and constructive. In their relationship with principals, school communities are also seen as slightly subordinate, resistant, distant, and directive, but somewhat demanding. They are quite accepting, supportive, and constructive, although the mean for the last trait, at 3.5, is among the least constructive assessed. It would appear that the demands expressed by communities are either generalized and ill-formed, or

Table 11–2
Mean Response and Standard Deviation of Response for Character of Seven Relationships
(N = 217)

Character of Relationship	A M	A SD	B M	B SD	C M	C SD	D M	D SD	E M	E SD	F M	F SD	G M	G SD
Subordinate	2.9	1.1	1.4	0.8	1.7	1.1	2.6	1.1	1.8	0.8	2.2	1.0	2.4	1.2
Demanding	2.5	0.9	2.7	0.9	3.2	1.1	2.5	0.9	2.8	0.7	2.7	0.9	2.2	0.8
Resistant	2.1	0.8	2.1	0.9	2.3	1.0	2.4	0.9	2.0	0.7	2.1	0.8	2.0	0.8
Distant	2.0	1.0	2.0	1.0	2.2	1.2	2.2	0.9	1.7	0.7	2.4	0.9	2.7	1.1
Directive	2.6	1.0	3.0	0.9	3.3	1.0	2.8	0.9	3.0	0.7	2.1	0.9	2.3	0.9
Accepting	3.7	0.9	3.6	0.9	3.5	1.0	3.4	0.8	3.9	0.8	3.8	0.7	3.4	0.8
Supportive	4.0	1.0	4.0	0.9	3.8	1.0	3.7	0.9	4.3	0.8	3.9	0.7	3.5	0.8
Constructive	3.9	1.0	3.9	0.9	3.8	1.0	3.7	1.0	4.1	0.8	3.9	0.9	3.4	0.9

Relationships:
A = Principals' to superintendents
B = Superintendents to principals
C = Director's to superintendents
D = Director's to school trustees
E = Principals' to teachers
F = Communities' to principals
G = Administration's to regional office of Ministry of Education

Scale:
1 = Not at all
2 = A little
3 = Somewhat
4 = Much
5 = Very Much

contradictory, and thus are not as directive or constructive as those from senior administrators and trustees.

Finally, the administrations' links to the regional Ministry of Education office are similar to the directors' relationship with trustees, but with an important difference. Local administrations are viewed as being slightly subordinate, demanding, resistant, and directive; somewhat distant, accepting, and constructive; and quite supportive. These are the most distant of all relationships investigated; they seem to lack the tension apparent in the others, with the lack of resistance combined with a relatively low level of acceptance compared to other relationships.

The degree of consensus among respondents on the character of the various relationships was estimated from the standard deviations of responses: The larger the standard deviation, the lower the consensus. The least consensus appeared on two items, one of which concerned the distance of the directors' relationship to superintendents. The distribution of scores was as follows: not at all, 28 percent; a little, 27 percent; somewhat, 17 percent; much, 9 percent; and very much, 3 percent. The mean was 2.2 and the standard deviation was 1.2. The most consensus appeared for several items with a standard deviation of 0.7. For example, the extent of demands placed by principals on teachers was distributed in this manner: not at all, 4 percent; a little, 22 percent; somewhat, 55 percent; much, 11 percent; very much, 1 percent. The mean was 2.8. Taken overall, there was greatest consensus about the principals' relationships with teachers, and the least about the directors' relationships with superintendents.

LEAST-EFFECTIVE RELATIONSHIPS

Respondents were asked which two of the seven pairs of relationships were, in their opinion, the least effective. All were nominated by at least 2 percent of respondents as being the least effective: (a) principals' to superintendents, 10 percent; (b) superintendents' to principals, 10 percent; (c) directors' to superintendents, 13 percent; (d) directors' to school trustees, 19 percent; (e) principals' to teachers, 2 percent; (f) communities' to principals, 42 percent; (g) administrations' to regional offices of Ministry of Education, 4 percent. Six were nominated for being the second least effective: (b) superintendents' to principals, 6 percent; (c) directors' to superintendents, 4 percent; (d) directors' to school trustees, 8 percent; (e) principals' to teachers, 2 percent; (f) communities' to principals, 10 percent; (g) administrations' to regional offices of ministry of Education, 69 percent.

It is apparent that the two relationships that are perceived as least effective are those that cross the boundary of the local school system, first to the school community, and second to the regional office of the Ministry of Education. Since formal organizations, by their very nature, internally integrate through an administrative structure, it is not surprising that internal relationships are perceived to be more effective than those that involve parties on the outside. Still, it appears that the relationships most in need of attention are those linking school systems to the environment. That environment might be changing much more rapidly than is comfortable for those in school systems, thus giving rise to the opinions reported in our survey.

Maintaining links with the community was difficult for a number of reasons. One principal noted there was no distinct parent organization for the school; often both parents are working outside the home, so more time is needed to deal with problems. As a result, rather than being proactive, schools are reactive. Another felt that too many principals don't take the time to develop community relationships; but, as one noted, the task is difficult: "There is real difficulty in obtaining feedback from a cross-section of the community in order to determine the feeling of the community about the school and the job it is doing." Part of the reason for this is that "the immediate community of the school is now larger, more fragmented and more diverse in many ways and thus the relationship is not as effective as it might be." Unfortunately, schools are "unable to adequately articulate their goals to the community to explain changes in pedagogy and the like in the face of unreasonable expectations." Often "the community does not know how to get involved in the school, and there is a fear from the school that the community will try to control the school." There are "increasing demands on the part of some parents' groups for greater control (i.e., governance) of the school curriculum and school affairs." One director summed up the issue as follows: "Our principals don't really know how to involve parents in schools so that parents have some real involvement in the education of their children. Administration doesn't know how to teach principals to do this. Parents don't know how to be involved without taking over, haranguing, or whatever. So we cultivate pleasant social relationships, share fund-raising activities, exchange some information and fight the odd fire. So far we are getting away with it, but one wonders how long."

Relations with the regional office of the Ministry of Education brought forth more general, often negative, comments about the ministry's approach to dealing with school boards. The problem, one director indicated, was the "Ministry's general lack of understanding of what it is like in the real world." A principal expanded, "They are at a distance geographically and removed from the schools; they need to slow down changes to allow boards to conduct in-service and implement programs more effectively." Several suggested that the ministry had assumed more of an "authority" role in recent years: "Communications always seem to be one-way and a credibility problem has developed; no one seems to be listening when we express concerns." One factor, a director indicated, is that "the Ministry does not believe in the concept of a Regional office. The Ministry is still suffering from a scheme for centralized control" even though directions appeared inconsistent: "The Ministry seems lost. The right hand doesn't talk to the left. It is subject to frequent changes and is too concerned with politics to give real educational solutions. Unfortunately, the field often can't wait for Ministry involvement as an integral part of action." "My only correspondence from the Ministry of Education is directive," responded one principal; "you can never get a clear-cut decision to a problem. The only direct contact is for audit purposes." One concluded with a plague-on-all-their-houses type of comment: "There is a lack of trust in the decisions of the MOE based on a lack of their understanding of education in the classroom. The present trustees are too interested in politics, are distrustful of the senior administration, and are always bickering among themselves. Lawsuits are prevalent. They don't listen to the director."

Returning to the original assessment of relationships, it is worth repeating that overall relationships between both principals and communities, and between board administrations and the Ministry of Education regional offices, were generally positive. The summary of comments diagnosing specific problems is largely negative because we asked about the nature of the problems that did exist. In the closing part of the paper, we discuss methods suggested for improving relationships.

ACTUAL AND PREFERRED DISTRIBUTION OF
DECISION-MAKING AUTHORITY

Who does make decisions about what goes on in schools? The description of school board structures, communication, and relationships already indicates that decisions do not occur at any one level, but often involve multiple levels. Problems between levels— delays, disagreements, excessive numbers of requests in both directions—suggest that some clarification may be possible about who does what, and who should do what. This section deals with these two issues.

Respondents were asked to indicate how much influence different individuals or groups had on key decisions in schools. The groups whose influence was assessed included (1) senior administration, (2) principals and vice-principals, (3) teachers, (4) students, (5) parents, (6) trustees, (7) the Ministry of Education, (8) the federal government, (9) teacher federations, (10) community or business groups, and (11) school councils (community groups that advise principals). The scale of influence ranged from "none" (coded 1) to "much" (coded 6). They could also indicate "not applicable."

The decisions focused upon were (1) the setting of school board goals, (2) the design of the curriculum, (3) types of instructional methods, (4) the hiring of teachers, (5) assigning teachers to schools, (6) the dismissal of teachers, (7) the number of teachers to be assigned to a school, (8) the number of support staff assigned to each school, (9) the amount of professional development for teachers, (10) the kind of professional development for teachers, (11) evaluation procedures for teachers, (12) evaluation procedures for students, (13) evaluation procedures for senior administrators, (14) spending priorities in the school board's budget, and (15) spending priorities in the individual school's budget.

These fifteen decisions can be grouped into four categories: resource allocation (items 7, 8, 9, 14, and 15), policies toward teachers (items 4, 5, 6, 10, and 11), instructional policy and practice (items 2, 3, and 12), and board-level policies and practices (items 1 and 13).

Tables 11–3, 11–4, and 11–5 provide a summary of respondents' perceptions. The first of these (table 11–3) concerns resource allocation decisions, which were perceived to be in the hands of senior administrators, backed up by trustees and the

Table 11–3
Mean Extent of Actual and Appropriate Influence of
Groups on Resource Allocation
(N = 217)

Individual Group[a]	NTS	NSS	APD	SBB	ISB
Senior administration	5.7	5.7	5.2	5.6	4.2
	5.3	5.2	5.0	5.3	3.8
Principals and VPs	3.9	3.8	4.5	3.5	5.4
	5.1	5.2	5.2	4.7	5.6
Teachers	2.1	2.1	3.8	2.4	4.0
	3.1	3.4	5.0	3.7	4.7
Students	1.3	1.4	1.3	1.4	1.8
	1.9	1.8	1.9	2.2	2.6
Parents	1.6	1.6	1.5	1.9	1.6
	2.0	2.2	2.0	2.9	2.4
Trustees	3.7	4.0	3.6	5.4	2.4
	3.5	3.7	3.5	5.0	2.4
Ministry of Education	2.5	1.9	3.2	3.9	2.3
	2.4	2.2	3.4	3.7	2.3
Federal government	1.1	1.2	1.2	1.9	1.1
	1.2	1.3	1.4	1.7	1.2
Teacher federations	3.7	2.3	3.4	2.3	1.6
	3.3	2.6	3.6	2.5	1.7
Community/business groups	1.1	1.2	1.3	1.6	1.4
	1.4	1.4	1.6	2.0	1.6
School councils	1.4	1.4	1.4	1.5	1.6
	1.8	1.9	2.0	2.1	2.3

[a]NT—Item 7, number of teachers to a school
NSS —8, number of support staff
APD—9, amount of professional development for teachers
SBB —14, spending priorities in school board budget
ISB—15, spending priorities in individual school's budget
"Actual" means are given above and "appropriate" means below
Scale: From 1 = none to 6 = much influence

Ministry of Education. Only on spending priorities within schools did another party, the principals and vice-principals, apparently have most say. As far as respondents' views on the appropriate levels of influence are concerned, a somewhat different pattern emerged. There was a shift toward school site administrators and teachers as being desirable, with diminished influence from central office authority. There was only very weak support for the provision of additional levels of influence to members of the community; the strongest support for a change of this sort advocated that parents be somewhat more involved in setting school board spending priorities.

Policies regarding teachers—hiring, assigning, dismissing, developing and evaluating—seem to be shared about evenly between senior administrators and building-level administrators (table 11–4). The latter had a bit more say in the hiring of teachers than central administrators did, but less say about subsequent assignments of teachers to schools. Central officials also directed professional development and the evaluation of teachers. In general, as with resource allocation, the respondents approved of allocating greater levels of responsibility to the school level, particularly in the professional development and the evaluation of teachers. They saw teachers taking a greater part in that process themselves. Indeed, they looked to teacher federations and the ministry for some additional input into the process. There was weak support for crossing the boundary between the school and the community to provide advice on these matters, although both parents and students were considered to have valuable insights.

Policies about curriculum, instructional methods, and student evaluation (table 11–5, columns 1 to 3), seemed to be influenced in subtley different ways. The ministry played the lead role in curriculum development, with implementation shared fairly evenly between central administrators, site administrators, and teachers. More appropriate, in the view of respondents, would be more equal partnering with the ministry, and more involvement at the local level with students, parents, and others. Instructional methods were primarily guided by teachers, with direction and support from principals, administrators, and others. Again, a more equal partnering seems to be preferred, with stronger input from administrators, the ministry, and federations. Student evaluation was considered to be a matter for teachers within a provincial framework: Directors and principals answering the questionnaire

Table 11-4
Mean Extent of Actual and Appropriate Influence of
Groups on Teacher Policy
(N = 217)

Individual Group[a]	HT	AT	DT	KPD	ET
Senior administration	4.8	5.1	5.5	5.0	5.5
	4.5	4.7	5.6	4.8	5.2
Principals and VPs	5.2	4.7	5.2	4.8	5.0
	5.6	5.5	5.6	5.3	5.4
Teachers	2.5	2.3	1.8	4.3	3.8
	3.4	3.1	2.4	5.4	4.9
Students	1.3	1.2	1.6	1.3	1.5
	1.8	1.6	1.9	2.0	2.5
Parents	1.3	1.2	1.9	1.4	1.4
	1.9	1.9	2.0	2.1	2.3
Trustees	2.3	1.9	3.3	2.5	2.8
	2.4	1.9	3.3	2.9	3.0
Ministry of Education	1.7	1.1	1.9	2.8	2.5
	1.8	1.2	2.2	3.2	3.0
Federal government	1.1	1.0	1.1	1.2	1.1
	1.2	1.1	1.1	1.3	1.2
Teacher federations	2.0	2.0	3.5	3.2	3.6
	2.0	1.8	3.2	3.6	3.7
Community/business groups	1.2	1.1	1.2	1.3	1.2
	1.5	1.3	1.3	2.0	1.6
School councils	1.3	1.2	1.4	1.1	1.3
	1.8	1.6	1.6	2.2	1.9

[a]HT = Item 4, hiring of teachers
AT = 5, assignment of teachers
DT = 6, dismissal of teacher
KPD = 10, kind of professional development for teachers
ET = 11, evaluation procedures for teachers
Scale: From 1 = none to 6 = much influence

appeared to feel this was appropriate, perhaps with stronger guidance from principals and the ministry.

The two board-level policies considered were the setting of school board goals and evaluation practices for senior administrators (Table 11–5, columns 4 and 5). Senior administrators and trustees, with significant direction from the provincial government, were important in both these areas. There was a desire for wider involvement in the setting of goals from all levels of the community. For the evaluation of administrators there was support for a modest increase in direction from central authorities.

For patterns of influence within school boards, it is helpful to break down the responses for influence on decision making by the role of the respondent: director, elementary principal, and secondary principal. Table 11–6 reports increases or decreases in influence that each of these three groups believed appropriate for senior officials and principals in the 15 decision areas. For example, all three groups felt that senior administrators should have less influence and that principals should have more. In curriculum development, all agreed that senior administrators had about the right influence, but that the influence of principals should increase. Disagreements were evident in a few areas—the hiring of teachers, assigning teachers to schools, and deciding on the number of teachers. On these issues, principals felt that senior administrators should have less influence while principals should have more. The directors agreed that principals should influence these matters more, but they did not see diminished influence for senior administrators. Nevertheless, the overall pattern of this evidence suggests a shared indication that there is desire to shift more power to the school.

CONCLUSION

This assessment of administrative structures in Ontario school systems by those employed within them provides insight into both past trends and future directions. The trends identified include progressive flattening of administrative hierarchies as senior officials assume broader roles both in the administration of schools and in functional areas. Administrative councils at central offices are increasingly likely to include principals as well as senior administrators, implying a more collaborative management style

Table 11–5
Mean Extent of Actual and Appropriate Influence of
Groups on Instructional and Board Level Policy and Practice
(N = 217)

Individual Group[a]	CD	IM	ES	BG	EA
Senior administration	4.4	3.9	4.3	5.5	5.0
	4.5	4.3	4.3	5.3	4.9
Principals and VPs	4.2	4.7	5.1	3.8	2.0
	4.9	5.3	5.4	4.9	3.9
Teachers	4.5	5.2	5.3	2.8	1.5
	5.2	5.4	5.5	4.3	3.1
Students	2.1	2.6	2.3	1.8	1.1
	3.6	3.9	3.5	3.5	1.6
Parents	1.9	2.1	1.9	2.7	1.3
	2.9	3.0	3.1	3.9	2.2
Trustees	2.4	2.1	2.3	4.9	4.6
	3.0	2.6	2.7	4.9	4.8
Ministry of Education	5.1	3.7	3.5	4.5	2.6
	4.7	4.0	3.7	4.1	3.4
Federal government	1.9	1.4	1.1	2.1	1.2
	2.1	1.7	1.3	2.3	1.3
Teacher federations	2.9	2.9	2.4	3.2	1.5
	3.3	3.3	2.9	3.4	2.3
Community/business groups	2.1	1.8	1.3	2.4	1.3
	3.2	2.5	1.8	3.4	1.7
School councils	2.1	1.9	1.5	2.4	1.2
	3.2	2.8	2.1	3.6	1.9

[a]CD = Item 2, curriculum design
IM = 4, instructional methods
ES = 12, evaluation of students
BG = 1, school board goals
EA = 13, evaluation procedures for senior administrators
Scale: From 1 = none to 6 = much influence

Table 11–6
Mean Preferred Change in Influence on Making Decisions by Roles

Decision	Roles	Preferred Change in Influence*	
		Senior Administration	Principals
Establishing school board goals	D (N = 21)	-.429	.381
	EP (N = 57)	-.386	1.339
	SP (N = 58)	-.121	1.068
Curriculum	D	.095	.571
	EP	-.035	.741
	SP	.000	.559
Establishing instructional methods	D	.429	.667
	EP	.414	.390
	SP	.186	.621
Hiring teachers	D	.000	.048
	EP	-.305	.593
	SP	-.363	.305
Assigning teachers to schools	D	.048	.333
	EP	-.542	1.051
	SP	-.421	.561
Dismissal of teachers	D	.050	.300
	EP	.000	.448
	SP	.000	.293
Deciding number of teachers	D	.250	.737
	EP	-.379	1.707
	SP	-.431	1.017

Table 11–6 (continued)

| Decision | Roles | Preferred Change in Influence* | |
		Senior Administration	Principals
Deciding number of support staff	D	.048	.286
	EP	-.550	1.850
	SP	-.712	1.424
Deciding amount of professional development for teachers	D	-.190	.381
	EP	-.172	.931
	SP	-.456	.695
Deciding the kind of professional development for teachers	D	-.143	.238
	EP	-.327	.636
	SP	-.424	.458
Deciding evaluation procedures for teachers	D	-.048	.381
	EP	-.351	.421
	SP	-.356	.458
Deciding evaluation procedures for students	D	-.143	.238
	EP	-.351	.421
	SP	-.356	.458
Deciding evaluation procedures for senior administrators in school boards	D	-.048	1.143
	EP	-.283	1.846
	SP	-.291	1.982
Deciding the spending priorities of the school board's budget	D	-.048	.619
	EP	-.333	1.491
	SP	-.431	1.052

Table 11–6 (continued)

| Decision | Roles | Preferred Change in Influence* | |
		Senior Administration	Principals
Deciding the spending	D	-.238	-.048
priorities of the individual school's	EP	-.357	.250
budget	SP	-.517	.103
Total mean scores	D	-.024	.418
	EP	-.240	.929
	SP	-.288	.732

(D: Director; EP: elementary principals; SP: secondary principals)
Note: Preferred changes in influence were calculated by subtracting "appropriate influence" from "actual influence." A negative score implies respondents would prefer to see the influence of the target group reduced.

and a desire to ensure that the perspectives at the center reflect the views of those who deliver front-line services to the public.

While both directors of education and principals were reasonably well satisfied with existing administrative structures, seven problem areas were identified for improvement: communication, administrative barriers, knowledge about both elementary and secondary programs, personal competence, workload, politics, and school-level authority. Difficulties in the authority relationships could be a primary source of many of these problems, a possibility addressed by assessing the character of these relations among various parties.

Three positive characteristics of authority relationships (accepting, supportive, and constructive) tended to dominate, in the view of respondents. Relatively less common were what might be considered negative characteristics: subordinate, demanding, resistant, distant, and directive. There seemed to be an overall acceptance of the legitimate authority of the various parties, with inherent tensions worked out in ways that built peoples' capacity, rather than ensured their compliance. Problems were most likely to be cited in relations that crossed boundaries—relations between schools and their communities, or between school systems and the ministry. Even these relations were not judged to be bad, but they did seem to be the more frequent source of difficulty and in need of development.

Problems in authority relationships can often be traced to disputes over "decision rights"—who has the authority to make a decision. Individuals at one level might feel they are burdened with too many decisions, or that they lack the authority to make decisions that are necessary for them to meet their responsibilities. To explore this issue, we assessed who was perceived to influence various types of policy decisions concerning (1) resource allocation, (2) teachers, (3) instructional matters, and (4) systemwide administration. There seemed to be a desire for more coherent policy at all levels, while shifting as much influence as possible to the school, with greater involvement by teachers and less by senior administrators, on pedagogical and managerial matters. Complementing this was a soft, but nevertheless clearly evident, support for greater influence from the ministry and the teachers federation in leading the development of policy.

The suggestion that the ministry might do more, paired with the low level of support for more involvement from the community, in some ways runs counter to the expectations generated by the analyses of relationships. Although not perceived as poor, school and community relationships were perceived as weakest among those assessed. Yet in none of the decision areas studied was there much more than modest support for a greater role for the community. It is difficult to say from the data, but there may be some fear and uncertainty about increasing community influence, perhaps due to the risk that special interest groups might exploit an opportunity to harass or control a school. On the other hand, fear is a poor excuse for reaching out when a need is perceived.

An internal assessment alone is not an adequate basis for undertaking reform of administrative structures and practices. More data are needed on the perceptions that others have. One such assessment was provided in the Report of the Commission on Private Schools (Shapiro 1985), in which the commissioner, Bernard Shapiro, wrote, "Expressed criticism of the board schools tended to focus on the perceived bureaucratization of the schools and the extent to which they are perceived to have become primarily instruments of the state and the professional experts rather than partnerships between the government and the professionals on the one hand and both parents and local communities on the other. Indeed, parents and local community representatives often are seen as the real casualties of both school districts' consolidation and the province's emphasis on control through professionalization, specialization and standardization" (pp. 57–58). He concluded by recommending each school have a "School Committee including the principal and elected parents and teachers in a minimum ratio of two to one. The tasks of this Committee would be to communicate, through the principal, with the school board so that the board is informed as to the community's priority concerns with regard to the school's policies and programs and the community is similarly informed with regard to the board" (Shapiro 1985, pp. 58–59, Recommendation 34).

Although Shapiro subsequently became Deputy Minister for Education and three other provinces (Quebec, Alberta, and British Columbia) adopted legislation creating such school councils, Ontario has taken no such action.

Combining Shapiro's report on the Ontario public perception, trends elsewhere, and the perceptions and preferences expressed by respondents to our survey suggests the direction for future change: an evolutionary renewal of individual school authority within a carefully constructed set of guidelines that would allocate decision rights in a clear-cut manner. The exact design of such a system is complex, and simple solutions are unlikely to succeed. Systematic experimentation is needed: Various types of decisions might be allocated to schools, different types of school administration might be tried, and various forums for community input—provincial, local, and school—could be assessed. Using the existing system as a secure foundation, such adaptive responses may well provide the mechanism that will provide for continuous improvement of our administrative apparatus for delivering education.

REFERENCES

Deming, W. E. (1986). *Out of the crisis.* Milwaukee, WI: ASQC Quality Press.
Hickcox, E. S., & Ducharme, D. J. (1972). Administrative staffing patterns in Ontario school districts. *Alberta Journal of Educational Research, 18*(2), 100–110.

Lawton, S. B. (1992). Implications of school-based management for school finance: An international survey. *School Business Affairs,* *58*(12), 4–11.

Lawton, S. B. (1993). *School board structures: A comparative analysis.* Manuscript, Department of Educational Administration, OISE, Toronto.

Osborne, D., & Gaebler, T. (1992). *Reinventing government: How the entrepreneurial spirit is transforming the public sector.* New York: Addison-Wesley.

Peters, T. J., & Waterman, R. H. (1982). *In search of excellence.* New York: Harper & Row.

Shapiro, B. J. (1985). *The report of the Commission on Private Schools in Ontario.* Toronto: Commission on Private Schools in Ontario.

Wang, S. (1991). *Board-school authority relationships in the Ontario systems.* Master's thesis, University of Toronto.

Merriam-Webster's Collegiate Dictionary, (1993) 10th ed. Springfield, MA: Merriam-Webster.

Weick, K. E. (1976). Educational organizations as loosely coupled systems. *Administrative Science Quarterly, 21,*1–19.

CHAPTER 12

Toward a More Comprehensive Appreciation of Effective School District Leadership

Kenneth Leithwood

So that's it. What effective district leadership entails and how, through such leadership, politics gets transformed into education. At least that's it for now, because the ten studies reported in previous chapters represent early days in this kind of inquiry. Nonetheless, they've helped us understand much better how effective superintendents manage the transformation. There are two purposes for this concluding chapter. The first is to provide a broad and somewhat impressionistic synopsis of what these chapters have taught us: I entitle this the "two faces of CEOs' politics." The second is to summarize, more analytically, what has been learned and where it would be productive to focus subsequent study.

THE TWO FACES OF CEOs' POLITICS

Perhaps some people began reading this book with the impression that occupants of the organizational apex in school districts sat in pristine offices buffered from the push and pull of real school life. Perhaps they thought that CEOs remained aloof from the messiness that seems so much a part of how most of us negotiate our days—that they delegated the mess to others. As a minimum, these chapters put the lie to that impression. A CEO's life appears to be a long series of overwhelmingly interpersonal negotiations and compromises punctuated with occasional episodes of planning

and goal setting. As often as not, this work is done in collaboration with many others. Several chapters hint at this. But a study
carried out (in parallel with those reported in chapters 3 and 4) by
Hickcox (1992) found that ten effective CEOs spent, on the average, *five hours per day* in meetings. Furthermore, the occasional
episodes of planning and goal setting are often in response to
someone else's agenda, that of the board, the province or state, the
teachers union, a "back-to-the-basics, parents-for-quality-educa-
tion" group, and so on. Most likely all of these at the same time.
So while Cuban (1989), for example, is correct in asserting a
"managerial imperative" for superintendents, this imperative is
enacted in a highly political context.

It is not so much the case that CEOs are a kind of organizational "tabula rasa" on which everyone else writes; they do appear
to give high priority to envisioning and direction setting on behalf
of their organizations, as Holdaway and Genge (see chapter 2)
found. But this has quite a different meaning in a school district
organization than it does in private enterprise. It is different in two
respects. First, as long as Steinberg's food stores, for example,
were managed by its founder, his vision was the only one that
counted: Through good times and bad times, there was never any
question about where the big policy decisions got made—at the
(very) top, as is the case in many single-owner enterprises. In his
metaphor of organizations as brains, this is the extreme archetype
of what Morgan (1986) means by organizations "with brains."
Intelligence on behalf of the organization is, almost literally, centered in the head of its owner. The rest of the organization exists
only to carry out directions from the head.

School district organizations, in contrast, may well be one of
the more extreme archetypes of what Morgan (1986) means when
he speaks of organizations "as brains." In such organizations,
responsibility for big policy decisions is widely distributed.
Among whom? Actually, that question is harder to answer than a
quick pass at it might suggest. Certainly, the elected board has
responsibility for policy decisions, at least those decisions left over
from state or provincial policy efforts. After reading Townsend's
account of the number of policies enacted at that level over a few
short years in one province, a fairly modest estimate of the policy
discretion remaining for boards seems warranted. Furthermore,
since board members face the electorate pretty frequently, their
sensitivity to the interests of powerful groups with a stake in the

education system is often exceptionally fine-tuned. So it is probably accurate to describe the intelligence used by school boards in
direction setting as widely distributed among many other stakeholders: The board will itself usually function as a conduit, organizer, and occasional booster (or dampener) of the power of that
intelligence.

And the CEO's role with the board? How about the CEO as
safari guide? Been there before. A rough map of the terrain in
mind. Some sense of the preparation required. Armed with a
machete to clear the sometimes impenetrable underbrush. But trying to help the members of the safari find the game of their choice,
within a very narrow menu of possibilities dictated by the terrain
in which they travel and the outer limits of what the animal rights
activists will tolerate (cameras only, no guns). We could go on; it
has possibilities.

There is a second way in which initiatives by superintendents
to plan, envision, and direction-set for their districts are different
from what they have typically been in private enterprise. The first
difference is due to the permeability, indeed vulnerability, of school
districts to "turbulence in the external environment" (a euphemism
for chaos, favored by organizational learning theorists). This turbulence requires the CEO to work at transforming "large p" and
"medium p" politics into education. The second difference is due
to the characteristic nature of school districts' internal environments and requires the CEO to work at transforming "small p" or
micropolitics into education. This is an altogether subtler, less visible, and less well understood aspect of what CEOs do. When it is
done right, some think of it as transformational *leadership*—see
Musella's chapter, for example, or Coleman and LaRocque (1991).

Now there is widespread, fundamental misunderstanding
about the internal environment of school districts. And this is
nowhere more evident than among the advocates of such "restructuring" initiatives as school-based decision making and teacher
empowerment. These folks appear to start from the premise that
schools and districts are heavily bureaucratized, centralized, and
managed from the top down: The task of restructuring is to create
flatter organizations in order to push decisions down to the level
of those with the best information. Our attention is directed, by
these folks, to the model efforts of large, rapidly changing, private-sector companies, and we are admonished to emulate their
example.

Do you know how many managerial job category levels Esso had before it began downsizing in about 1988? Over forty! Now they are "flattened" to only about fifteen. Do you think Esso was any different than IBM, GE, Ford, and others? No. How many categories of professional jobs are to be found in schools? Maybe two or three in your typical elementary school. Add one more for department heads in most secondary schools and perhaps another three or four layers at the district level.

The irony of this is a bit preposterous, actually. The so-called first wave of reform during the 1980s in the United States (e.g., Murphy 1989) included a number of efforts, career ladders for example, to "unflatten" the educational organization, on the grounds that this would increase incentives to teachers. Apparently the first wave was whipped up by a bunch of transactional types who believed overwhelmingly in the power of contingent reward, exchange theory, external incentives, and the like. Fortunately, the first wave crested out of sight of the mainland, although it did wash up on the shores of several islands doing some serious but not permanent damage. So now schools are being asked to change into what they have always been, with the help of corporate models that are less well-developed than are most school districts already. And no one seems to have noticed. At least I haven't heard or read any comment on the matter.[1]

What is my point, you ask. Actually, I have two points. The first is that the internal environment of school districts in which CEOs plan, direction-set, and the like is, on the one hand, driven by a set of regularities and conditions that severely limit the range of initiatives available to even the most creative teacher or principal. Everyone whines about secondary teachers teaching subjects, not kids, for example. You try "teaching kids" when you are confronted with maybe 150 or 200 of them every day—14-year-olds, at that. Secondary teachers aren't bad people. Most of the ones I know are pretty bright, quite like their students, and are fairly committed to their own professional growth. Contrary to popular belief, they are as interested in innovative instructional techniques as your average elementary teacher. But the organizational structure (and not the flatness of this structure) within which they work inexorably rejects some practices and makes it sensible to engage in others.

My second point is that teaching kids is not the same as manufacturing Clorox bleach, microchips, painkillers, or automobile tires. Edward Demings's advice, for example, to build quality into your products, in part by working with your suppliers to ensure consistency in your raw materials (Sashkin and Kiser 1992), requires more creativity to apply in school districts than I'm capable of, at least. But, to push the analogy along just a little, most teachers have a strong concern for continuously adjusting what they are doing in light of feedback from the student. Discretion. A flexible repertoire. Building on kids' interests. These are among the hard-won tools teachers have come to value in performing a job that most of their critics haven't the faintest feeling for and that would turn their psyches to mush in a matter of months.

In sum, then, CEOs plan and direct school districts whose internal environments are, on the one hand, already defined by extraordinarily hard-to-change regularities[2] and are, on the other, coped with best by the exercise of considerable discretion at the level of service delivery. Under these conditions "micropolitics" seems quite appropriate as a description of CEOs' leadership: Building on what those in the trenches consider to be possible, knowing that you can easily be ignored if those in the trenches don't consider your plans and directions possible. How can CEOs be ignored in this way, you ask. Easy. They lead and manage what are already about the flattest public or private organizations one can imagine, organizations that defy close supervision, even if close supervision seemed like a good idea.

In sum, then, the two faces of CEOs' politics include, first, the largely explicit politics of the school district's external environment and its legitimate demand to have its invariably diverse and often conflicting values reflected in the goals and plans for educational programs in the district. The second face includes the usually much subtler politics of the school district's internal environment and its power to insist that at least any plans likely to be realized in practice have to be "do-able" within the framework of some very hard to change organizational regularities and the need for considerable judgment to be exercised by those who actually do the teaching.

IMPLICATIONS FOR FUTURE RESEARCH

After an extensive review of more than three thousand leadership studies, Stogdill complained:

Four decades of research on leadership have produced a bewildering mass of findings. . . . The endless accumulation of empirical data has not produced an integrated understanding of leadership. (Quoted in Yukl 1989, p. 267)

Lack of a widely accepted theory, or "integrated understanding," is commonly cited as an obstacle to further progress in almost all areas of social science research. Most of us nod in agreement and carry on regardless, perhaps in the belief that it is an unrealistic option.

To date, empirical research concerning the superintendency has resulted in substantially less than a "bewildering mass of findings" and, as I noted in chapter 1, only a handful of studies specifically address the meaning of effectiveness in the superintendency. It does not require unmanageably large amounts of data, however, to appreciate the utility of an integrative framework. Such a framework would be helpful as another, more analytic way of summarizing what the ten studies reported in this book add up to and what they imply for future inquiry. In this section of this chapter, I describe one possible framework, significant elements of which are based on my own work, and use it as a tool for such purposes.[3] Figure 12–1 displays the central constructs and relationships in the framework.

The construct *leadership practices* may be considered a kind of fulcrum, for our purposes. What it means to be an "effective superintendent" is a question, first of all, about such practices. But a comprehensive appreciation of effective school district leadership also demands an explanation of how effective practices come about (their causes). Figure 12–1 suggests that such an explanation is to be found most directly in the thoughts and feelings of superintendents (internal processes); less directly, leadership practices can be explained by the kinds of influences from the external environment that superintendents choose to think about. That is,

Figure 12–1
A Framework for Understanding School District Leadership

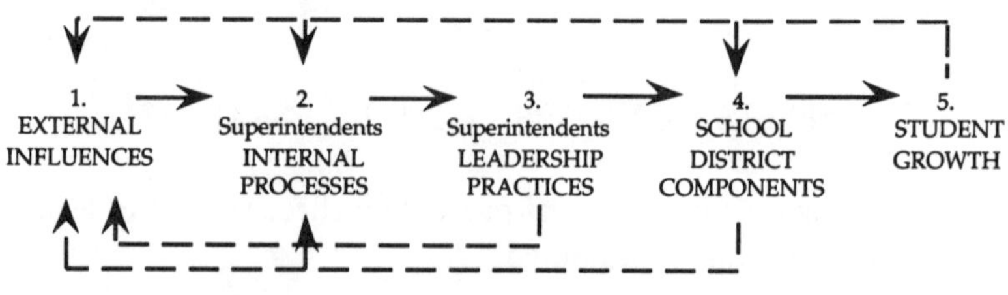

superintendents' interpretations of state mandates, for example, along with their own sense of what is important to do in their districts, give rise to the forms of leadership in which they overtly engage.

Leadership practices almost always have indirect effects on such basic organizational outcomes as the goals we aspire to for students in schools. Ignoring those aspects of the organization through which superintendents' leadership practices are connected to the outcomes aspired to for students (*school district components*) is to treat both district and school organizations as black boxes. Indeed, it might be claimed that for those in relatively remote leadership roles, like superintendents, finding elements of their organization that they can influence and that will in turn impact on something that will impact on "the bottom line" is their major challenge.

At this level of abstraction, the framework in figure 12–1 closely approximates the product of other efforts to better appreciate leader practices and their antecedents and consequences. For example, Yukl (1989) has proposed a variant on this framework to guide leadership research in general; Bossert and colleagues (1982) offer a version to explain the principal's role in instructional management. My colleagues and I have proposed several increasingly elaborate variants to explain the principal's role in school improvement (Leithwood and Montgomery 1986; Trider and Leithwood 1988; Leithwood, Begley and Cousins 1990).

While each of these frameworks shares in common most of the constructs in figure 12–1, at least a significant portion of the variables associated with each construct are different in each case and have been specified in some detail so as to acknowledge the unique features of the domain within which the research is taking place. Without such further specification, the value of these frameworks, including figure 12–1, would be pretty questionable. For this reason, the subsequent discussion of this figure includes identification of one set of variables within four of the five constructs that seem promising in the particular domain of the superintendent's leadership for school improvement.

The sets of variables that I propose within each construct can be justified, but they remain open to dispute (as would alternative sets). And this is the point. At least a major portion of future research in this domain ought to be driven by such well-framed dispute, in my view. There will be dispute about the most productive theories for describing each construct and its relationship with other constructs. For example, within the construct *leadership practices* potentially are to be found such contemporary grand leadership theories as path-goal theory (e.g., Vroom and Yetton 1973), situational leadership theory (e.g., Yukl 1989), appreciative leadership theory (e.g., Srivastva and Cooperrider 1990), moral leadership theory (e.g., Sergiovanni 1992), and the like. Each of these theories offers an opinion about preferred leadership practices. Most also spell out some propositions about the effects of those practices on others—*school district components* in figure 12–1. Some also attend to those *external influences* that ought to be considered by leaders (for example, "task structure" in the case of situational leadership theory).

This analysis, however, is not about the development of grand leadership theory: Indeed, the pursuit of that purpose may be the source of Stogdill's opening complaint. Its aim, more modestly, is to impose some conceptual order on the evidence provided by ten studies and offer some direction for future work concerned, in particular, with effective school district leadership in the contemporary context of North American schooling. Assumptions about that context are critical and are part of the discussion concerning external influences.

External Influences

Figure 12–1 assumes that what superintendents do (their practices) depends on what they think, their internal processes. These internal processes are partly shaped by the meaning and significance attributed by superintendents to the people, events, and other aspects of the external environment of which they are aware.

What aspects of their external environment do effective superintendents pay attention to, and how do these things influence their thinking? Evidence from chapters in this book and from prior research highlight at least five aspects: the community, the elected board, the school district itself, mandates from national and provincial or state governments, and general social trends.

First, as chapters 2 and 3 reveal so clearly, the elected board is by far the greatest external influence on superintendent thinking: this is consistent with almost all earlier relevant evidence (e.g., Allison 1991; McLeod 1986). Several case studies by Wirt (1991) suggest that this influence can sometimes completely overshadow other influences, as when a superintendent is hired specifically to settle a strike in terms favored by the board. But this dominance is inconsistent with how effectiveness has been conceived of in this book; politics does not get transformed into education in any meaningful way when the board's influence is allowed to completely overshadow other considerations.

With respect to the community, secondly, superintendents in Wills and Peterson's study (chapter 5) were influenced in their responses to state mandates by their perceptions of economic and social change in the community. Elsewhere, Crowson and Morris (1992) reported that they were "frankly surprised . . . by the degree to which superintendents' [of unknown effectiveness] discourse involved a lengthy discussion of their surrounding community." Hord, Jolly, and Mendez-Morse's (1992) portrait of superintendents in small rural districts shows most of them to be indistinguishable from their communities in terms of origin, values, or lifestyles (Holmes's chapter suggests that value conflicts might well arise in larger districts, however). In chapter 2, effective superintendents were reported to use "public satisfaction" as a central criterion for judging their district's progress.

Third, a number of these same studies have indicated that superintendents pay close attention to the internal features of their own schools and district organizations, as well. Chapter 5, by Wills and Peterson, and chapter 6, by Murphy, clarify which internal features receive most of the superintendent's attention. For example, in Wills and Peterson's study the districts' human and fiscal resources were of central concern as superintendents shaped their responses to state mandates. Also of concern to these superintendents, as well as to the Kentucky superintendents in Murphy's study, was the structure of decision making within their districts—how participative it could become before it overburdened staff or disenfranchised the superintendent. Lawton, Scane and Wang (chapter 11) show how such decision-making structures have gradually been flattened in one provincial jurisdiction. District size appears as a critical factor in shaping the thinking and practices of superintendents: Variations in district size, for example, powerfully affect the resources available to superintendents and the range of problems that they must cope with personally.

Studies reported in this book and elsewhere suggest two sets of external influences in addition to district, board, and community. Wills and Peterson's superintendents were influenced in their thinking about how to respond to state mandates by their perceptions of economic and social change. Hallinger and Edwards (1992) found, in their one case study, a superintendent thinking about the consequences of "economic competition" for the education of students in his district, a "society-at-large" category of influence. Superintendents are also sensitive to trends in the profession (e.g., the professionalization of teaching—Hallinger and Edwards 1992) and mandates from different levels of government, especially the state or province (e.g., chapters 5, 6, and 7).

Among the more promising questions still to be addressed in efforts to better appreciate effective school district leadership are these: How much priority is typically awarded each of the categories of external influence about which we now have evidence (and others that may be salient) in the thinking of effective superintendents? Are there differences among effective superintendents in the awarding of such priorities, and, if so, what accounts for these differences? Under what circumstances do some external influences rise or fall in priority?

Internal Processes

Figure 12–1 implies the not very surprising claim that what superintendents do (their practices) is a function of how they feel and think, their *internal processes*. It also implies that, in the absence of a better understanding of such processes, the roots of superintendents' leadership practices and the basis for change in such practice will remain opaque. Attitudes, values, beliefs, problem-solving processes and domain-specific knowledge make up the meaning to be given to *internal processes* (traits and dispositions might also be included). This construct has been less directly and less commonly addressed than the others in figure 12–1 by research on leadership and administration in education. Nevertheless, variables associated with the construct have received considerable attention in education with respect to teachers (e.g., Calderhead 1987; Stromnes and Sovik 1987). Outside education comparable attention is evident—for example, in Yukl's (1989) framework, in the now-substantial bodies of work on the strategic thinking of executives (e.g., Schwenk 1988; Srivastva 1983), and in research concerning the role of executive values in problem solving and decision making (e.g., Hambrick and Brandon 1988;

Toffler 1986). Indeed, attention to internal processes and how they influence behavior substantially encompasses what Sims and Lorenzi (1992) refer to as the "new leadership paradigm."

While much less attention has been devoted to this construct in efforts to understand educational leadership, growing interest is evident in recent reports, well represented in a recent text edited by Hallinger, Leithwood, and Murphy (1993), for example, focused on school leaders. A chapter in the recent compilation of research on superintendents by Leithwood and Musella (1991) applied this focus to the superintendent, and chapter 4 in this text is a direct extension of that application. The framework used in this research consists of six components making up a model grounded in evidence concerning the problem-solving processes of both principals and superintendents (Leithwood and Steinbach 1991). Three chapters in this text (chapters 4, 5, and 10) provide evidence related to this model. The six components are these:

- *Interpretation.* A superintendent's understanding of the specific nature of the problem, often in situations where multiple problems could be identified. Hallinger and Edwards (1992), for example, report the superintendent in their study interpreting the problem facing his district as including "economic competitiveness, improved higher order thinking, more flexibility in instructional delivery, professionalization of teachers." Wills and Peterson (chapter 5) show how variations in superintendents' beliefs about, for example, their own futures, the motivation for state mandates, accountability, and the availability of human and fiscal resources affected their interpretation of the problem of implementing the state mandate. The effective superintendents in Leithwood, Steinbach, and Raun's study (Chapter 4) helped their colleagues interpret problems by showing the relationships between the immediate problems being addressed and the larger mission and problems of the district.
- *Goals.* The relatively immediate purposes the superintendent is attempting to achieve in response to her or his interpretation of the problem. Once again, in Hallinger and Edward's (1992) case study, for example, the superintendent set such goals for his problem solving as formally

involving school-level professionals and parents in decision making that influences teaching and learning. Leithwood, Steinbach, and Raun framed the goals being pursued by their effective CEOs as transforming ideas into organizational reality and fostering organizational learning.

- *Principles/values.* The relatively long-term purposes, operating principles, fundamental laws, doctrines, and assumptions guiding the superintendents' thinking. Crowson and Morris (1992) identified a number of values strongly held by the superintendents in their study: honesty, respect for staff, patience, and control ("risk management"). Furthermore, their evidence shows such values to be a central pillar in their problem solving, often acting, as Leithwood and Stager (1989) have suggested, as substitutes for knowledge. Raun and Leithwood (1993) as well as Leithwood, Steinbach, and Raun (chapter 4) found superintendents' problem solving guided by values they labeled "participation," "pragmatism" and "duty." When Holmes (chapter 10) inquired about the educational philosophies of CEOs, he found them to be substantially more progressive than those of other educators, nurses, and engineers. This raises the dilemma of what status CEOs' own values should have when providing leadership to their districts.

- *Constraints.* "Immovable" barriers, obstacles, or factors severely narrowing the range of possible solutions superintendents believe to be available. The central office staff in Corbett and Wilson's (1992) study were concerned to avoid being viewed as "heavy handed." Holdaway and Genge's effective superintendents (chapter 2) cited constraints arising from the board, lack of time, lack of money, and excessive numbers of problems to be solved.

- *Solution processes.* What the superintendent does to solve a problem in light of his or her interpretation of the problem, principles, and goals to be achieved and constraints to be accommodated. Most of the leadership practices described in the next section can be viewed as specific solution processes in this framework.

- *Mood.* The nature of the emotion or affect displayed during problem solving, and its intensity. Little explicit evidence has been reported about superintendents concerning this component. On the other hand, there are few reports of emotional anxiety, either, suggesting that many superintendents are, for the most part, reasonably calm and confident in the face of their problems. Showers and Cantor (1985) claim that such states contribute to flexible problem solving. Blumberg's (1985) study comes closest to identifying stressful emotional states in CEOs, but similar evidence from subsequent studies has been meagre.

A central question suggested by this model of "internal processes" for further research on the superintendents' leadership for school improvement is, What is the nature of the internal processes giving rise to effective superintendent leadership practices? (e.g., How are problems interpreted? How are goals set, and what are they? What values are central to the thinking of effective superintendents, and how are they used in problem solving?)

Leadership Practices

The construct in figure 12–1 that I described earlier as being the fulcrum is leadership practices: the overt, observable actions taken by effective superintendents to maintain and improve the quality of education in their districts. Our chapters by Wills and Peterson, Musella, and Holdaway and Genge address such practices quite directly. But the dramatic differences evident in how such practices were framed across these three studies illustrate how useful it would be to have an integrative perspective with which to better appreciate their combined significance. Although not entirely satisfactory, transformational leadership theory might serve this purpose; it is a framework that has been applied in several previous efforts to understand the work of exceptional superintendents (e.g., Powers 1985; Coleman and LaRocque 1991). Musella also makes some explicit use of transformational leadership concepts in chapter 9.

Proposed in a mature form by Burns (1978), such theory subsequently has been extended considerably by Bass and his associates (e.g., Bass 1985; Bass and Avolio 1989; Bass et al. 1987) as well as others in noneducational contexts (e.g., Podsakoff et al. 1984; Podsakoff et al. 1990; Ehrlich, Meindl, and Viellieu 1990). Efforts to better appreciate the manifestations of transformational leadership in education have just begun and largely are focused on school-level leaders (e.g., Sergiovanni 1990; Leithwood and Stein-bach 1991; Sashkin and Sashkin 1990; Leithwood and Jantzi 1990).

Transformational leadership actually encompasses two distinct sets of practices, one set referred to as "transformational" and one set as "transactional." Transactional forms of leadership are premised on exchange theory; various kinds of rewards from the organization are exchanged for the services of the employee, who is seen to be acting at least partly out of self-interest. Superintendents' transactional leadership practices, for example, help school administrators recognize what needs to be done in order to reach a desired outcome. According to the theory, this increases principals' confidence and enhances motivation as well. The two primary dimensions of transactional leadership identified in Bass's formulation of the theory (adapted to the superintendents' leadership) are these:

- *Contingent reward.* The superintendent tells staff what to do in order to be rewarded for their efforts. Two previous studies provide some evidence that superintendents do this. Hallinger and Edwards (1992) observed the use of both incentives and disincentives by the superintendent in their study to foster use of a shared-decision model. One of the superintendents in the study by Hord, Jolly, and Mendez-Morse (1992) rewarded *students* for specific achievements. Superintendents in Murphy's study expressed difficulty in shifting from this way of working toward more facilitative forms of practice.

- *Management by exception.* The superintendent intervenes with staff only if standards are not being met. Prior evidence suggests that feedback resulting from superintendents' monitoring of school improvement may be the most frequent manifestation of this leadership dimension (see Hord, Jolly, and Mendez-Morse 1992; Corbett and Wilson 1992). In addition, Crowson and Morris (1992) reported the dramatic case of a superintendent himself rewriting the constitution for student government in a school in order to avoid further instances of racial discrimination.

Bass and associates consider transactional leadership practices to be a necessary but not sufficient basis for organizational leadership. Such practices do not motivate people to do their best or to maintain peak effort. Nor do they encourage people, as teachers are now being encouraged through current restructuring efforts, to assume more leadership responsibility themselves. Adding on transformational leadership practices encourages people to work for transcendental goals, to be self-motivating, and to seek sources of self-actualization in their workplace.

Podsakoff and colleagues (1990) captured most of the practices currently associated with transformational leadership in six dimensions. The following are those six dimensions adapted to research on the superintendent:

- *Identifying and articulating a vision.* Behavior on the part of the superintendent aimed at identifying new opportunities for her or his district, and developing, articulating, and inspiring others with her or his vision of the future. This is a relatively common practice, according to prior evidence and also appeared among the practices of effective superintendents in chapters 2, 5, and 9.

- *Providing an appropriate model.* Behavior on the part of the superintendent that sets an example for staff to follow and that is consistent with the values the superintendent espouses. Many studies report superintendents modeling what they believe in. For example, the district staff in Corbett and Wilson's (1992) study modeled new forms of instruction; a superintendent in Hord, Jolly, and Mendez-Morse's (1992) study stood in the school halls at changing time to demonstrate the importance he attached to schools having a "caring climate." Holdaway and Genge (chapter 2) and Musella (chapter 9) also report evidence of this practice.

- *Fostering the acceptance of group goals.* Behavior on the part of the superintendent aimed at promoting cooperation among staff and assisting them to work together toward a common goal. Like articulating a vision, this set of practices seems common to superintendents, judging from prior evidence. For example, Crowson and Morris (1992) reported trustee-superintendent interaction designed to negotiate a set of shared goals for change. District office staff in Corbett and Wilson's study promoted goal consensus through their consistent messages about the priority to be awarded instructional improvement. Chapters 2, 4, 5, 6, and 9 add support to the claim that this practice is both common and critical to the work of effective superintendents.

• *High performance expectations.* Behavior that demonstrates the superintendent's expectations for excellence, quality, and/or high performance on the part of staff. The two superintendents in Musella's study provided evidence of this dimension of practice. Coleman and LaRocque's (1990) effective superintendents worked to establish within their districts norms of accountability and high standards of student achievement, especially in core subjects:

> The norm of accountability subsumed a concern for high expectations: it was not enough to try to meet community demands; continual efforts to improve and to achieve (and preferably exceed) certain standards of achievement were clearly called for. (p. 106)

Hallinger and Edwards (1992) as well as Hord, Jolly, and Mendez-Morse (1992) also describe high expectations being expressed in the feedback superintendents provided various staff groups as a result of careful monitoring activities.

• *Providing individualized support.* Behavior on the part of the superintendent indicating respect for staff and concern about their personal feelings and needs. Three studies in the text illustrate (or at least hint at) superintendents' practices that provide individualized support. As Holdaway and Genge's study (chapter 2) indicated, effective superintendents give high priority to good communication and the maintenance of cordial relations with their staffs and others: they considered "being supportive" one of their key influence strategies. The importance these superintendents attached to the people with whom they worked emerged as one of the key themes in this study. In the context of group problem solving, effective superintendents in Leithwood, Steinbach, and Raun's study (chapter 4) indicated close attention to the professional growth of their senior administrative colleagues. As one said: "I cheer him on . . . this chap has come a long way." Evidence from Musella's two case studies (chapter 9) portrays the superintendents as "approachable, friendly, caring, and good communicators" in the minds of those with whom they worked. While we are not told what practices gave rise to this impression, it seems to have been largely responsible for the creation of norms, in the two districts, of people helping each other on the job and with personal problems. Respondents believed that their districts were "supportive" and "people oriented."

This dimension of transformational leadership shines a spotlight on the essential humanness of district organizations and the powerful influence a leader's consideration and respect for the hopes, beliefs, and capacities of individual colleagues can have on their commitment to the success of the organization. Studies of school leadership have repeatedly demonstrated the potency of this dimension of transformational leadership (e.g., Leithwood, in press), which Blase (1989) conceptualizes as being micropolitical. Micropolitical perspectives, as he explains,

> have emphasized the dialetical, interactive, multidirectional, strategic, conflictual, ideological and interpretive/perceptual aspects of the organization as they relate to the use of power. (p. 378)

• *Intellectual stimulation.* Behavior on the part of the superintendent that challenges staff to reexamine some of their assumptions about their work and rethink how it can be performed. Musella's study provides the clearest examples of practices that constitute intellectual stimulation. Among the qualities their staffs attributed to the two new CEOs in this study were the "provision of initiative" and the expression of a "fresh outlook on education"; these superintendents also increased inservice for teachers, provided more resource persons for schools and decentralized decision making, a practice likely to increase the issues with which school-based people would grapple. All these practices illustrate what it means to provide intellectual stimulation and likely accounts for the opinion expressed by staff that their districts were challenging places to work. Something of a paradox, noted explicitly by Hallinger and Edwards (1992), is that in spite of a substantial movement toward school-site management in many states and a few provinces, district staff are often the source of ideas during improvement efforts. This is also evident in the data provided by Musella (chapter 9) as well as Leithwood, Steinbach, and Raun (chapter 4).

From the perspective of transformational leadership theory, promising questions to pursue in future research on effective superintendents include these: Do the transformational practices of effective superintendents result in the extra effort by staff toward district and school improvement that appears to occur in noneducational contexts (see, e.g., Ehrlich, Meindl, and Viellieu 1990)? What mix of transactional and transformational practices by superintendents best serves the purposes of school improvement? Do variations in organizational context (e.g., district size, sense of crisis) influence the optimum mix of transformational and transactional practices by superintendents? What range of specific superintendent practices are interpreted by district and school staffs as manifestations of transformational and transactional leadership? Can transformational leadership provided at the district level be distributed across the district staff, or is it crucial that it also be provided by the superintendent? Are there predictable patterns of development in the acquisition of transformational leadership practices by superintendents?

School District Components

Figure 12–1 encompasses the assertion made, metaphorically, in chapter 1 that superintendents, even very effective ones, cannot have other than indirect effects on the learning of students in their districts. Were it otherwise, we would bear witness to successful alchemy. Furthermore, as we observed about the study by Peterson, Murphy, and Hallinger (1987), when superintendents do attempt to tightly control what happens in the classroom, the results can be spectacularly wrongheaded. So what are the organizational avenues through which superintendents' practices might eventually be expected to contribute to the quality of education provided by their districts? At least five of the chapters in this book provide pieces of the answer to this question. These results take on more meaning, in my view, when placed within a framework of some normative value.

Several recent reports concerned with variables accounting for districtwide changes recommend an organizational design framework as a basis for bringing greater coherence to the school district components construct in figure 12–1. Originally proposed by Galbraith (1977) in relation to noneducational organizations, this framework has been modified and applied to school districts by Jones and Leithwood (1989), Leithwood and Jantzi (1990), and Leithwood and Musella (1991). As in figure 12–2, the framework specifies six components of a district that are open to superintendents' influence and plausibly linked to student growth (column 1). These dimensions provided an exhaustive set of categories for school district components identified in the five relevant studies in this text (column 2). As well, there is other evidence which supports the salience of these dimensions for superintendents attempting school improvement, evidence exemplified by the references in column 3.

Organizational design theory suggests several promising questions for future research concerning the superintendents' leadership for school improvement: Are some district components a more productive focus than others for superintendents' district and school improvement initiatives? (The selection of "information collection and decision-making processes" by a number of high-profile superintendents—see Hallinger and Edwards 1992 and Wissler and Ortiz 1988—suggests that this might be the case.) What possible characteristics of each school district component offer greatest support for the improvement efforts of school staffs?

CONCLUSION

Aside from general curiosity, why would anyone have enough interest in effective superintendents to expend the effort required for this compilation of studies? Admittedly, it seems a bit late to raise this question. Some readers, furthermore, may consider the answer obvious: so that superintendents-to-be or not-so-effective superintendents can learn from the example. After all, it was that straightforward premise that fueled the use of effective-schools research in its "second coming" as the basis for fostering school improvement. "Implement the correlates of effective-schools research," said the high-profile drumbeaters, "and you too can have above average standardized achievement test scores in your schools." It

Figure 12–2
Components of the School District Providing a Focus for Superintendents' Leadership Practices

1. School District Components	2. Examples of Components Identified in the Five Studies	3. Examples of Other Evidence Supporting the Components as a Focus for Superintendents
1. The goals for students pursued by the district	• District mission • School and district goals	Powers 1985
2. The tasks required of staff to achieve District goals	• Specification of staff roles • Strategic planning • Providing appropriate programs	McPherson 1988
3. Resources and organizational structures	• Time for planning • District structure • Resources for professional development • Delegation of responsibility • School buildings	Louis 1987
4. Personnel policies and procedures	• Board policies • Professional development of principals, teachers, senior administrators • Incentives for change	Murphy, Peterson, and Hallinger 1986

1. *School District Components*	2. *Examples of Components Identified in the Five Studies*	3. *Examples of Other Evidence Supporting the Components as a Focus for Superintendents*
5. Information-collection and decision-making processes	• Informal information-search processes • Participative decision-making processes • Monitoring of implementation • Quality of communication • Providing information to Stakeholders • Monitoring student achievement	Wissler and Ortiz 1988
6. Organizational culture	• District culture (norms, etc.) • School culture	Coleman and LaRocque 1991

took a few years to figure out that this was not the straightforward task it appeared to be at first blush. The "correlates" (e.g., strong instructional leadership) turned out to be a bit light on practical details. School contexts dissimilar to those in which the research was conducted often seemed to require a kind of medicine unlike the correlates. The correlates themselves had nothing to say about processes that would be helpful for their implementation. And so on. Indeed, what some have concluded is that the correlates themselves are really not so helpful after all! What are helpful are the principles on which the correlates are premised. Murphy (1989), describing these principles as the "legacy" of the effective-schools movement, cites the educability of learners, a focus on outcomes, taking responsibility for students, and attention to consistency and coordination throughout the school community.

When it comes to effective superintendents, there is nothing analagous to the superficially well-developed correlates of effective schools. But perhaps the studies in this text, along with the other related research touched on in this chapter, provide some tentative clues to principles of effective school district leadership. For starters, we could probably justify commitment to increasingly expert individual and group problem-solving processes; and commitment to keeping foremost, in political deliberations, the consequences for students of those decisions taken. Also justifed would be commitment to the professional growth of school and district staff, and taking responsibility for continuous efforts to design the district organization so as to make full use of staff capacities. As a final principle, CEOs should also take responsibility for continuous efforts to establish, review, and clarify the central directions to be taken by the district organization, in collaboration with the entire community of legitimate stakeholders. These principles begin to explain the basis on which effective CEOs transform politics into education.

NOTES

1. There has been much talk of schools as loosely coupled organizations, of effective schools as more tightly coupled, and of the advantage of simultaneous loose-tight coupling characteristics. But this work seems not to have had much influence on the current push toward decentralization.

2. We might claim that changing these regularities is what CEOs really ought to be about. I tend to agree, but that is a problem for another book.

3. I used this framework, in the role of guest editor, also to summarize the results of five studies reported in two consecutive issues of the journal *School Effectiveness and School Improvement* (Leithwood 1992a, 1992b)

REFERENCES

Allison, D. (1991). Setting, size and sectors in the work environment of chief education officers. K. Leithwood and D. Musella (Eds.), *Understanding School System Administration* (pp. 23–4). London: Falmer Press.

Allison, D. J., & Nagy, P. (1991, April). *A study of principal problem spolving: An introduction to the study.* Paper presented at the annual meeting of the American Educational Research Association, Chicago.

Bass, B. M. (1985). *Leadership and performance beyond expectations.* New York: Free Press.

Bass, B. M., & Avolio, B. J. (1989). Potential biases in leadership measures: How prototypes, lenience, and general satisfaction relate to ratings and rankings of transformational and transactional leadership constructs. *Educational and Psychological Measurement, 49,* (3), 509–27.

Bass, B. M., Waldman, D. A., Avolio, B. J., & Bebb, M. (1987). Transformational leadership and the falling dominoes effect. *Group and Organizational Studies, 12,* (1) 73–87.

Blase, J. (1989). The micropolitics of the school: The everyday political orientation of teachers toward open school principals. *Educational Administration Quarterly, 25*(4), 377–407.

Blumberg, A. (1985). *The school superintendent: Living with conflict.* New York: Teachers College Press.

Bossert, S. D., Dwyer, D., Rowan, B., & Lee, G. (1982). The instructional management role of the principal. *Educational Administration Quarterly, 19*(3), 34–64.

Burns, J. M. (1978). *Leadership.* New York: Harper & Row.

Calderhead, J. (Ed.) (1987). *Exploring teachers' thinking.* London: Cassell.

Coleman, P., & LaRocque, L. (1990). Reaching out: Instructional leadership in school districts. *Peabody Journal of Education, 65*(4), 60–89.

Coleman, P., & LaRocque, L. (1991). *Struggling to be good enough.* New York: Falmer Press.

Corbett, D., & Wilson, B. (1992). The central office role in instructional improvement. *School Effectiveness and School Improvement,* 3(1), 45–68.

Crowson, R., & Morris, V. C. (1992). The superintendency and school effectiveness: An organizational hierarchy perspective. *School Effectiveness and School Improvement,* 3(1), 69–88.

Cuban, L. (1989). The district superintendent and the restructuring of schools: A realistic appraisal. In T. Sergiovanni & J. Moore (Eds.), *Schooling for tomorrow: Directing reforms to issues that count.* Boston: Allyn & Bacon.

Ehrlich, S. B., Meindl, J. R., & Viellieu, B. (1990). The charismatic appeal of a transformational leader. *Leadership Quarterly,* 1(4), 229–48.

Galbraith, J. R. (1977). *Organization design.* Reading, MA: Addison-Wesley.

Hallinger, P., & Edwards, M. (1992). The paradox of superintendent leadership in school restructuring. *School Effectiveness and School Improvement,* 3(2), 131–49.

Hallinger, P., Leithwood, K., & Murphy, J. (Eds.). (1993). *Cognitive perspectives on educational leadership.* New York: Teachers College Press.

Hambrick, D. C., & Brandon, G. L. (1988). Executive values. In D. Hambrick (Ed.), *The executive effect.* London: JAI Press.

Hickcox, E. (1992). *Practices of effective CEOs: A preliminary discussion.* Mimeo, Ontario Institute for Studies in Education, Toronto.

Hord, S., Jolly, D., & Mendez-Morse, S. (1992). The superintendent's leadership in school improvement: A rural perspective. *School Effectiveness and School Improvement,* 3(2), 110–30.

Jones, L., & Leithwood, K. (1989). Draining the swamp: A case study of school system design. *Canadian Journal of Education,* 14(2), 242–60.

Leithwood, K. (1992a). Qualitative studies of superintendents' leadership for school improvement. *School Effectiveness and School Improvement,* 3(1), 42–45.

Leithwood, K. (1992b). Editor's conclusion: What have we learned and where do we go from here?, *School Effectiveness and School Improvement,* 3(2), 173–184.

Leithwood, K. (in press). Leadership for school restructuring. *Educational Administration Quarterly.*

Leithwood, K., Begley, P., & Cousins, B. (1990). The nature, causes and consequences of principals' practices: An agenda for future research. *Journal of Educational Administration,* 28(4), 5–31.

Leithwood, K., & Jantzi, D. (1990). Transformational leadership: How principals can help reform school cultures. *School Effectiveness and School Improvement,* 1(4), 249–80.

Leithwood, K., & Montgomery, D. (1986). *Improving principal effectiveness: The principal profile.* Toronto: OISE Press.

Leithwood, K., & Musella, D. (1991). *Understanding school system administration.* New York: Falmer Press.

Leithwood, K., & Stager, M. (1989). Expertise in principals' problem solving. *Educational Administration Quarterly, 25*(2), 126–61.

Leithwood, K., & Steinbach, R. (1991). Components of chief education officers' problem-solving processes. In K. Leithwood & D. Musella (Eds.), *Understanding school system administration* (pp. 127–53). New York: Falmer.

Louis, K. (1987). *The role of school districts in school innovation.* Paper prepared for the conference, Organizational Policy for School Improvement, OISE, Toronto.

McLeod, G. (1984). The work of school board chief executive officers. *Canadian Journal of Education, 9*(2), 171–90.

McPherson, R. B. (1988). Superintendents and the problem of delegation. *Peabody Journal of Education, 65*(4), 5.

Morgan, G. (1986). *Images of organization.* Beverly Hills: Sage.

Murphy, J. (1989). *Restructuring schools: Capturing and assessing the phenomena.* New York: Teachers College Press.

Murphy, J., Peterson, K., & Hallinger, P. (1986). Administrative control of principals in effective school districts: The supervision and evaluation functions. *The Urban Review, 18*(3), 149–175.

Peterson, K., Murphy, J., & Hallinger, P. (1987). Superintendents' perceptions of the control and coordination of the technical core in effective school districts. *Educational Administration Quarterly, 23*(1), 79–95.

Podsakoff, P. M., MacKenzie, S. B., Moorman, R. H., & Fetter, R. (1990). Transformational leadership behaviors and their effects on followers' trust in leader, satisfaction and organizational citizenship behaviors. *Leadership Quarterly, 1*(2), 107–42.

Podsakoff, P., Todor, W., Grover, R., & Huber, V. (1984). Situational monitors of leader reward and punishment behaviors: Fact or fiction? *Organizational Behavior and Human Performances, 34*, 21–63.

Powers, N. C. (1985). Transforming leadership: A process of collective action. *Human Relations, 38*(11), 1023–46.

Raun, T., & Leithwood, K. (1993). Pragmatism, participation and duty: Values used by CEOs in their problem solving. In P. Hallinger, K. Leithwood, & J. Murphy (Eds.), *Cognitive perspectives on educational leadership* (pp. 54–74). New York: Teachers College Press.

Sashkin, M., & Kiser, K. (1992). *Total quality management.* Seabrook, MD: Duchocon Press.

Sashkin, M., & Sashkin, M.G. (1990, April). *Leadership and culture building in schools*. Paper presented at the annual meeting of the American Educational Research Association, Boston.

Schwenk, C. R. (1988). The cognitive perspective on strategic decision making. *Journal of Management Studies, 25*(1), 41–56.

Sergiovanni, T. J. (1990). *Value-added leadership: How to get extraordinary performance in schools*. New York: Harcourt Brace Jovanovich.

Sergiovanni, T. (1992). *Moral leadership: Getting to the heart of school improvement*. San Francisco: Jossey-Bass.

Showers, C., & Cantor, N. (1985). Social cognition: A look at motivated strategies. *Annual Review of Psychology, 36*, 257–305.

Sims, H., & Lorenzi, P. (1992). *The new leadership paradigm: Social learning and cognition in organizations*. Newbury Park, CA: Sage.

Srivastva, S. (1983). *The executive mind*. San Francisco: Jossey-Bass.

Srivastva, S., & Cooperrider, D. (1990). *Appreciative management and leadership*. San Francisco: Jossey-Bass.

Stromnes, A., & Sovik, N. (Eds.). (1987). *Teachers' thinking*. Trondheim, Norway: Tapir.

Toffler, B. L. (1986). *Tough choices: Managers talk ethics*. New York: Wiley.

Trider, D., & Leithwood, K. (1988). Exploring the influences on principals' behavior. *Curriculum Inquiry, 18*(3), 289–312.

Vroom, V., & Yetton, P. (1973). *Leadership and decision-making*. Pittsburgh: University of Pittsburgh Press.

Wirt, F. (1991). The missing link in instructional leadership: The superintendent, conflict and maintenance. In P. Thurston & P. Zodhiates (Eds.), *Advances in educational administration: Vol. 2. School leadership*. London: JAI Press.

Wissler, D. F., & Ortiz, F. I. (1988). *The superintendent's leadership in school reform*. New York: Falmer Press.

Yukl, G. A. (1989). *Leadership in organizations* (2d ed.). Englewood Cliffs, NJ: Prentice Hall.

SUBJECT INDEX

NAME INDEX